The Ultimate Irrelevant Encyclopaedia is neither irrelevant to your enjoyment nor to your bookshelf. It is, however, *the* source book to a wealth of information you never thought to ask about or knew existed.

In its comprehensively illustrated and cross-referenced pages you will discover all you need to know about:

* **The initiation rite of the Aborigine**
* **The world's smallest underpass – for badgers**
* **The philosopher who considered it better to eat dead bodies than bury them**
* **The king who died in a fall – from a toilet seat**
* **The use of herrings to cure malaria**
* **The world's first oil slick**
* **The pipe 'smoking' habits of Josef Dzhugashvili**
* **The inspired judgment of the electric light bulb by a British Parliamentary Committee**

There has never been an encyclopaedia so rich in bizarre, extraordinary and mind boggling items of information. Whether you dip into it, follow the fascinating (and infuriating) cross-references or simply look up your chosen subject, you will be entertained, entranced and amused. You will certainly be armed to dazzle, or bewilder, any acquaintance with a gem of irrelevant information.

THE
ULTIMATE
IRRELEVANT
ENCYCLOPAEDIA

THE
ULTIMATE
IRRELEVANT
ENCYCLOPAEDIA

BILL HARTSTON
—— AND ——
JILL DAWSON

London
UNWIN PAPERBACKS
Boston   Sydney

First published in Great Britain by George Allen & Unwin 1984
First published by Unwin Paperbacks 1985

UNWIN®PAPERBACKS
40 Museum Street, London WC1A 1LU, UK

Unwin Paperbacks
Park Lane, Hemel Hempstead, Herts HP2 4TE, UK

George Allen & Unwin Australia Pty Ltd,
8 Napier Street, North Sydney, NSW 2060, Australia

Unwin Paperbacks with the Port Nicholson Press
PO Box 11-838 Wellington, New Zealand

© Bill Hartston and Jill Dawson 1984, 1985

ISBN 0 04 827148 9

Printed in Great Britain
by Hazell Watson and Viney Limited,
Member of the BPCC Group, Aylesbury, Bucks

IT IS A VERY SAD THING THAT
NOWADAYS THERE IS SO LITTLE
USELESS INFORMATION.

Oscar Wilde (1854–1900)

Acknowledgements

The compilation of an encyclopaedia of irrelevant information is a task which would have been insurmountable but for the efforts of those pioneers who have trodden the paths of useless knowledge before us, those junk junkies whose blinkered inspiration has enabled them to ignore all but the most truly worthless of facts. To them we owe a great debt of thanks, as also to our numerous friends and colleagues who have offered us the scrapings from their personal dustbins of data. Our aim has been primarily to organise these diamonds of dross, these nugatory nuggets, into a format wherein they may shine more brightly and be more accessible to the dedicated searcher after true irrelevance.

The works which we have consulted in collecting and checking information are too numerous to list in their entirety, but the following brief bibliography will be found to contain most of the relevant irrelevancies which formed our source material.

General Reference Works:
Harmsworth's Universal Encyclopaedia (1922)
Brewer's Dictionary of Phrase and Fable (1921 edition)
Lemprière's Classical Dictionary (Routledge 1879 and 1949)
The Smith and Jones World Atlas (Mitchell Beasley 1983)

Fact Collections:
The Book of Facts by Isaac Asimov (Hodder and Stoughton 1980)
The Hamlyn Book of Amazing Information (1979)
The Fact-a-Minute Book by Paul Jones (Arrow 1982)
The Amazing Almanac by Gyles Brandreth (Pelham 1981)
The Book of Lists by Wallechinsky, Wallace & Wallace (Cassell 1977)
Tolstoy's Bicycle by Jeremy Baker (Sphere 1983)
Would You Believe It? by Sanders, Sanders, Girling & Davies (Coronet 1974)
Would You Believe It About Animals? by Runeckles, Runeckles, Girling & Sanders (Futura 1977)
Curious Facts by John May (Secker and Warburg 1981)
Man Bites Man by George Ives (Penguin 1981)
A Day in the Life of the World by A. Bailey (Hutchinson 1983)
Amazing Times by Stephen Winkworth (Allen & Unwin 1982)

Oddly Enough by John Hall (Granada 1979)
Fancy That by John Hall (Thornhill Press 1976)
The Incredible Quiz Book by Ian Messiter (Unwin Paperbacks 1983)
The Shocking Book of Records by M. Guinness (Sphere 1983)

More Specialist References:
Famous Last Words by Jonathon Green (Omnibus Press 1979)
What a Way to Go by Peter Bowler and Jonathon Green (Pan 1983)
Punishments of Former Days by E. W. Pettifer (1939)
and numerous esoteric papers including:
Mummy as a Drug by W. R. Dawson (Proc. Roy. Soc. Med. 1927) and Polar Bears in the Middle Ages by T. J. Oleson (Canad. Hist. Rev. 1950).

And a final word of thanks to Campkins of Cambridge for their extremely helpful and efficient service processing the photographs which serve to illustrate this work.

A

AARDVARK

(From the Dutch: *aarde*, earth; *vark* pig.) When eating termites, the aardvark keeps its nostrils closed. But ants really do get up its nose.

ABORIGINE

The initiation rite for membership of an Aborigine tribe is to jump out of a tree, have two front teeth knocked out, and drink some blood. A simple method might perhaps be to knock out one's own teeth and swallow a mouthful of blood when falling clumsily out of a tree.

In 1957 a Darwin University research project set out to discover why Aborigines stand on one leg to rest. An orthopaedic specialist interviewed some Aborigines and attempted to train whites to adopt the same resting posture. No firm conclusions were reached, but several white trainees are believed to have fallen over.

Storks also like to take a rest standing on one leg.

☐ See also: *eating, manslaughter.*

ABORTION

In North America, beavers' testicles were formerly believed to be of value in inducing an abortion. They also cured toothache and added a delicate flavour to tobacco when minced. The first country to legalise abortion was the USSR in 1920.

ABRAHAM

☐ See **CONVEYANCING.**

ABYSSINIA

The official name of Abyssinia is now **ETHIOPIA.**

☐ See also: *electric chair.*

ACCIDENTS

Most serious accidents in the home occur in the kitchen in England. In France, however, the bedroom is statistically the most dangerous room.

In England, Benjamin Disraeli further diminished the chance of bedroom accidents by leaving the legs of his bed in bowls of salt water in order to ward off evil spirits. Meanwhile, back in France, Louis XIV owned 413 beds. If these were passed down even unto the fifth generation, it might help explain why his great-great-great-grandson, Louis XVI, did not consummate his marriage to Marie Antoinette until seven years after their wedding. Perhaps it took that long before they met in the same bed.

☐ See also: *railways.*

ACNE

According to the results of a 1969 study, it is a total myth that chocolate makes you spotty. Sixty-five acne sufferers were given a daily dose of chocolate for a month; after this period 46 reported no change, 10 were better and 9 claimed that their symptoms had worsened. A control group was fed with something looking and tasting like chocolate, but not the real thing. They reported 5 improved cases, 7 deteriorations and 53 much the same.

The nature of the chocolate substitute was not specified, but there is a Brazilian butterfly with the colour and smell of chocolate.

During adolescence 66.4 per cent of boys and 69.4 per cent of girls will at some time suffer from acne.

☐ See also: *eunuch.*

ACRONYM

Around 4,000 Chicago homes have their cookers fuelled by methane gas produced from cow dung. The company providing this valuable service is called the Calorific Recovery Anaerobic Process Inc.

ACTING

First place in the voting for Best Actor of 1926 was taken by Rin-Tin-Tin. He died only six years later, at the age of 14, in the arms of Jean Harlow.

ADAMS, Douglas (*b.* 1952)
☐ See **FORTY-TWO.**

ADAMS, John (1735–1826)

The second President of the United States of America.

☐ See **INDEPENDENCE.**

ADDAMS, Charles (*b.* 1912)
☐ See **CARTOONS.**

ADOLESCENCE

Ten-year-olds were allowed to marry in England in 1576, the lowest the age of consent has ever been. In 1875 it rose from 12 to 13, then from 13 to 16 in 1885, since when no further change has taken place. In California, the age of consent was raised to 18 in 1913.

In 1785 90 per cent of those hanged in Britain were under 20 years of age.

ADRIAN IV

Pope Adrian IV (born Nicholas Breakspear) was the only English pontiff. Henry II asked for his permission to conquer Ireland.

☐ See **DEATH.**

ADULTERY

In the reign of King Canute, the penalty for an adultress was to forfeit 'both nose and ears'. The crime was evidently considered only half as serious in ancient India, where an adulterer of either gender could get away with having only a nose cut off.

The sixteenth-century astronomer Tycho Brahe lost his nose in a fight at the age of 19 in 1565. For the remainder of his life he wore an artificial nose made of silver and gold, attached with a pot of cement which he always carried on his person. Many surgeons of that time were highly accomplished in skin-grafting techniques to rebuild noses lost in forfeit for crimes.

AESCHYLUS (525–456 BC)

Writer of tragedy.

☐ See **DEATH.**

AFGHANISTAN

The minaret of Jam in Afghanistan is the second tallest minaret in the world.

☐ See also: *philately, radio, sport.*

AGATHOCLES (361–289 BC)

Son of a potter who rose to become Tyrant of Syracuse.

☐ See **FIRE OF LONDON.**

AGE OF CONSENT

Although it was only just over a century ago that 12-year-olds could marry (see **ADOLESCENCE**), nowadays no boy of 1

Afghan national dance

or less can even be accused of a sex offence. You have to be 14 before the law presumes you to be capable of committing one.

Louis XIII of France married Anne of Austria when both were 14. They consummated their marriage three years later when a couple of friends showed them how.

AIRCRAFT

A Jumbo jet weighs as much as sixty-seven African elephants. Despite this, elephants continue to be discriminated against in aviation law. It is forbidden, for example, to lead one's elephant through the approach tunnels of London's Heathrow Airport.

In Milwaukee it is decreed that a pet elephant must be kept on a lead when taken for a walk on public streets.

☐ See also: *xylocopid.*

ALASKA

American state purchased from Russia in 1867 for $7,200,000.

☐ See **ESKIMO.**

ALBANIA

Atheistic state which issued a postage stamp in honour of its leading smoker, Ahmed Zog I, who puffed his way through 240 cigarettes a day. He might have been better off in the Hunza tribe of north-west Kashmir; they do not suffer from cancer. Long before smoking was identified as a health risk, the belief was held among Indonesian natives that smoking through cigarette holders made of dugong tusks gave protection against bullets.

☐ See also: *demography, execution, Sweden, uniqueness.*

ALBATROSS

Name given to the genus *Diomedea* of the zoological order Tubinares. The young albatross, after leaving the island of its birth, may fly for two years before touching land again An albatross can fly all day without once flapping its wings. By adopting this clever high-flying strategy, albatrosses must have generally avoided capture by the ancient Romans who made a

special glue to spread on trees in order to catch birds.

ALBERT I, King of Belgium (1875–1934)

King Albert I of Belgium was killed in a climbing accident. His last reported words were: 'If I feel in good form, I shall take the difficult way up. If I do not, I shall take the easy one. I shall join you in an hour.'

The precise nature of the difficulties which he encountered are not known, but it should be noted that in 1977 12-year-old Emma Disley climbed Mount Snowdon on stilts.

ALCHEMY

☐ See **JAMES IV.**

ALCOHOL

(From the Arabic: *al*, the; *koh'l*, a fine powder of antimony used to stain the eyelids. Nowadays more often taken orally.) During the reign of Catherine I of Russia, the law prohibited women from getting drunk. This led to a great increase in the number of female transvestites seen at Moscow balls when the wine flowed freely. Catherine's predecessor, Peter the Great, had the lover of one of his mistresses executed and his head preserved in alcohol. The head was kept by his bedside as a warning to others.

☐ See also: ***anaesthetics, ant, bequests, canary, homosexuality.***

ALECTRYOMANCY

Divination by cock is called alectryomancy. Grains of corn are arranged in a circle, each grain covering one letter of the alphabet. A cock is placed at the centre of the circle and spells out its predictions according to which grains it pecks at. The succession of the Roman Emperor Theodosius was thus predicted by a couple of smart alectryomancers.

Setting off from base camp the hard way

ALEXANDER, King of Greece (1893–1920)

Nephew of Kaiser Wilhelm II.

☐ See **DEATH.**

ALEXANDER THE GREAT (356–323 BC)

On capturing the city of Thebes, Alexander the Great was still peeved that the enemy had refused to surrender without a fight, so he ordered the city to be razed to the ground. Being a man of culture, however (see **PITT, William**), he spared the house in which Pindar the Poet had lived more than a century before. Just as Alexander paid his respects to the poetry of Pindar, so it is said did Napoleon pay homage to the music of Haydn. On entering Vienna, Napoleon's first act is reputed to have been to dispatch soldiers to make sure that the old composer was well and secure.

ALEXANDRIA

Founded by Alexander the Great in 332 BC, the city of Alexandria was the site of the first coin-operated slot machines. They functioned as holy water dispensers. Alexander the Great was an epileptic. According to Pliny the Elder, an attack of epilepsy can be warded off by placing the placenta of a she-ass under the nose of the sufferer. She-ass placentas were not available from Alexandrian slot machines.

ALFONSO XIII, King of Spain (1886–1941)

His last words were 'Spain, My God!' which seems to permit several interpretations according to the intonation.

☐ See **CAREERS.**

ALFRED THE GREAT, King of England (849–901)

Actually he was only really King of Essex, Kent and Wessex, and overlord of the rest of the kingdoms in the land.

☐ See **BAKING.**

ALGERIA

☐ See **LITERACY.**

ALLAH

There is no god but Allah and Mahomet is the prophet of Allah.

☐ See **INCOMPETENCE.**

ALLEN, Woody (b. 1935)

Woody Allen's one regret in life is that he is not somebody else.

☐ See **WATERPROOFING.**

ALLIGATOR

(From the Spanish: *El lagarto*, the lizard.) The bellow of an alligator can be heard up to a mile away. A small pair of bellows (not those of crocodiles) formed part of Mr

White's Halitosis Detector, patented in 1925. This was a device to trap the human breath while exhaling. Reversed and squeezed, the bellows expelled the breath, allowing its producer to have a sniff.

☐ See also: ***musical appreciation.***

ALLITERATION
☐ See **BICYCLE, LONDON.**

ALPHABET
☐ See **CAMBODIA, CAMEROON, GEOGRAPHY, HAWAII.**

AMAZON
The River Amazon carries more water than the next eight largest rivers in the world put together. With this Amazonian act of

GIANT AMAZON QUEEN

selfishness, it should hardly be surprising that there are no rivers at all in the Cayman Islands.

☐ See also: ***arithmetic, communication.***

AMBISEXUALS
☐ See **OYSTER, PHILIPPINES.**

AMMONIA
A colourless, pungent-smelling gas, whose name is derived from the ancient Egyptian god Ammon. Its chemical formula is NH_3.

☐ See **LIZARD.**

AMPUTEES
Perhaps the most extraordinary cricket match in history was played at the Montpelier Tea Gardens on 9 and 10 August in 1796. All the players were old Greenwich pensioners who had lost an arm or a leg. One side comprised entirely one-armed cricketers, their opponents all sported wooden legs. The match attracted 5,000 spectators and resulted in a victory for the 'timbertoes', as one contemporary account styled them, by 103 runs.

AMSTERDAM
(Latin *Amstelodamum*; formerly Amstelredam, the dyke or dam of the Amstel.)

☐ See **OHIO, TULIP.**

AMUSEMENT
A dummy hanging as an exhibit in the Amusement Park at Long Beach, California, had been there for at least five years before it was discovered in 1976 that it was a mummified human corpse.

ANACHRONISM
The right place but the wrong time.

☐ See **CLOCK, POTATO, TURKEY.**

ANACREON (563–478 BC)
A lyric poet who wrote in the Ionic dialect, lived a long life of pleasure and debauchery

and was deeply enamoured of a youth called Bathyllus.

☐ See **FIRE OF LONDON.**

ANAESTHETIC

The Chinese physician Hua T'o used to render his patients unconscious with alcohol. He plied his merry trade around AD 140. After his demise (perhaps the origin of the expression Hua T'o-day, Gone T'o-morrow) no significant improvement in anaesthetics came until 1844 when nitrous oxide was first used for dental operations.

Some still prefer Hua's recipe, but it is harder to get on the National Health.

☐ See **DRUNKEN DRIVING** for a modern example of the anaesthetic powers of alcohol.

ANAGRAM

A way of jumbling and mixing up words to change the meaning.

☐ See **KINNOCK.**

ANAXAGORAS (*c.* 500–428 BC)

Greek philosopher exiled from Athens in 435 BC for making the outrageous suggestion that the sun was a glowing rock 100 miles across, when everyone knew that it was a shining disc. His last words were: 'Give the boys a holiday.'

ANDORRA

The principality of Andorra is constitutionally ruled by two co-princes, the Bishop of Urgel in Spain and the President of France. They share a payment of about £12 every two years for carrying out their princely duties; the President of France takes the larger share. In Andorra you have to wait longer to vote than anywhere else on earth. There is no vote for anyone under 25, the highest age of majority in the world.

ANGLING

Anglers must watch their step in Muncie, Indiana, where it is illegal to carry fishing tackle in a cemetery. If they manage to avoid cemeteries and take their catch back to Oklahoma, opportunities to have a good time will still be severely curtailed by a law which prohibits getting a fish intoxicated. In culinary circles, this law is generally circumvented by killing the fish before marinating.

☐ See also: *fishing.*

ANGOLA

Angola is one of the worst places on earth to be working as a weather forecaster. There is over six times as much rain in Cabinda in northern Angola as there is in Lobito in the south. The expression 'raining cats and dogs' is thus more likely to be heard in the north of the country. 'Cats and dogs' appears to derive from the Greek words *kata* and *doxein* meaning 'full' and 'receptacle'. Hence 'cats and dogs' = bucketfuls. This pun loses a great deal when translated into Bantu or Portuguese, the languages of Angola.

ANKLE

☐ See **BONE.**

ANNE, Queen of Great Britain and Ireland (1665–1714)

Queen Anne produced seventeen children, of whom only one (William, Duke of Gloucester) survived infancy, and he too died at the age of 10 while his mother was still alive. In terms of royal procreation she was considerably less successful than Catherine de Medici who was married to one French King (Henry II), reigned for a time herself as Queen, and produced three more French Kings (Francis II, Charles IX and Henry III) all of whom took the throne in her lifetime.

☐ See also: *scrofula.*

ANNULMENT

'Women using false hair, iron stays, high-heeled shoes or bolstered hips to entice a husband shall lie under the penalty of the law against witchcraft and the marriage shall stay null and void' (decree of Elizabeth I).

ANT

A group of **INSECTS** belonging to the order Hymenoptera. The ant can lift fifty times its own weight, can pull up to 300 times its own weight, and always falls over on its right side when intoxicated.

☐ See also: ***aardvark, Edison, nose, slavery, Sri Lanka, Texas, Uganda.***

ANTARCTICA

The southern circumpolar continent. One way to reach Antarctica is to set off from Cape Beale in British Columbia, Canada, and sail due south. The next land you hit will be Antarctica. But if you only want to go there to see the snow, you might as well stay in Canada. The city of Montreal spent $32 million in the winter of 1979 keeping the streets clear of snow.

☐ See also: ***ice.***

ANTELOPE

A large group of mammals of the family Bovidae.

☐ See **DRAGONFLY, FIREFLY, PENGUIN.**

ANTIGUA

Island of the West Indies discovered in 1493 by Christopher Columbus and named by him after a church in Seville, Spain. Columbus died of syphilis. Magellan and Captain Cook were fellow-sufferers. Occupational hazard probably.

ANTI-SOCIAL BEHAVIOUR

In Indiana, it is illegal to ride on a bus within four hours of having eaten garlic. In Waterloo, Nebraska, barbers are breaking the law if they eat onions between the hours of 7 am and 7 pm. The record in English literature for consecutive, semantically independent, uses of the word 'onions' is held by Anthony Burgess in his novel 'Enderby

The antelope

Outside' with an unparalleled string of fo onionses: '. . . he had breathed on Hog Enderby, bafflingly (for no banquet wou serve, because of the known redolence onions, onions) onions. "Onions", sa Hogg . . .'

ANTONYMS

When used as verbs the words 'best' an 'worst' have the same meaning. 'Cleav can mean either to stick together or to sp apart. The writer must hope that th context will make the appropriate sens clear. More confusing still is the wo 'impassionate' which can mean either full passion or free from passion.

APARTHEID

In Chaucer's time it was illegal to sto French wine and Spanish wine in the san cellar. See **TENPIN BOWLING** for con parable regulations concerning und garments.

PE

An anthropoid monkey.

☐ See **BEE**.

PHRODISIAC

Japanese farmers used to drink a potion made from dead earthworms for its aphrodisiac qualities. For sensual stimulation this hardly seems to be a great advance on the old Aztec belief that cocoa had the power to enhance lustful thoughts. The melting point of chocolate is 89°C. The afternoon temperature on Mars (the planet, not the chocolate bar) only reaches 80°C, making it a perfectly safe place to store one's cocoa powder.

☐ See also: *shellfish.*

POLLONIA, St (3rd century)

St Apollonia is the patron saint of toothache therapy. Her teeth were believed to have the power to prevent toothache and were eagerly sought by sufferers. Fortunately for her, the great Apollonia tooth hunt only began after her death, but by the time of Henry VI in England so many of the saint's supposed dental relics were being peddled around the country that an attempt was made to gather them all in and put a stop to the trade. Several tons of teeth were amassed by the collectors. According to an old Cornish superstition, a child may be freed from ever having toothache if the first milk tooth it sheds is pushed down a mousehole.

POPLEXY

(From the Greek: *apo-* expressing completeness; *plessein*, to strike.) In the seventeenth century, tea was widely proclaimed to be a cure for apoplexy. This wondrous beverage was also thought to be effective against migraine, lethargy, vertigo, paralysis, drowsiness, epilepsy, catarrh, colic, consumption and gallstones. Dr Johnson used to drink more than forty cups of tea a day.

In Bhutan they drink tea with butter. The currency in Bhutan is the ngultrum. There are some grounds for believing that an apoplectic attack can be brought on by trying to pronounce ngultrum.

APPENDIX

A small blind prolongation of the caecum (in US cecum, pronounced *se'kəm*). They caecum here, they find 'em under **COMA** and **KOALA**.

APPLE

Tree of the order Pyrus malus (natural order Rosaceae).

☐ See **INSOMNIA, ORANGE**.

ARABIC

There are ninety-nine words to describe God in Arabic, but He is believed to feel no wrath at having so narrowly missed the century. If you want to learn Arabic, but do not like the idea of having to master the squiggly script, try Maltese, the only Arabic language written in Roman letters. The Eskimo language has more than twenty words for snow.

ARC DE TRIOMPHE

The Arc de Triomphe de l'Etoile, the larger of the two Parisian Arcs de Triomphe, is 162 feet high, 147 feet wide and 73 feet deep.

☐ See **INSOMNIA**.

ARCHANGEL

(From the Greek: *archi-*, chief; *angelos*, angel.) Russian seaport, English wildflower, or the highest order of Angel. There used to be seven in this angelic premier league, but Raphael, Uriel, Chamuel, Jophiel and Zadkiel were relegated to the Apocrypha.

☐ See **JOHN**.

ARCHERY

In 1349, in order to boost the war effort and ensure a state of preparedness for any

conflict, Edward III declared all sports other than archery to be illegal for the common people. By the sixteenth century archery lessons were compulsory for all males from the age of 7 upwards.

☐ See also: *Canada.*

ARGENTINA

Isabel Peron, second wife to Juan Peron, was president of the Argentine from 1974–6. She is the only president this century not to have held the title either of General or Dr.

Eva Peron, Isabel's predecessor to the title of Mrs Peron, holds the Argentine all-comers record for posthumous travel. She died in Argentina in 1952, was buried in Italy in 1955, exhumed and moved to Madrid in 1971 and finally in 1976, on the orders of Isabel, flown back to Bueno Aires to join the family crypt.

☐ See also: *cowboy, dentistry, football, Kinnock.*

ARISTOTLE (384–322 BC)

(Aristoteles to his friends.) From the tim of Aristotle until 1688, it was general believed that animals sprang from mud an rotting flesh. Aristotle also believed, no unreasonably, that pointed eggs containe male chicks while eggs with rounded en would produce females.

☐ See also: *Pitt, William.*

ARITHMETIC

(From the Greek: *arithmos*, number.) the language of the Yancos tribe of t Amazon, the highest number for whi there is a specific word is called poetta rarorincoaroac. It means 'three'.

ARMADILLO

(From the Spanish diminutive of *armad* armed.) Diminutive armed mammal of th family Dasypodidae.

☐ See **BIRTH, CONGO, FLEA.**

ARMLESSNESS

☐ See **AMPUTEES, CERVANTES, DRUNKEN DRIVING, SEURAT.**

ARPOCRAS

Perhaps the greatest glutton of ancie Roman times. At one sitting, Arpocras said to have consumed four tablecloths ar a broken glass. He was then given perm sion to leave the table.

ARSON

(From the Latin: *ardere*, to burn.) Scotland (where they are less hot on Lati arson is known as fire-raising.

☐ See **STORK.**

RT

According to the United States customs office at Baltimore, 'paint placed on a canvas by a sub-human animal' is not a work of art and hence cannot be allowed to enter their country free of duty. This definitive delineation of the boundaries of art was necessitated by an attempt in 1950 to import paintings produced at London Zoo by the chimpanzee artist Congo. They were heading for an exhibition of monkey art. Congo's initial reaction at having been profoundly insulted may have been mollified by a further comment by the customs spokesman: 'If we did not know they were produced by an animal we would have thought they were good modern art.'

Henri ('Le Douanier') Rousseau was a customs officer. Many of his colleagues would have thought his paintings to be good art had they not known they were painted by a customs official.

☐ See also: *caterpillar, fine art, monkey.*

ARTAXERXES

There were three Persian Kings called Artaxerxes. The first (reigned 464–424 BC) was the son of Xerxes and had one hand longer than the other. They called him Longimanus. The second was the son of Darius II and had a remarkable memory. They called him Mnemon and he married two of his own daughters, reigned from 404–358 BC, had 150 children from his 350 concubines (but only four legitimate sons) and died at the age of 94. The third Artaxerxes, surnamed Ochus, was the son of the second. He put nearly all his family to death, broke his father's heart, and was finally poisoned by a physician. His flesh was afterwards devoured by cats and his bones were used for sword handles.

ARTHUR

Semi-mythical King or chieftain of Britain.
☐ See **AUSTRIA**.

ARTIFICIAL LIMBS

The first artificial limb was made in 1551 by Ambroise Paré in order to enable a handless man to ride a horse. More recently a flamingo named Pedro from Banham Zoo in Norwich was fitted with an artificial leg, fashioned from a piece of plastic tubing, after it had broken its own leg in a fall. A consultant dentist had to be called in at London Zoo to repair a toucan's beak with artificial alloy and plastic skin. The original beak had had a chunk bitten off during a lover's tiff by a bad-tempered lady toucan.

☐ See also: *barrel-organ, Bernhardt, careers, emergency, Goering, rubber, Seurat.*

ARTISTIC APPRECIATION

When Henri Matisse's painting, 'Le Bateau', was hung, by accident, upside down at the Museum of Modern Art in New York in 1961, it was forty-six days before anyone noticed.

When the 'Mona Lisa' was stolen from the Louvre and was missing for two years between 1911 and 1913, more people visited the art museum in order to view the blank space on the wall than had ever come to see the picture. During the period of its absence, six Americans are known each to have parted with $300,000 for their own 'original' 'Mona Lisa'.

☐ See also: *orange.*

ARTISTS

Painters tend to have a hard life. Pablo Picasso was abandoned by the midwife at his birth as stillborn. He was revived by a physician uncle who happened to be present, by breathing cigar smoke into his lungs. Vincent van Gogh was another late starter. He began to draw only at the age of 27 and is known to have sold only one painting during his lifetime. Camille Pissarro was more successful and his mummified remains can still be seen in Lima cathedral. And while you are in Peru, don't miss the opportunity to taste the camu-camu fruit, which has sixty times the vitamin C content of the orange.

ASPARAGUS

Genus of plants of the order Liliaceae. *Asparagus officinalis* is the most common.

☐ See **KNOWLEDGE, THEOLOGY.**

ASS

One of the four divisions of the genus *Equus*. (Horse, zebra and quagga are the others.)

☐ See **BALDNESS, WEASEL.**

ASSASSINATION

The Assassins were a secret Syrian sect of the eleventh to thirteenth centuries, noted for their unquestioning obedience to orders from their chief. These orders usually involved murdering somebody. The name is a c.rruption of *Hashishin* (hashish-eaters) which gives an indication of their preferred state for assassinations.

☐ See also: *euphemism.*

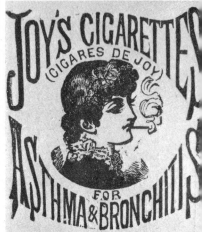

ONE OF THESE CIGARETTES
gives immediate relief in cases of Asthma, Hay Fever, Chronic Bronchitis, Influenza, Cough, and Shortness of Breath, and their daily use affects a complete cure. The contraction of the air-tubes, which causes tightness of chest and difficulty of

The attempted assassination of George III

STAIRE, Fred (*b.* 1899)

☐ See **INSURANCE**.

STHMA

Russian folklore offers two alternative remedies for asthma: either take two tablespoons of fresh ox blood every day until relief is obtained, or inhale the steam from well-boiled potatoes.

During the Second World War, Germany planned the construction of bombs packed with Colorado beetles to be dropped on England to destroy the British potato crop. Hitler's fiendish mind was doubtless toying with the idea of a surprise attack catching us unprepared while we were all wheezing asthmatically, unable to boil potatoes to alleviate the symptoms. But he had forgotten about our massive reserves of ox blood.

STONISHMENT

King penguins living on uninhabited islands have been known to fall backwards with surprise on seeing a human being for the first time.

STROLOGY

Astrologer Girolamo Cardano predicted that he would die on 21 September 1576. When he woke up feeling perfectly well, he may have harboured some doubts about whether his calculations had been correct. But he need not have worried, for he killed himself later the same day.

☐ See also: *calendar, conjunction, flood, sneezing, syphilis.*

STRONAUT

(From the Greek: *astron*, a star; *nautes*, a sailor.)

☐ See **FARTING, FISH**.

STRONOMER

Man with stars in his eyes.

☐ See **ADULTERY**.

ATHANASIUS (*c.* 297–373)

Bishop of Alexandria now believed not to have written the Athanasian creed.

☐ See **SEGREGATION**.

ATHLETICS

That fine Welsh athlete Griffith Morgan (1696–1732) ran 12 miles in fifty-three minutes on the last day of his life. After the achievement of finishing the race in such a fine time, he was awarded 100 gold sovereigns, but a further congratulatory slap on the back caused him to keel over and die.

It is illegal to run a three-legged race for money in British Columbia.

ATLANTIC CITY

Popular resort of New Jersey, USA, 56 miles south-east of Philadelphia.

☐ See **MONOPOLY**.

ATLANTIC OCEAN

The Atlantic is the second largest ocean on earth.

☐ See **PANAMA, SECRETS, SNOW**.

ATTILA, King of the Huns (*c.* 400–53)

Attila died on his wedding night, of an 'uncommon effusion of blood'. Some say the excitement was too much for him, others maintain that he was slain by another of his jealous wives.

☐ See **WILLIAM THE CONQUEROR**.

ATTLEE, Clement Richard (1883–1967)

☐ See **CHURCHILL, R.**

AUCTION

Eighteen thousand mummified cats were offered for sale at a Liverpool auction in March 1890. One of them was used as the auctioneer's hammer. They were sold at a rate of £3 13s 9d a tonne (working out at about ten cats a penny) to be used as fertiliser.

When cats have intercourse, withdrawal of the male organ is painful for the female. Probably not half as painful, however, as being mummified.

☐ See also: ***Mussolini, shaving, torture.***

AUGUSTUS CAESAR (63 BC–AD 14)

In 8 BC Augustus Caesar, disappointed not to have a month of his own, renamed the month of Sextilis 'Augustus'. Realising also that his new month would still be one day shorter than that of uncle Julius, he seized a day from February to add to August.

Of course, when all this happened nobody knew that it was really 8 BC at the time. In fact nobody knew what year it was at all until around AD 700 when the Venerable Bede had the bright idea of dating events from the birth of Christ.

The Princess Augusta, whose name was very similar to that of the Roman Emperor

AURAL SEX

The doctors of Henry VIII thought tha he had contracted syphilis when Cardina Wolsey whispered in his ear. The ear of th locust is in its abdomen. Henry VIII had re hair.

AUSTEN, Jane (1775–1817)

Jane Austen's name never appeared on th title pages of her books during her lifetim⊕ When it did appear in print in The Qua⊕ terly Review of 1821 it was misspelt.

☐ See **DOLPHIN.**

AUSTRALIA

Mount Isa in Queensland, Australia, is th largest city in area in the world, being abou the same size as Switzerland. But Switze land can offer a taxi service by hang-glide which Mount Isa has yet to inaugurate.

If all the wool produced in a year i Australia were to be knitted into a singl scarf of average width, it could go round th world ten times.

☐ See also: ***Barbados, Borneo, emu,*** ***gluttony, misunderstanding, seaside.***

AUSTRIA

Emperor Maximilian I of Austria believe himself to be a direct descendant of Kin Arthur (of round table fame). A statue ⊙ King Arthur can be seen defending the lat Emperor's tomb in Innsbruck, in the com pany of other distinguished ancestor Maximilian married the daughter ⊙ Charles the Bold, was chosen to be King ⊙ the Romans, recovered Vienna from th Hungarians and overthrew the Turks a Villach in 1492. Yet can any of these fea⊕ really compare with that of a later Austria⊕ Johann Hurlinger, who walked on h hands from Vienna to Paris in fifty-five day at an average speed of 1½ mph?

☐ See also: ***avalanche, Italy.***

AUTOMOBILE

At the end of 1925, there were 24,564,57

Fig. 1.

Fig. 2.

CARRIAGE WITHOUT HORSES.

cars in the world, of which 21,094,980 were American.

☐ See also: *Malaysia, population, Somalia, theft.*

AVALANCHE

(From the Latin: *ad*, to; *vallis*, valley.) In December 1916, during the First World War, an Austrian commander in the Alps gave his men the order to open fire with their cannon. Several thousand of his own troops were killed by the avalanche which the noise started. In those days, the effects and the precise measurement of noise were improperly understood. Many years later, however, experts at a court in Freiburg-im-Breisgau testified that ten quacking ducks make as much noise as three motor lorries with trailers.

AXOLOTL

Gyrinus edulis (pronounced *aks'o-lot-l*), the larval form of Amblystoma.

☐ See **QUETZAL.**

AYER, Sir Alfred J. (*b.* 1910)
☐ See **PHILOSOPHY.**

AZTEC
☐ See **CANNIBALISM, JAGUAR, SCIENCE.**

B

BABBAGE, Charles (1792–1871)

Founder of the modern **COMPUTER**.

☐ See **POETIC LICENCE**.

BABOON

Monkey of the genus *Cynocephalus* (dog-headed). The female gelada baboon has nipples so close together that her baby can feed from both at the same time.

☐ See also: *sedative.*

BABYLONIA

The ancient Babylonians had a highly effective and fair system for ensuring that all their daughters were married off. The attractive girls were sold to potential husbands at auction and the proceeds were used as dowries for the ugly ones who attracted no bidders.

☐ See also: *gardening.*

BACCHANALIA

(After Bacchus, the Roman god of fertility and wine, known to the Greeks as Dionysus.)

☐ See **STOCKS**.

BACHELOR

James Buchanan is the only bachelor ever to have served as President of the Unit States. No only child has ever become American president. Among the Briti Prime Ministers, Ramsay MacDonald a Stanley Baldwin had no siblings. Rams MacDonald is the only premier of eith England or the United States whose fath was a bachelor. William the Conqueror w a bastard too.

☐ See also: *healing, marriage.*

BACON, Sir Francis (1561–1626)

☐ See **DEATH**.

BADGER

(*Meles taxus*, mammal of the order Car vora, but eating mainly insects and root What is claimed to be the world's smalle underpass was constructed beneath the M motorway. It is only one foot in width a was built to enable badgers to have sa passage across the busy road.

BAKING

King Alfred was not the only monarch w was into cakes in a big way. In 1730 Ki William I of Prussia ordered a cake to baked which would feed his army of 30,C men. The recipe included 5,000 eggs, 1 t of butter, 36 bushels of flour and 200 gallo of milk. The resulting cake measured feet long, 24 feet wide and 2 feet high.

BALDNESS

Pliny the Elder had a cure for baldness using the ashes obtained by burning the genitals of an ass. These are pounded up with oil in a leaden mortar and applied to the shaven head. This treatment also prevents the onset of greyness. Modern theory does not support Pliny's remedy, maintaining instead that the only proven method of avoiding baldness is castration. A trifle drastic perhaps, but more popular with asses than the older remedy.

☐ See also: *genetics, Germany, Kenya, Paul I, vanity*.

BALDWIN, Stanley (1867–1947)

British Prime Minister.

☐ See **BACHELOR**.

BALZAC, Honoré de (1799–1850)

French writer who had a weakness for fortune-tellers and to whom music was a greater delight than literature.

☐ See **GLUTTONY**.

BANANA

(*Musa sapientum*) The banana is the largest known plant without a solid trunk; botanically it is a herb. According to a Mexican folk remedy, the best thing you can do for tonsillitis is to wrap a hot buttered banana skin around your throat, just over the tonsils, and eat ground dog excrement mixed with butter. On the other hand, you might prefer tonsillitis. The President of Zimbabwe is Dr Canaan Banana.

☐ See also: *Burma, Handel, Honduras*.

BANGKOK

Capital and chief seaport of Thailand (formerly Siam). The world record for vasectomies was claimed in Bangkok in December 1983, when fifty doctors held a nine-hour marathon snip-in, dealing with 1,190 patients. A gramophone record of a song called 'I've been vasectomised' reached number one in the Thai hit parade the same year.

Kite-flying is a big-league sport in Thailand.

BARBADOS

The eggs of the flying fish of Barbados are too heavy to float so this bright little fish lays them on mats of seaweed which provide the necessary support. In Australia a folk remedy for boils is to cover the affected area with the wetted skin of a boiled egg. Ordinary hen's eggs are usually prescribed, but it might be worth trying Barbadian flying fish eggs on special occasions. Sixty per cent of the population of Barbados are women.

BARBERS

(From the Latin: *barba*, a beard.) In 1909 in

London, Robert Hardie, barber extraordinary, shaved six men in one minute then, blindfolded, shaved another in twenty-seven seconds. A competent vet can castrate a cat in five minutes, but Napoleon's surgeon, Baron Dominique Larrey, could amputate a man's leg in fourteen seconds. At that rate he could amputate twenty-one legs and be halfway through the next one before our poor moggy has realised what the vet is up to.

☐ See also: *haircut, surgery.*

BARGAINING

Samuel Tapon, a Frenchman, committed suicide in 1934 after losing £50,000 in unwise speculations. At the shop where he went to buy the suicide rope, he haggled over the price and succeeded in saving himself a few centimes. He left more than £1½ million. There is, on average, one suicide every twenty minutes in the United States.

BAROMETER

(From the Greek: *baros*, weight; *metron*, measure.) Instrument to measure the pressure of the atmosphere. They come in three types: mercury barometers, aneroid barometers, and frogs. Frogs only croak when the pressure falls.

BARREL-ORGAN

A barrel-organ, a case of butterflies, 5,630 umbrellas and a glass eye were among the items left on the trains of the LMS Railway in 1946. A snake in London Zoo was once fitted with a glass eye, but there is every reason to believe that it was custom built rather than picked up second hand at a lost property office. It was a closely kept secret that Theodore Roosevelt was blind in his left eye.

BARRISTER

The reason barristers wear black is because they are still mourning for Mary, wife of William III, who died in 1694. The 'little gentleman in velvet' is not a barrister, b[ut] the mole, celebrated in Jacobite toast[s] whose hole was responsible for unhorsin[g] and killing William III in 1702.

BASEBALL

A sport believed to have derived from a[n] early American school game called On[e] Old Cat and its later developments calle[d] Two Old Cat, Three Old Cat and Four O[ld] Cat. Running out of old cats, they called th[e] next version Baseball.

☐ See **DOLPHIN.**

BASINGSTOKE

Town in Hampshire, England, and not [a] good place to die. In 1675 the town [of] Basingstoke was fined £100 for negligenc[e] when it was discovered that a woman ha[d] been buried alive.

BASKETBALL

☐ See **ELEPHANT, SALIVATION.**

BASTARD

(From the French: *bâtard*: late Latin *bastum*, a pack-saddle. The old Frenc[h] term was *fils de bast*, son of a pack-saddl[e] perhaps referring to the morals [of] muleteers.)

☐ See **BACHELOR.**

BASTILLE

(From the old French: *bastir*, to build.)

☐ See **BUCKINGHAM PALACE, POETIC JUSTICE.**

BAT

Any member of the order Cheiroptera[.] The bat is the most efficient flying machin[e] known to man. Of the 4,000 or so know[n] species of mammal on earth, about 1,50[0] are bats. In 1943 approximately 30 millio[n] bats were collected by the US Army Corp[s] and 2 million dollars invested in th[e] development of a bat bomb. Each bat wa[s] to carry an incendiary device on a delaye[d] action fuse. They would be released over Germany and create havoc and conflagration. By 1945 this new fearsome weapon was declared operational, but the whole plan was abandoned after some of the kamikaze bats escaped and detroyed an aircraft hangar and a general's car.

☐ See also: *parsley, vampire.*

BATH

Architecturally stunning spa situated in the Avon valley. In Kidderminster it is an offence to own a bath without a watertight plug. Quite apart from the water saved, it is a matter of simple respect to the natural sponge which, it should be remembered, takes fifty years to grow to bath size.

When the South Eastern Gas Board urged couples to save fuel by bathing together, a member of parliament described the suggestion as 'deplorably vulgar'. Mrs Ida Jones (who had won £10 for the idea) commented: 'There is nothing wrong with it. It is better than having a rubber duck.'

☐ See also: *cleanliness, Taft, waterproofing.*

BAUDELAIRE, Charles Pierre (1821–67)

French poet, son of a civil servant and odd character who was packed off to India by relatives because of his early extravagant behaviour. Whereas Coleridge found his creative temperament stimulated by opium, Baudelaire preferred hashish. Another thing which differentiates these two poets is that only Baudelaire ever dyed his hair green.

☐ See also: *forgiveness.*

BEANS

Seed of plants of the natural order Leguminosae, and a much maligned vegetable. Hippocrates thought that they injured the eyesight, Cicero believed that they corrupted the blood and inflamed passions, while the Pythagorean philosophy forbade their consumption altogether; it was thought that some souls were transformed into beans after death.

BEANS (BAKED)

The total weight of Heinz baked beans sold each year in Britain is equivalent to that of approximately 20,000 African elephants.

☐ See also: *treacle.*

BEAR

In 1499 a bear was put on trial in Germany on a charge of terrorising local villages. The start of the trial was delayed while considering a defence plea that the defendant had the right to be tried by a jury consisting of his fellow bears. At the turn of the century (twentieth, not sixteenth), every tenth house in St Petersburg would have at least one pet bear cub during the season. They were kept until aged about three months when, according to a contemporary account, 'they exhibit certain signs of familiarity which to the average man in the street seem rather uncalled for'. They would then be either presented to the bear-pits or eaten.

☐ See also: *bee, Byron, elephant, Gloucester, pregnancy.*

BEAR-KEEPING

There is an old English belief that any child

force two on the Beaufort Scale. No Beaufort readings are available for the mode of kissing preferred by the Tinguian tribe of the Philippines: with lips close to but not touching, each other's face, the kissers take sharp inhalations of breath.

BEAUTY

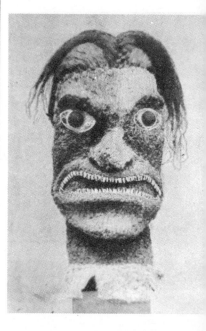

who has ridden on a bear will never have whooping cough. This may have been just a smart advertising gimmick spread about by bear-keepers who would keep their coffers full by charging for rides. On the whole, the parent might have been best advised to save money, let the child catch whooping cough, then treat it with another folk remedy: a nest of mice tied round the child's neck in a bag.

BEATLES
□ See **CHICAGO, COMA, MUSICAL APPRECIATION.**

BEAUFORT, Margaret (1443–1509)
□ See **PRECOCIOUSNESS.**

BEAUFORT SCALE
Device for recording the strength of the wind at sea. Normal breathing registers

King Philip the Fair of France applied the same high standards of fair good looks to his subjects as he evidently enjoyed himself. He declared any skin disease to be a punishable offence and lepers were sentenced to death. The scientific unit of beauty is the millihelen, defined as the amount of beauty required to launch one ship. An Arab chief once offered twenty-three camels for Diana Dors. (His estimate of her beauty must therefore have been twenty-three desert millihelens.)

□ See also: ***dogshow, Japan, Kenya.***

BEAVER

Genus of large rodents. Before eating a beaver an American forest Indian will ceremonially remove its kneecaps and burn them. Unlike its kneecaps, the teeth of a beaver never stop growing throughout its life. Sharks' teeth do not keep growing in size, but they produce a non-stop supply of new teeth on a sort of dental conveyor belt to replace old worn ones. By the time it is 10 years old a shark will have bitten and gnawed its way through about 24,000 teeth.

☐ See also: *abortion, hat, yak.*

BED

A warm and restful place where we all feel relaxed and secure.

☐ See **ACCIDENT, ALCOHOL, BOMBING, COOKERY, RABIES, VICTORIA.**

BEDBUG

(*Cimex lectularius*) Mating is no fun for the female bedbug. The male pierces a hole in her back with a spike which grows on his penis. Sperm is then ejaculated directly into the bloodstream through the puncture and is then carried by the blood to her ovaries. She does not seem to enjoy a good meal all that often either; a female bedbug has been known to go 565 days without food. And to add to her troubled life, in 1898 Frank Racher of New York patented an electric bedbug exterminator. It was designed to deliver an electric shock to any bug climbing up the legs of the bed, thereby either killing the bug or causing it to think again and reverse back down the leg towards the floor.

BEDE, The Venerable (c. 673–735)

Historian and priest who spent his whole life in a Benedictine monastery. Continued his translation of St John's Gospel until his dying hour. Not quite good enough for canonisation, but he was entitled 'Venerable' in the ninth century.

☐ See **AUGUSTUS CAESAR.**

BEDTIME

King Philip the Handsome of Spain died in 1506 but his wife kept his body in her bed for the next three years. Queen Victoria's loyalty to Albert after his death lasted longer, but was not expressed in quite such a close manner. For forty years she continued to have his evening clothes laid out each day in Windsor castle.

Research indicates that women are less likely to fall out of bed than men. Shah-Yin, a Chinese princess of the Sung dynasty, was probably unaware of that piece of information when she had a bed specially made to be able to accommodate her together with thirty lovers.

BEE

On average the effort expended in producing a single pound of **HONEY** involves 50,000 bee miles flown and 4 million flowers visited. Bears have been observed to climb telegraph poles in their search for honey, mistaking the buzzing sound for that of bees. Such errors presumably happen less frequently in Ottawa, where the buzzing of bees is prohibited by anti-noise legislation. More people die each year from bee stings than from snakebites. It is illegal, incidentally, to eat snake in Iraq on a Sunday. The Italian for bee is *ape.*

☐ See also: *eye, insect, motorcycling, xylocopid.*

BEER

Octopuses in Monterey Bay in California have been seen making their homes in discarded beer cans. In Germany, however, there is a type of **FLEA** which lives and breeds only in beer mats. The consumption of beer in a privy, toilet or lavatory is forbidden in Manitoba, Canada.

'Octopodes' is the other correct plural form of 'octopus'.

☐ See also: *Italy, John, lovesickness, nutrition, paternity, saints.*

BEETHOVEN, Ludwig von (1770–1827)

Beethoven liked to stimulate his brain by

having iced water poured over his head. Hemingway preferred a more traditional method – alcohol, cigarettes and coffee, while Proust ascribed one particularly productive period to the effects of eating a cake dunked in tea, a beverage he seldom drank. The results of his inspiration were not called 'reflections on tea-times past', but 'Swann's Way'.

☐ See also: *Da Ponte.*

BEETLE

(From the Anglo-Saxon: *bitan*, to bite.) Member of the insect order Coleoptera.

☐ See **CRIME, FLAMINGO, FUSSINESS, THEOLOGY, UMBRELLA.**

BELGIUM

The largest iceberg ever sighted was in the South Pacific in 1956. It covered an area greater than that of Belgium. Even an average iceberg weighs 20 tons.

☐ See also: *Albert I, caterpillar, Cuba, dogshow, Napoleon III, rabbit, saints, vegetables.*

BELIZE

The State of Belize in Central America gets its name from a Mayan Indian word meaning 'muddy water'. The arteries in the human body get their name from a Greek word meaning 'windpipe'. Since no blood flows through the arteries after death, the early Greek physicians found them empty when they performed dissections, so jumped to the conclusion that their function was to carry air through the body. The spines of sea urchins have been used in the manufacture of artifical arteries.

BELL, Alexander Graham (1847–1922)

At that historic moment when he uttered the first message ever to be transmitted by the telephone, Alexander Graham Bell chose the poignant and memorable lines: 'Mr Watson, come here; I want you.' Samuel Morse had a little more panache

when he inaugurated the electric telegraph in 1884. His chosen message: 'What God hath wrought.' Rather flowery, but he had been a portrait painter before he decided to invent the Morse code.

☐ See also: *Garfield.*

BELLOWS

(From the Anglo-Saxon: *baelig*, a bag.) A windbag.

☐ See **ALLIGATOR, RHEUMATISM.**

BENEDICT IX (*d.* 1055 or 56)

Pope from 1032–46, being deposed and returning several times in that period.

☐ See **PETER I.**

BEN HUR

A book, a film and a stage play.

☐ See **PETER I.**

BENIN

Previously known under the more homely name of Dahomey, this Central African state was annexed by France in 1894 and became independent in 1958. It was most fun in the pre-French days, when a man could be executed for failing to recite without error the names of the kings of Dahomey.

Now one of the best things to do in Benin is to suffer from leprosy. The country has the proud claim of having more leprosy clinics than hospitals.

BENNETT, Enoch Arnold (1867–1931)

British novelist and playwright whose last words were: 'Everything has gone wrong, my girl!'

☐ See **DEATH, STAMMERING.**

BENTHAM, Jeremy (1748–1832)

British philosopher Jeremy Bentham went to Queen's College, Oxford, at the age of twelve, graduated when he was fifteen and later founded Utilitarianism. Perhaps through a desire to be posthumously utilitarian, he willed his estate to University College Hospital on condition that his body be preserved and placed in attendance at all board meetings. The offer was accepted and his embalmed corpse, adorned with a wax model of his head, attended every meeting of the board for ninety-two years after his death.

Another star to be stuffed and mounted had, during his active days, the ability to count up to twenty and to untie knots with his teeth. He was Roy Rogers' horse Trigger. Jeremy Bentham could probably have untied knots with his teeth had he put his mind to it.

BEQUESTS

Mrs Myrtl Grundt, the widow of a fur dealer from Perth, Australia, left one million Australian dollars to a pair of polar bears in the local zoo. Another useful benefactor to society was the Rev. John Gwyon, rector of Bisley in Surrey, who hanged himself in 1929, leaving £9,976 to establish a fund to provide knickers for boys of the district.

Others have encouraged a more competitive spirit among potential legatees. John Orr, a nineteenth-century Scot, left a sum of money to provide an annual sum of £30 for the tallest, shortest, oldest and youngest brides to have married that year in the town of St Cyprus, Scotland. Rather more was demanded from anyone wishing to inherit from Charles Vance Millar, who died in Canada in 1927. Among a number of unusual bequests he left a substantial prize to be awarded to the Toronto mother who gave birth to the most children in the ten-year period following his demise. The race was close and frantic with $568,106 finally shared out among four mothers, each of whom had produced nine healthy offspring. Consolation prizes were awarded to two applicants with ten births; one was considered unworthy of the top honour because five of her children had been illegitimate, while the other runner-up counted four stillbirths among her ten.

Several people have left bits of their own bodies as bequests. Juan Potomachi gave 200,000 pesos to the Teatro Dramatico in Buenos Aires in 1955 on the sole condition that his skull be preserved and used as Yorick in Hamlet. Oddly enough, this desire for a posthumous stage career had already occurred once before, when John Reed, a nineteenth-century gaslighter at the Walnut Street Theatre in Philadelphia, similarly willed that his head be severed from his corpse and prepared for the same role. Even more touching was the bequest of the poet Paul Whitehead, who died in 1774, leaving his heart to Lord De Spencer. So moved was De Spencer that he had the heart buried in his own family mausoleum. Unfortunately the tomb was plundered sometime in the nineteenth century and Whitehead's heart stolen.

Henry Durrell of Bermuda was either rather playful or simply a ditherer. Unable to decide which of three nephews should inherit his palatial mansion after his death in 1921, he stipulated, in a spirit of total fairness, that the matter be decided by the roll of a dice. There is no doubt, however, that Ian Fleming was inspired by a feeling of fun when he bequeathed £500 to each of three friends, provided they spent the money 'on some extravagance'.

Even when men leave their estate to their wives, their motives may be less than totally honourable. German poet Heinrich Heine left all his assets to his wife on the one condition that she remarry 'because then there will be at least one man to regret my death'. William Shakespeare was perhaps still less generous; he left his wife his second best bed. And finally, David Davis of Clapham, in 1788, left the sum of five shillings to Mary David, precisely calculated to be enough 'to enable her to get drunk for the last time at my expense'.

☐ See also: *Britannia, Cromwell, generosity, Jesus Christ.*

BERLIN

Former capital of a united Germany, now two cities divided by a wall.

☐ See **OHIO.**

BERMUDA

About 300 islands, only twenty of which are inhabited.

☐ See **MALAYSIA, MOTORCYCLING.**

BERNE

Swiss city justly famous for its bears.

☐ See **CANNABIS.**

BERNHARDT, Sarah (1845–1923)

Actress Sarah Bernhardt did not trust banks and insisted on being paid in gold. She was very fond of animals and brought back from Australia a koala bear, some possums and a St Bernard dog called 'Auckland'. Sometimes she slept in a satin-lined rosewood coffin upon which lay layers of her lovers' letters. In later life she had a wooden leg, but acted on.

☐ See also: *thespians.*

BERTHA OF THE BIG FOOT

Alias Berthe au Grand Pied, alias Queen Bertrada, club-footed wife of King Pepin of the Franks. Died at an advanced age in 783.

☐ See **BREEDING.**

BESTSELLER

The Onliest and Deepest Secrets of the Medical Art was an enormously successful book by Hermann Boerhaave, Dutch physician and chemist. On Boerhaave's death in 1738, the sole copy of the work was found sealed shut. Such was his reputation, that it fetched the equivalent of $20,000 in gold. When the seal was then broken, the book was found to comprise ninety-nine blank pages and only one with printing on it. The message read: 'Keep your head cool, your feet warm, and you will make the best doctor poor.' Since so much of the body's heat escapes through the head (see **HEADGEAR**), the most efficient way to ensure that your feet keep warm is to wear a hat.

BHUTAN

The state of Bhutan, between Bangladesh and China, once issued a stamp which was a miniature gramophone record of its national anthem. The capital of Bhutan is Thimbu (or Thimphu) though formerly the winter capital was Punakha and Tasichozong the summer capital. It may be the only place on earth where the stamps are better to listen to than the radio stations; eight of the ten stations broadcast only flood warnings. Tourists to Bhutan might like to acquire a smattering of Dzongka, which is the main local language, a Tibetan dialect. But take some friends – tourists are only admitted to Bhutan in groups of six.

☐ See also: *apoplexy, calendar.*

BIBLE

There are more acres in Yorkshire than words in the Bible. But there are more than thirty times as many bottles of Coca-Cola drunk every day throughout the world as there are letters in the Bible. There are 50 per cent more deaths on the road every year in the United States than the number of verses in the Bible. There are 1,189 chapters in the Bible, but the nineteenth chapter of the Second Book of Kings is identical to chapter 37 of Isaiah. The French for 'Behold Behemoth!' is 'Voici l'hippopotame!'.

☐ See also: *Carroll, European Economic Community, girl, John, reindeer, slavery, vocational guidance, wife-hater, witches.*

BICYCLE

(From the Latin: *bis*, twice, and the Greek: *kyklos*, circle.) This fashionable mode of transport was denounced by a Baltimore preacher in 1896 as a 'diabolical device of the demon of darkness'. His reason for condemnation was not on the perfectly justifiable grounds that the word is an ugly Latin–Greek hybrid (etymological purists would only ride a dicycle) but simply because too many of his parishioners were lured away from church on pleasant Sunday afternoons by the temptation of a bike ride. Perhaps because they are aware of the potential corrupting danger to moral standards, British Columbia has imposed a 10 mph limit for tricycles.

☐ See also: *Israel, Tolstoy.*

BIFOCALS

Bifocals were invented in 1785 by Benjamin Franklin. The inspiration came from a desire to be able to enjoy his dinners fully, able to see both what he was eating and the companion to whom he was talking. Franklin was also responsible for the invention of the rocking-chair.

BIKINI

The first known appearance of that ultimately erotic garment the leather bikini was in third-century Roman entertainments. The connection with Bikini atoll in the Marshall Islands, scene of many atomic tests, is obscure. One might conjecture that it has something to do with so much of it having been blown away.

BILLIARDS

The invention of the game of billiards dates back to 1591, exactly 200 years before the death of Mozart (see **FINGERPRINTS**). Early exponents of the game, if this illustration of Henry, Prince of Wales, is typical, had trouble with their cueing action. Henry was the son of James I, but died in 1612.

BIRMINGHAM
☐ See **ITALY, NURSING.**

BIRTH

The great dwarf lemur of Madagascar always gives birth to triplets. This can hardly impress the nine-banded armadillo, which always produces quadruplets, all of the same sex. This remarkable creature can also inflate its intestines to give extra buoyancy in water, and it is the only animal other than the human to suffer from leprosy.

The Indian Chencha tribe believe that night-time sex produces blind children. An old German belief maintains that sex in the rain produces girl babies while fine-weather conception guarantees a boy.

☐ See also: *Aristotle, children, Churchill, W., coincidence, Congo, Peter I, reproduction.*

BIRTHDAY

King John III, seventeenth King of Poland, was born, crowned, married and died all on 17 June. Nobody sang 'Happy Birthday to You' on any of these occasions since he died long before it was written in 1935. The song is still in copyright.

☐ See also: *celibacy, horror.*

BIRTHMARK

According to a superstition of the Pennsylvania Germans, an unwanted birthmark may be removed by rubbing it with the hand of a corpse. Either hand will do, but if you use the right hand, you could save the left for the **BUTTER.**

BLACKBIRD

(*Turdus merula*) One of the most musical of British birds.

☐ See **BURIAL.**

BLADDER

A hollow organ twixt kidneys and urethra.

☐ See **NAPOLEON III.**

BLOOD

Each red blood cell travels round the

uman body about 43,000 times a month.
Vith this hectic lifestyle, it is hardly
urprising that 8,000 such cells are des-
royed every hour and their life expectancy
only four months. Grasshoppers have
hite blood.

] See also: ***asthma, colour-blindness,
   entrepreneurs, flamingo, giraffe, goat,
   Julius Caesar, kidney, leech, Morocco,
   salmon, Tanzania, tax, vampire.***

OOD DONOR

A person who sheds blood for honourable
notives.

] See **DUELLING.**

OOD VESSEL

A vein or artery.

] See **BELIZE, COLUMBUS.**

ÜCHER, Gebhard Leberecht von 742–1819)

Prussian soldier and greatest ally of
Wellington at the battle of Waterloo.

] See **STRING.**

AR, Wild

(*Sus scrofa*) Progenitor of the pig.

] See **MUMMY.**

DY

Two-thirds of an average person's body
weight is made up of water. Despite that,
rom the remainder, there are 20 sq. ft of
kin, enough fat to make seven bars of
oap, enough phosphorus to make the
eads of 2,000 matches, enough iron to
nake one nail, enough carbon to make the
eads for 9,000 pencils and enough potas-
ium to explode a toy cannon. Queen
Christina of Sweden kept a toy cannon with
niniature cannonballs which she used to
re at fleas.

HEMIA

The *Winter's Tale*, by W. Shakespeare; Act
, Scene 3:

Bohemia, a desert country near the sea.
Enter Antigonus with a Child and a
Mariner.
Ant. Thou art perfect, then, our ship hath
touch'd upon the deserts of Bohemia?

Well no, actually. The Bard hath made a
geographic slip. Bohemia lieth totally inland. The nearest coast is eight-score miles
away.

BOILED EGG

(Oeufs à la coque.)

□ See **CROSSWORD.**

BOILS

First catch your field toad, for an ancient
Egyptian treatment for boils. Place the toad
on a stick facing the rising sun until it has
dried out. Take the toad limb correspond-
ing to the part of the body suffering from
boils and tie it to the ailing limb. If there is
no toad about, various remedies from
Texas might be tried using fat bacon (left on
overnight), ripe berries (eat one on the first
day, two on the second, and so on for nine
days), a fried road runner bird (eat it) or
cow manure (apply hot, externally).

□ See also: ***menstruation.***

BOLEYN, Anne (1507–36)

Daughter of Thomas, earl of Wiltshire,
direct descendant of Sir Geoffrey Boleyn,
Lord Mayor of London in 1457, second wife
of Henry VIII. After she was beheaded,
Anne Boleyn's heart was stolen. It was
taken to a church in Thetford, Suffolk, and
lay hidden there for three centuries. It was
finally found again in 1836, buried under
the organ. When Henry's first wife, Catherine of Aragon, married him, she was
already both a widow and a virgin.

□ See also: ***France.***

BOLIVIA

Colombia is the only South American
country with beaches onto both the Atlantic
and Pacific oceans. This arouses much
resentment in Bolivia and Paraguay, where

there are no coastlines at all. But Bolivia did have three different presidents in the course of one day on 3 October 1970.

BOMBAY

The chief seaport of western India, situated on the island of Bombay (18°53′N and 72°52′E).

□ See **METEMPSYCHOSIS.**

BOMBING

The Finnish air force is forbidden by international law to have bombers or any aircraft capable of carrying bombs. This may limit Finland's capacity to retaliate in case of attack, but the Finns may always take comfort in the knowledge that they have more hospital beds per head of population than any other country. Sufferers from clinophobia ought, therefore, to be advised to avoid Finland. Clinophobia is a morbid fear of beds. Fear of teeth is called odontophobia.

□ See also: *bat, illiteracy.*

BONES

Human babies are born with 350 bone some of which later unite to leave the adu with only 206, half of which are to be foun in the wrists, ankles, hands and feet. Th other important difference between babi and adults is that babies can breathe ar swallow at the same time, which adul cannot manage.

BOOKS

'Never lend books', advised Anato France, 'for no one ever returns them; th only books I have in my library are boo that other folk have lent me.' Despite th observation betraying rare perspicacit Anatole France was found after his death t have had one of the smallest human brai ever recorded.

BOREDOM

The female giraffe has frequently been see to wander off absent-mindedly in mi copulation, leaving a frustrated and u stable male tottering to the ground. Th

Typical ornithophobia

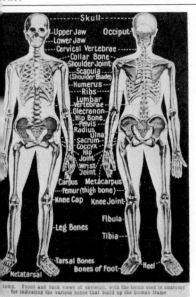

tomy. Front and back views of skeleton, with the terms used in anatomy for indicating the various bones that build up the human frame.

oes not happen with wild mice, which take nly five seconds to copulate.

☐ See also: ***emulsion.***

RNEO

he largest island of Singapore, where ead-hunting used to be the main pastime. During the Borneo border war, the Aus- ralian army dropped a detachment of five ats in order to clear a forward post of rats. he brave felines, outnumbered and in- leed outsized by their enemies, gave their ives for their country after fierce fighting. Military experts among the Borneans were ighly critical of the whole strategy; they aid that pythons would have been much nore effective.

☐ See also: ***foreplay.***

STON

he state capital of Massachusetts, USA, ut not a pleasant place for a tea party cf. **HATTO**).

☐ See **STOCKS.**

BOTSWANA

The vast majority of human males are diorchid, but most Botswana bushmen, having only one testicle each, are monor- chid.

BOTTOM

According to a recent survey by the jeans industry, the shape of someone's bottom carries considerable importance in how their character is judged by others. People with small, neat bottoms are thought to be intelligent, active and determined, but not sexy. Bigger bums score high on sex appeal, as well as being considered extrovert, easy-going and kind. Skinny rears are viewed as a sign of neuroticism, tidy botties are prudish, while flabby means lazy. The most desirable shape was considered to be on the fleshy side but not flabby; the fullness being confined to the buttocks and not extending to the waist. There should be a small gap visible between the thighs. Useful adjectives to remember: callipy- gean (fair-buttocked), steatopygous (fat- buttocked).

☐ See also: ***bumph, Charles VII of Sweden.***

BOUNTY HUNTERS

A supermarket in Osaka, Japan, offered about 2½p for each dead cockroach brought in by customers. They collected 98,499 in a week. The champion bounty hunters were a team of two women who killed 1,351 in their own home. This sport is less popular in Vietnam, where it is con- sidered bad luck to kill a cockroach. In Japan, only the cockroaches consider it unlucky.

BOURNEMOUTH

Seaside resort of Hampshire, England, which had the first electric tramways in the country.

☐ See **CAPITAL PUNISHMENT.**

BOWEL

(From the late Latin: *botellus*, a little sausage.)

☐ See **CHOPIN, WILLIAM THE CONQUEROR.**

BOXING

The only heavyweight boxing champion ever to have lectured on Shakespeare at Yale University was Gene Tunney.

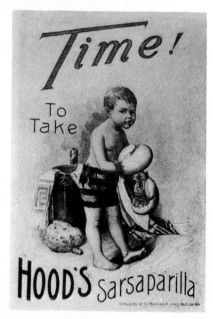

BRAHE, Tycho (1546–1601)

Danish astronomer, astrologer and scientist, lucky enough to have been given an island by King Frederick II of Denmark from which to observe the sky.

☐ See **ADULTERY.**

BRAILLE, Louis (1809–52)

Blinded at the age of 3, Louis Braille

invented the alphabet named after hi when he was only 15. It was not until 191 however, that Richard Hardy patented t musical toilet-roll holder.

☐ See also: *Edison.*

BRAIN

The fully grown human brain weighs abo three pounds. This compares well with t gorilla's brain which checks in at arou $1\frac{3}{4}$ pounds. Unlike the gorilla, the hum sometimes sleeps on his back. He is the on animal to do so, apart from a gelding nam Rodger owned by Mr P. Davis. Rodge habit of taking a nap lying on his back wi his feet in the air and mouth open made necessary for Mr Davis to erect a sign in window. The sign read: 'This horse is n dead'.

☐ See also: *books, breathing, brontosaurus, canary, cockroach, dove fishing, hare, intelligence, Julius Caesa water, wind.*

BRAIN DAMAGE

☐ See **SHOPLIFTING.**

BRANDING

(From the Anglo-Saxon: *brand*, burning In France until 1832 galley-slaves we branded on the shoulder with a fleur-de-l or the letters TF (travaux forces, force labour). Branding had been abolished Great Britain in 1829, except of course fe deserters from the army and soldiers notoriously bad character, who had to bea the letters D or BC until 1879.

☐ See also: *ear, torture.*

BRASSIÈRE

The modern brassière was invented in 19 by Mary Phelps Jacob, who was pained whalebone corsets. Though Ms Jacob pro ably did not realise it, a blue whale's pe can be 7 or 8 feet long.

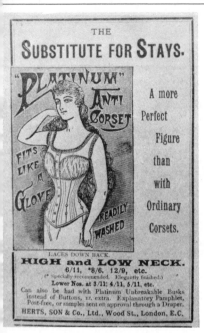

BRAT

(From the Old English: *bratt*, a brat.) On her eighth birthday, Shirley Temple received 135,000 presents.

BRAVERY

When Spain declared war on the United States in 1898, the immediate American response was to declare war on Spain, and to backdate their declaration by three days because they thought it looked braver if they had done it first. The name of Spain comes from a Carthaginian word meaning 'land of rabbits'.

BRAZIL

(Republica Federativa do Brasil.) In 1978 a new cemetery was being built in the Brazilian town of Sao Joao de Meriti. While work was progressing, the authorities found themselves obliged to publish advertisements stressing that the cemetery was not yet open and requesting murderers kindly not to dump their victims' bodies on site as had frequently happened.

☐ See also: *acne, business, Ceylon, crime, dentistry, fertiliser.*

BREAD

(From the Anglo-Saxon; *bread*, *breod*, bread.)

☐ See **FATALITIES, FLEA, MOTORING, SEGREGATION.**

BREASTS

The mammary glands of the female. Marie Antoinette had the same bust measurement as Jayne Mansfield. Jane Russell's bosom, however, so impressed Howard Hughes that he wrote four pages of notes on the subject. He was working on the problem of designing a cantilever support structure for it. A Victorian recipe for breast enlargement recommended bathing in twenty pounds of strawberries. Even if that failed in its object of adding to the size, it might enhance the flavour.

☐ See also: *crockery.*

BREATHING

Twenty per cent of the oxygen we inhale is used to keep the brain functioning. If the human lungs are spread out flat, they cover the same area as a tennis court. That might seem worth considering if you are desperate for a game of tennis, but it is not recommended if you want to continue breathing as well.

BREEDING

(From the Anglo-Saxon: *bredan*, to nourish.) Frederick William I of Prussia built up an élite squad of soldiers, the Potsdam Grenadiers, an army of giants, each of whom was around seven feet tall. He would bribe, cajole and occasionally kidnap suitable conscripts for this force. He also tried to ensure a continuing supply of gawky grenadiers by marrying off its members to exceptionally tall women.

An example of physical characteristics which were not inherited is the Emperor Charlemagne. His father was Pepin the Short, King of the Franks, who stood a proud 4 ft 6 in., and his mother was Bertha of the Big Foot.

BRIGHTON

Formerly Brighthelmstone, fashionable watering-place of Sussex, England. Brighton was popular even with Adolf Hitler, who gave specific orders to the Luftwaffe to take special care if they bombed the town. He wanted Brighton Pavilion preserved to be his headquarters when he landed to take charge in Britain.

BRIGID, St (452–523)

One of the busiest of all patron saints, St Brigid is called upon by cows, fugitives, midwives, newborn babies and Irish nuns. She is in greatest demand among runaway Irish nuns delivering newborn calves. She also appears just off Fleet Street as St Bride, and should not be confused with St Bridget (1302–73), daughter of the governor of Upland, Sweden.

BRITANNIA

The lady who modelled for Britannia on centuries of British coinage was Lady Frances Teresa Stewart (1647–1702), afterwards Duchess of Richmond and Lennox. Said by a contemporary commentator to have 'less wit than beauty' she liked to spend her time playing blind man's buff, or building houses of cards. She left her fortune to the upkeep of her cats.

BRITISH COLUMBIA

Western province of Canada.

☐ See **ANTARCTICA, ATHLETICS, BICYCLE, CAMEL.**

BRONTOSAURUS

(From the Greek: *bronte*, thunder; *sauros* lizard.) Belonging to the sub-order Sauropoda of the order Dinosauria, the brontosaurus weighed around 35 tons, but its brain was only one pound. The tyrranosaur was also not renowned for its intellectual capabilities, but its mouth was so big that one bite would contain enough food to feed a human family for a month. This fact was never put to practical use since, firstly, a tyrranosaur's mouth at mealtimes is not the safest place to go shopping or scavenging and secondly, there were no human families around at the time anyway.

BROTHEL

(From the Anglo-Saxon: *breothan*, to go to ruin.) A place to make money through the exploitation of immorality and weakness.

☐ See **ECONOMICS, SURGERY.**

BROWNING, Robert (1812–89)

The critic, poet and translator, Edward Fitzgerald, famed for his version of the Rubaiyat of Omar Khayyam, once displayed his lack of gallantry by writing in disparaging tones of the poetry of Elizabeth Barrett Browning (1806–61). Coming across the article years later, Robert Browning made a special trip to Boulge in Suffolk in order to dance upon Fitzgerald's grave.

BRUSSELS

(Bruxelles to the French.) The old capital of the duchy of Burgundy.

☐ See **VEGETABLE.**

BUCHANAN, James (1791–1868)

American president, born on St George's day.

☐ See **BACHELOR.**

BUCKINGHAM PALACE

Royal residence designed by a Dutchman and built in 1703 over a cesspool. Carnaby

Street lies on the site of a former plague pit. A 'hospital for fourteen leprous maidens' was demolished to make way for St James's Palace, built for Henry VIII.

Where the Bastille used to be in Paris, there is now a children's roundabout. With typical French perversity it rotates anti-clockwise.

☐ See also: *Marble Arch.*

BUCKLAND, William (1784–1856)

By profession William Buckland was canon of Christ Church (1825) and Dean of Westminster (1845), but his main interest was always geology. He stole Ben Jonson's heel bone from Westminster Abbey, and at dinner one evening swallowed an object which purported to be the embalmed heart of King Louis XIV of France. He died not long after. Louis XIV had a stomach twice the size of that of an average man.

BUDDHA (*c.* 623–543 BC)

(From the Sanskrit 'the enlightened'.) Also known as Prince Siddhartha or Gautama or Sakyamuni. One of Buddha's teeth has been preserved in a temple in Ceylon for the last 2,500 years. On special occasions it is paraded through the streets in a sacred casket. The length of the nose of the great bronze Buddha at Kamakura, Japan, is 3 ft 9 in.

☐ See also: *last words.*

BUDGERIGAR

(From the Aborigine: *budgeri*, good; *gar*, cockatoo.)

☐ See **PETS.**

BUILDING

A fundamental law of economics may underlie the findings of a recent piece of research: calculations indicate that the amount of money spent on financing research into construction methods in Britain is approximately the same as the amount of money spent on providing tea for builders on construction sites.

BULGARIA

Although the Mongolian government is trying to dissuade the rest of the world from using the word 'mongol' to indicate a sufferer from a type of mental deficiency, the Bulgarians have voiced no such official reservations about the use of the word 'bugger'. Bagarap is pidgin for disaster.

When a Bulgarian nods his head, he means 'no'.

☐ See also: *sugar.*

BULL

Male animal of the Bovidae family.

☐ See **COLOUR-BLINDNESS, NUDITY, SPERM.**

BULLFIGHTING

As can be seen from the poster overleaf, fight's will have in the after-noons and the undertakings wich have taken these spectacles at theirs expences have made all short of sacrifices for make them correspondents to this city and the border's greaters affected.

BUMPH

The derivation of the word 'bumph' comes from a Second World War slang expression for toilet paper, viz: bum-fodder. Toilet paper itself was in fact invented in 1857 by Joseph C. Gayetty, though the first known flush toilets date back to the palace of Knossos in Crete over 4,000 years ago. Four thousand years is a long time to have had to wipe one's bum on old newspapers. The average United States family of four, incidentally, wipes its way through 50,000 sheets of toilet paper a year.

BURGESS, Anthony (*b.* 1917)

British novelist.

☐ See **ANTI-SOCIAL BEHAVIOUR.**

BURIAL AT SEA

An ordinance was passed in California in 1966 making it legal to have one's ashes scattered 3 miles out to sea.

BURIAL

There is more to burial than just digging a hole in the ground and dumping a corpse in it. Among those who preferred a more individual treatment, we should like to exhume the following from the archives of burial lore: Georges Clemenceau, French Premier, whose last words were: 'I wish to be buried standing – facing Germany.' His wishes were carried out. Major Pierre Labellière went one better, choosing to demonstrate his disenchanted view of the world by being buried vertically upside down. Of course, one takes up less room with a vertical interment. Such an orientation might have been an alternative solution to Ben Jonson's dilemma. His plot in Westminster Abbey's Poets' Corner was too small for a conventional laying to rest. He finally took his place in a sitting position. India's eunuchs (known as hijras) are traditionally buried vertically, supported by a frame of sticks.

None of these gentlemen took much other than their pride with them to their graves, but others have shown that sometimes it is not only the good which men do which is interred with their bones. Blackbird, chief of the Omaha tribe, was buried astride his favourite horse. The same theme was followed by Mrs Sandra West, buried in San Antonio on 19 May 1977 exactly as stipulated in her will: '. . . next to my husband, in my lace nightgown . . . in my Ferrari, with the seat slanted comfortably'. Fortunately her husband was already dead, but the burial was accompanied by elaborate precautions to prevent grave-robbers exhuming the car, still in excellent working order. The Ferrari was blue.

Coffins have contained other things besides cars. In 1776 Margaret Thompson was buried in a coffin full of snuff, with the six greatest snuff-takers of the parish acting as pall-bearers, while Aimee Semple McPherson (1890–1944) had a telephone installed in her coffin. She had been a practising spiritualist and was hoping to carry on her work after death. But delivering the 'phone bills must have been a problem.

Another who was able to socialise posthumously was Shah Khan Jahan (reigned 1627–58), who was buried in a conical tomb with his hand stuck through the wall. Every visitor to the tomb paid his respects by shaking hands with the late Mogul Emperor. This practice continued for forty years until the appendage was too withered for further friendliness.

Of course, there is no reason why a little ceremony like burial should put an end to one's civic duties. Czar Peter III of Russia was murdered in 1762 after a brief reign of only six months. He had not had time even for a proper coronation, but this was remedied thirty-five years later, when the coffin was specially reopened to crown the late Czar.

Coffins can be a bit of a problem sometimes, since they are not really designed to be opened. The German poet, Hans von Thummel, bypassed this difficulty by being buried in an oak tree. Anyone else worried by a pressing need to escape from their coffin could well utilise one of the twenty or more devices patented to prevent the dangers of premature burial. The first such was in 1862 when Franz Vester produced a design incorporating a vertical tube, a ladder and a bell, to permit the alarm to be raised and an exit made by anyone waking up to find himself interred. In 1882 a refinement of Vester's apparatus was constructed by the appropriately named Albert Fearnaught. In Fearnaught's coffin, any hand movement by the putative corpse would release a spring and a flag of distress would be raised above the grave. Such devices are believed to have gone down well in **BASINGSTOKE.**

URMA

An intelligent use for mud has been discovered by Burmese elephants. These bright beasts have been observed to silence the bells hung around their necks by clogging them with mud in order not to be noticed when they are stealing bananas.

❏ See also: *carpentry, charity, Kipling, names, snakebite, sport.*

URNS, Robert (1759–96)

Plunging a burn into cold or icy water does far more good than rubbing butter on it.

❏ See **SPITTING.**

BUSINESS

The business with the biggest annual financial turnover in Turin is Fiat Cars. The second biggest is prostitution. Italy produces 32 per cent of the world's olives; Brazil produces 17 per cent of the world's bananas.

❏ See also: *gerbil.*

Best plunged into icy water

BUTTER

If you want rich, creamy butter, all you have to do is dip the left hand of a dead man into the cream during the churning process. (Old Irish recipe.)

□ See also: *apoplexy.*

BUTTERCUP

(*Ranunculus*) Perennial herb of the order Ranunculaceae.

□ See **DONKEY.**

BUTTERFLY

A general name for any of the dayligh Lepidoptera. The butterfly tastes with i hind feet. Sea urchins walk on the tips their teeth. (Or possibly they chew wi their legs; it depends which way you look it.) The Nile catfish swims upside down.

□ See also: *acne, barrel-organ, California eye, spoonerism.*

BUTTON

(From the French: *bouton,* a button Though known to the ancient Egyptia and even in prehistoric times, when th button was rediscovered in Europe in th fourteenth and fifteenth centuries, it wa used only as decoration. The practical us came later. The Duffel coat originated the Dutch town of Duffel. 'Buttons' mea sheep's dung.

BYRON, George Gordon Byron, 6th Baron (1788–1824)

Lord Byron (Dulwich, Harrow and Trinit College, Cambridge) had a club foo though authorities differ as to whether th was his left or right foot. At Cambridg he was not permitted to keep a dog in h rooms, so he had a pet bear. On leavin University, he entertained visitors at Nev stead Abbey, serving them wine in human skull.

□ See also: *computer, Ecuador, last words, Sophocles.*

C

CABBAGE

(From the Latin: *caput*, head.) A hardy biennial vegetable of the natural order Cruciferae and genus *Brassica*. During the First World War, to counter the bad effect which anti-German feeling was having on sales, sauerkraut was re-named 'liberty cabbage'.

☐ See also: *Churchill, J., water.*

CAGE, John (*b. 1912*)

American composer.

☐ See **RADIO, SILENCE, VEXATIONS.**

CALENDAR

(From the Latin: *calare*, to summon; *calendarium*, account book.) In Bhutan in the eastern Himalayas the calendar is carefully altered each year in order to avoid those days with bad astrological prognoses. In extreme cases, even a whole month may be omitted if the stars are inauspicious. In such circumstances, another month will simply be repeated in its place.

In 1751 the days between 25 March and 4 April were skipped in England when the calendar changed from the Julian to Gregorian system. Use of the faulty calendar had caused an eleven-day error to accumulate over the centuries. The following year, when America decided the time was ripe to catch up, George Washington changed his birthday from 11 February to 22 February in order not to miss the party. In two months in 1790 he was to spend $200 on ice cream.

☐ See also: *jaguar.*

CALIFORNIA

Anyone threatening, killing, or otherwise disturbing a monarch butterfly in Pacific Grove, California, is committing a misdemeanour (or more likely a misdemeanor) and may be fined $500 under City Ordinance 352.

☐ See also: *adolescence, amusement, beer, burial at sea, Christmas, extra-terrestrial, longevity, worms.*

CALVIN, John (1509–64)

(Not from the Latin: *calvus*, bald.) French Protestant theologian.

☐ See **PITT, William.**

CAMBODIA

(Also known as Democratic Kampuchea.) The Cambodian alphabet has seventy-two letters.

☐ See also: *frog.*

CAMBRIDGE

University city of England and intellectual capital of the civilised world.

☐ See **BYRON, CHAMPAGNE, CREATION, CROMWELL, FILMS, NOBEL, RATS.**

CAMEL

(From the Hebrew: *gamal*, a camel.)
Group of even-toed, ungulate, ruminating
mammals. The backbone of the camel is
perfectly straight. It has no gall bladder.
Hunting camels is illegal in Arizona, but if
you should capture one elsewhere, remember that you are not permitted to ride it on
the roads of British Columbia.

☐ See also: *beauty, cream, hospital,*
musical composition, road safety, Saudi
Arabia, Siberia, Somalia.

CAMEMBERT

(From Camembert in Normandy, or your
local cheese shop.) The eighth annual
camembert eating championships were
held in Paris in 1983 and won by Michel
Beaufils, who consumed eight whole
camemberts in fifteen minutes.

CAMEROON

Republic, of which the capital is Yaounde,
located by geographers just below the
bump on the left-hand side of Africa
Women of the Fali tribe in the Cameroon
may be identified by their rats' tee
earrings and their habit of wrapping the
legs in cotton rope. Cameroon is the onl
country in Africa where French and Englis
are the two official languages. When Japa
ruled Korea between 1910 and 1945, th
Korean language was banned. This migh
have been in sheer desperation at having t
cope with an alphabet possessing ten vowel
and only fourteen consonants.

CAMPANOLOGY

(From the Latin: *campana*, bell; and th
Greek: *logos*, discourse.) The science or a
of bell-ringing. A court in Sicily in 198
ruled that the Duke of Gualtieri Avarn
had every right, if he wished, to ring the be
of his private chapel whenever he ha
sexual intercourse. His family had com
plained of the noise, with bells ringing at a
times of the day and night. The Duke wa
64.

CANADA

Although no longer a part of British North America, it is clear that Canada retains a sense of decorum. It is illegal, in the streets of Winnipeg, to use a bow and arrow.

☐ See also: *Antarctica, beer, gerbil, pumpkin, saints, seaside.*

CANARY

(From the Spanish: *canario*, an inhabitant of the Canary Islands.) The brain of the canary shrinks by about 20 per cent during the winter months. The portion of it which shrivels away to nothing includes the area which controls its singing. It grows back again in the spring, when the bird learns a completely new repertoire of songs.

In humans, chronic alcoholism shrinks the left-hand side of the brain. In severe cases the brain has been found to be up to 20 per cent smaller than normal. But experimental evidence suggests that alcoholism in humans in no way inhibits the desire to sing.

We await with interest the results of possible future research on the brains of alcoholic canaries.

☐ See also: *nightingale.*

CANCER

A genus of edible crab, a constellation, a carcinoma.

☐ See **ALBANIA, ROOSEVELT, F. D., SYPHILIS.**

CANNABIS

A narcotic substance which can severely hamper the growth of caterpillars. Experiments have shown that a caterpillar egg fed on cannabis can take nine months to develop into a chrysalis, compared with the normal time of nine weeks.

In 1921 at the Museum of Fine Arts in Berne, an exhibition was held of water colours by Leo-Paul Robert. All 300 exhibits were paintings of caterpillars.

CANNIBALISM

(Anthropophagy is the nice word for it.) Each year the Aztecs sacrificed about a quarter of a million people (one per cent of the total population) to the gods. The bodies were then eaten by the masses. Such meals have been considered to provide an important protein source in the national diet. An 11-stone man has enough meat to provide a meal for seventy-five not too greedy cannibals.

In Mexico they eat ants, which have more protein than beef, chicken, fish or eggs. Smoked caterpillar is preferred in some African countries. It is as nutritious as ants and far less fattening.

☐ See also: *kuru, Scotland, wedding customs.*

Preparing the spit-roast

CANUTE, King of England (*c.* 994–1035)

The son of Sweyn Forkbeard, King of Denmark, Canute claimed the English throne at the age of 19 on Sweyn's death. He was a sensible and modest ruler but a man with a poor grasp of public relations. Now remembered chiefly for his attempt to hold back the waves, he should have taken greater pains to ensure that history never forgot that the demonstration was for the benefit of his courtiers. Canute was simply reprimanding them for their sycophantic folly in believing that he had such a power.

☐ See also: *adultery.*

CAPITAL PUNISHMENT

In 1819 there were 222 offences on the English statute book punishable by death. Among these heinous crimes against humanity were: damaging shrubs in a public garden, larceny of property greater than a shilling in value, cutting a hop-bind in a hops plantation, and breaking down the head of a fishpond so that the fish might escape.

It is against the bye-laws in Bournemouth (though not punishable by death) to fish off the pier with two rods at the same time.

☐ See also: *Edward VI, guillotine, headache, sorcery, stork.*

Who's a silly Canute?

Auditioning at Bambridge for the job of wolf-scarer

CAPP, Al

□ See **CARTOONS**.

CARBON

Non-metallic element standing at number six in the atomic table and known in the world of chemistry as C.

□ See **BODY**.

CARDANO, Girolamo (1501–76)

Alias Hieronymus Cardanus. Italian mathematician, philosopher and physician, who was either the first man to be able to solve cubic equations or the man who stole the formula from a fellow mathematician named Tartaglia.

□ See **ASTROLOGY**.

CARDS

At one time, it was claimed that playing cards were introduced into Europe for the original purpose of diverting Charles VI of France from his melancholic disposition around 1390. From 1615 there was a duty on playing cards in Britain and in the eighteenth century there was a government monopoly on making them. In 1803 one Richard Hardy was hanged for 'issuing a playing card – the ace of spades'.

□ See also: *sex.*

CAREERS

King Alfonso XIII of Spain employed an Anthem Man whose sole duty was to tell the tone-deaf king when the national anthem was being played, so that he would know when to stand.

If you cannot find a tuneless monarch to act as employer, the railways offer an assortment of attractive posts. In Japan they employ Railway Pushers whose job it is to squeeze people into rush-hour trains so that the doors will be able to close. Another technological advance that led to the creation of jobs on the railways was the invention of bubble gum in 1928. New York Central Station found themselves obliged to employ a professional gum remover whose average daily harvest was 7 lb of the sticky menace.

Escalators have provided another source of rewarding careers. When the first such moving staircase was installed at Harrod's department store in London in 1898, attendants were posted at the top of the escalator with instructions to administer brandy and smelling salts to those passengers overcome by the experience. In 1911 Earls Court underground station installed its first escalators and employed a man with a wooden leg to walk up and down to prove how safe they were and to dispel the fear other passengers might have for these demonic devices.

Another disabled person was less fortunate in his choice of career. In 1977 a Yorkshire burglar came before the courts, facing his seventh conviction. He had a withered hand, an artificial leg and one eye was missing. He was urged by the judge to take up a 'more rewarding occupation'. He might have considered applying for the job of Official Wolf-Scarer to the village of Bambridge in Yorkshire, hired for a sum of £2 a year to keep wolves at bay with a blast on his buffalo horn.

In 1982 twelve people at Thatcham in Berkshire were employed to sniff the air outside their homes in order to estimate the smell from the nearby sewage works. But this trend towards specialisation is no recent phenomenon. In medieval Japanese armies certain troops had the specific job of counting the number of decapitated heads after each battle. The Amsterdam police have a similarly specialised task-force called the grachtenvissers, whose sole duty is to cope with motorists who have driven into canals.

If they were a typically Dutch profession, the Quatorzes were quintessentially French. They earned their living by being the fourteenth at dinner parties, thereby avoiding the bad luck which would surely strike if they had not come.

If the main occupational qualification of the Quatorzes was gluttony, Miss Edith King was a young American lady who turned another of the deadly sins to her professional advantage. Miss King was employed by the United States War Department in 1905 with the task of rounding up deserters. She collected $50 for each captive. Flirtation was her only weapon, but quite sufficient to lead 500 into court.

She must have been a charming and cheerful lady. For those of a more morose disposition, it is harder to recommend a modern career. The miseries may have been born too late. In Victorian times, a professional 'mute' would earn 6d an hour to mourn at funerals.

CARLISLE

English city, 299 miles NNW of London by rail, known to the Romans as Luguvallum.

□ See **DIVORCE.**

CARNABY STREET

□ See **BUCKINGHAM PALACE.**

CAROLINE (1768–1821)

Second daughter of Charles William Ferdinand, Duke of Brunswick, and Augusta, sister of George III, she married her cousin George (later George IV) in 1795. They were formally separated after only a year. Caroline had to be forcibly restrained from attending her ex-husband's coronation in Westminster Abbey in 1821. George's worry that she might gatecrash probably contributed to his need for thirty-nine handkerchiefs during the ceremony to mop perspiration from his face. On Napoleon's death later the same year, George IV was informed that his greatest enemy had passed on. His reaction was a gleeful: 'Has she, by God!' assuming the reference to be to Caroline.

CARP

Family of fresh-water fishes known as Cyprinidae.

□ See **RUMANIA.**

CARPENTRY

(From the Latin: *carpentum*, a carriage or wagon.) The carpenter frog has a croak which sounds like the blow of a hammer. Unlike the women of the Pedaung tribe of Burma, who stretch their necks to a length of up to 40 inches with brass rings, the frog has no neck. Tigers rarely attack frogs but when they attack Pedaung women they run the risk of breaking their teeth on the brass neck bands.

CARPET

The carpet-moth (of the geometrid family Larentidae) is so called after its carpet-like markings. It is not at all related to any species which feeds upon carpets.

☐ See **INCOMPETENCE.**

ARROLL, Lewis (1832–98)

Pseudonym of Charles Lutwidge Dodgson, English author and mathematician. In the last thirty-seven years of his life, he wrote 98,721 letters to friends. There are 3,586,489 letters in the Bible.

ARTER, James Earl, Jr (*b.* 1924)

James Carter was the first American president to have been born in a hospital. There is a hospital for fish in Japan. In many Japanese hospitals and hotels there are no rooms numbered 4 or 9, because the words for those numbers sound like the words for death and suffering. It is not known whether this restriction also applies in the fish hospital to the numbering of fishbowls.

ARTOONS

James Thurber was blinded in one eye at the age of six when his brother accidentally shot him while playing with a bow and arrow. He went totally blind at the age of 45, when he had to give up his secondary career as cartoonist and concentrate on humorous writing.

Al Capp (of Li'l Abner fame) was another cartoonist to suffer an early disability. He had to have one leg amputated above the knee after a streetcar accident at the age of 12.

Charles Addams (the Addams family and other ghoulish cartoons) married in 1980 at the age of 68. His bride, Marilyn Miller, was 53 and wore black. The ceremony took place with appropriate dignity in a dog cemetery.

ASANOVA, Giovanni Jacopo (1725–98)

Casanova used to eat fifty oysters for breakfast, and always used British contraceptives.

ASTRATION

(From the Latin: *castrare*, to geld.)

☐ See **BALDNESS, BARBERS.**

CASTRO, Fidel (*b.* 1927)

President of Cuba since 1959.

☐ See **DOMINICA.**

CAT

Carnivore of the genus *felis*. In the tenth century a kitten in England was worth one penny, or fourpence if a proven mouser. A thousand years later, Peter, the Home Office cat, was on the payroll receiving £6.50 a year for his services. When he was buried in 1964, a marble memorial was erected and a ceremonial goat joined the mourners.

The Romans used weasels to catch mice. If you have neither cat nor weasel, the most effective bait in a mousetrap has been found to be not cheese but lemon-flavoured boiled sweets. Milk chocolate is a close second.

☐ See also: *Angola, auction, barbers, Borneo, Britannia, Churchill, W., Cyprus, dormouse, Eisenhower, etiquette, impotence, lemur, mating, metempsychosis, mountaineering, mouse, musical composition, Napoleon III, pets, polar bear, recycling, sedative, Whittington.*

CATARRH

(From the Greek: *kata*, down; *rhein*, flow.) Inflammation of mucous membrane, particularly nasal.

☐ See **APOPLEXY.**

CATERPILLAR

(From the Old French: *chatte peleuse*, a hairy cat.) The caterpillar has over 2,000 muscles. So great appears to be the dread of the Belgians for this musclebound creature that the law in Brussels carries a possible penalty of imprisonment for anyone who fails to kill a furry caterpillar, given the opportunity to do so.

☐ See also: *cannabis, flying.*

CATFISH

(*Anarrhichas lupus*) A fish with cat-like

features also known as the wolf-fish.
☐ See **BUTTERFLY, ELECTRICITY.**

CATHERINE OF ARAGON (1485–1536)

First wife of Henry VIII of England,
daughter of Ferdinand and Isabella of
Spain, buried in Peterborough Cathedral.
☐ See **BOLEYN.**

CATHERINE DE MEDICI (1519–89)

The French have always been conscious of
fashion and decency. In the sixteenth
century, Catherine de Medici, Queen re-
gent of France, decreed that ladies at court
must have a 13-inch waist. Restrictions had
become considerably less severe by the
nineteenth century but a special permit was
still required from the Commisariat de
Police at that time if a lady wished to wear
trousers in public.

CATHERINE PARR (1512–48)

Sixth and last wife of Henry VIII.
☐ See **REMARRIAGE.**

CATHERINE I OF RUSSIA (c. 1684–1727)

Born in Lithuania, her father, a small-
holder, died when she was an infant. She
was brought up by a Lutheran pastor as a
foundling, and married a Swedish dragoon.
In 1702 the Russians captured the town of
Marienburg, where she lived, and she went
off with the Russian general Sheremetiev.
He sold her to Prince Menshikov, who
passed her on to Peter the Great. All this
time her name had been 'Martha' but she
changed it to 'Katerina Alexeyevna' before
becoming Empress of Russia. The rest is
history.

☐ See **ALCOHOL, INSOMNIA.**

CATHERINE DE VALOIS (1401–37)

Wife of Henry V of England, youngest
daughter of the mad king Charles VI of
France, grandmother of Henry VII.
☐ See **NECROPHILIA.**

CAYMAN ISLANDS

Group of three islands (Grand Cayma
Cayman Brac, Little Cayman) in the We
Indies.

☐ See **AMAZON, CIVILISATION.**

CELERY

(Not from the Latin: *celer*, quick; whic
would have made it the original fast foo
but from the Greek: *selinon*, parsley.)
☐ See **SLIMMING.**

CELIBACY

(From the Latin: *coelebs*, unmarried
Normally taken to be an absolute state, b
it seems that some can be more celiba
than others. King Mongkut of Siam, o
whose life was based the story of th
musical 'The King and I', had in his you
been a Buddhist priest and taken a vow o
celibacy. Perhaps thanks to this vow he ha
only twelve children when he acceded
the throne of Siam in 1851 at the age of 4
He lived for another sixteen years, produ
ing 82 more children from 27 of his wive
He is reputed to have been the first perso
in Thailand to have celebrated his birthda
each year. Now most Thais (particularly o
school Thais) follow his example. Rossi
(*qv*) was able to celebrate his birthday on
every four years.

CEMETERY

(From the Greek: *koimeterion*, a sleepin
place.)
☐ See **ANGLING, BRAZIL,
 CARTOONS, PAMPERED PETS.**

CENTENARIAN

One whose life is of great length.
☐ See **DWARF.**

CENTIPEDE

Order of the Myriopoda (many-legge
animals) some of which actually do hav
over a hundred legs, thus rendering the
less likely to fall foul of the Trad

Descriptions Act than are millipedes, none of which have more than about 700. All centipedes start life with six pairs of legs, but grow more later. There are about 3,000 different species, half of which have just fifteen pairs of legs, others have up to seventy-seven pairs. The world's biggest centipede is the 46-legged Scolopendra Gigantea of South America. It is 26 cm long and eats lizards, mice and insects. All centipedes are carnivorous. Millipedes are vegetarian.

ERVANTES, Miguel de (1547–1616)

In his youth Cervantes entered the service of Cardinal Julio de Acquaviva, papal legate to Spain. While page to the Cardinal, he killed the alguacil (sheriff) Sigura, in self-defence, but was still condemned to the loss of his left hand. Later he was wounded at the battle of Lepanto, which may have caused further injury to the left arm, but he eventually settled down and wrote Don Quixote single-handed. He died on the same day as Shakespeare, 23 April 1616.

CESSPIT

A place to find filthy, evil-smelling water.

☐ See **COLOGNE.**

CEYLON

(Now Sri Lanka.) Coffee was the original crop in Ceylon, and mainstay of its economy, but in the nineteenth century the plants were destroyed by disease. Tea was then grown in its place and quickly took over. The annual harvest of one coffee tree, after being dried and ground, only produces one pound of coffee. Brazil produces twice as much coffee as India produces tea.

☐ See also: ***Buddha, Sri Lanka.***

CÉZANNE, Paul (1839–1906)

French painter who denied that he was the father of Impressionism.

☐ See **MODESTY.**

CHAMELEON

(From the Greek: *chamai*, on the ground; *leon*, lion.) The tongue of the chameleon can be twice as long as its body. Tongues of frogs and toads and such creatures grow out of the front of their mouths to increase their range for fly-catching.

CHAMPAGNE

The correspondence columns of the British Medical Journal in 1981 featured an interesting debate on the relative dangers of corks and rubber bungs when ejected at speed from champagne bottles. One letter finally gave the correct, and safe, opening procedure for champagne: Hold the cork firmly with your dominant hand and twist the bottle with the other hand. The ideal angle of inclination at which to hold the bottle is between 45° and 60°. In Cambridge, more eye injuries are caused by squash balls than by champagne corks, but these are the two top ocular dangers.

☐ See also: ***Duncan, Frederick the Great, genius.***

A frog toying with its lunch (see Chameleon*)*

CHAPLIN, Sir Charles Spencer (1889–1977)

Charlie Chaplin was born on the same day as Adolf Hitler. At the height of his fame, he received 70,000 letters in two days. The extent of Herr Hitler's fan mail is not known.

CHARITY

In Burma, giving money to charity is interpreted as a confession of guilt and an indication of a desire for atonement. Queen Victoria made a charitable gesture in 1842 when she offered to pay income tax. The Department of Inland Revenue, in good Burmese style, refused her offer. When Elisa Bonaparte, sister of Napoleon I, lay dying in 1820, friends tried to comfort her by saying that there was nothing as certain as death. She replied: 'Except taxes', and expired.

CHARLEMAGNE (742–814)

The Emperor Charlemagne (or Charles the Great) had a more exciting life after death than most. He was embalmed in a sitting position and remained on his throne from 814 until 1215 when he was finally given a decent burial. Later Otto III, Duke of Saxony, broke into Charlemagne's tomb and found the body in good repair except for some apparent fingernail growth (more probably finger tissue shrinkage) and a decayed nose. He trimmed the nails and repaired the nose with gold.

☐ See also: ***breeding, illiteracy, Pitt.***

CHARLES I, King of Great Britain and Ireland (1600–49)

Even with his head attached, Charles I was only 4ft 7 in. tall. By a statute of 1835 it is illegal to wear fancy dress for advertising purposes within three miles of the statue of Charles I in Whitehall.

☐ See also: ***Henry Frederick, salt, shivering.***

CHARLES II, King of Great Britain and Ireland (1630–85)

Second son of Charles I.

☐ See **NAPKIN, PRAGMATISM, SCROFULA, THEATRE.**

CHARLES VI, King of France (1294–1328)

Called Charles the Well-beloved, son of Charles V, called Charles the Wise.

☐ See **CARDS.**

CHARLES VII, King of Sweden

King Charles VII of Sweden was executed in 1167. There is no record of there ever having been any Kings Charles I to VI. The Swedish are, however, a very superstitious people. Their actors believe it to be lucky to be kicked in the rear before a performance.

CHARLES VIII, King of France (1470–98)

King Charles VIII of France was one of the few fatalities caused by the game of tennis. Conducting his queen, Anne of Brittany, onto a tennis court, he bashed his head on the lintel and died of the fractured skull which he incurred. Another royal to meet a sporting end was Frederick, Prince of Wales, who was killed after being struck by a cricket ball in 1737.

☐ See also: *France.*

CHARLES THE BALD, King of Germany (823–77)

Half-brother of Louis the German, King of East France. Louis's son was Charles the Fat. They carved up **GERMANY** between them in the ninth century.

CHARLES THE BOLD, Duke of Burgundy (1433–77)

Fifteenth-century ruler of Burgundy, son of Philip the Good.

☐ See **AUSTRIA.**

CHEESE

Wholesome foodstuff from milk curd and the Latin *caseus.*

☐ See **MONET, RAT, UMBRELLA, ZOROASTER.**

CHEESEBURGER

This has no connection with any town named Cheeseburg in Germany.

☐ See **PSYCHIATRY.**

CHEETAH

(*Cynaelurus jubatus.*) Member of the cat family which purrs when stroked.

☐ See **MUSICAL APPRECIATION, SPEED.**

CHELSEA

District of London, England.

☐ See **LIBYA.**

CHEMISTRY

Formerly chymistry, the branch of science concerned with the composition of substances. A biochemist in the United States recently estimated the value of the ingredients in the human body (including small traces of rare chemicals) to be approximately 6 million dollars. Any latter-day Frankenstein wishing to compose a human from the basic ingredients would be advised to do his shopping somewhere other than in Zaire, where there are fewer chemists' shops per head of population than anywhere else on earth. If he likes mushrooms, the decision might be different. Zaire has the biggest mushrooms in the world.

☐ See also: *discovery.*

CHEROKEE

North American Indian tribe of Iroquoian stock.

☐ See **TREE.**

CHESHAM

For Chesham, change at Chalfont.

☐ See **LONDON.**

CHESS

Despite being born in 1937 with only three fingers on his right hand, Mikhail Tal won the World Chess Championship in 1960. When rooks make their nests high in trees, it is said to be a sign of a good summer, nests lower down presage cold, wet weather.

☐ See also: *universe.*

CHESTERFIELD

Market town of Derbyshire, England. In 1978 a team was engaged to dredge Chesterfield canal. They did an exceptionally thorough job, but had some difficulty shifting an old and rusty chain lurking on the bottom. After the job was completed and the dredgers had departed, complete with chain as trophy, the level of water in the canal gradually fell, until one and a half miles of waterway had completely disappeared. The chain which they had removed was attached to the plug for the canal. The River Idle had a busier day than usual coping with the outflow.

CHEWING GUM

A masticatory, dating back to the seventeenth century when it was prepared from isinglass, but popularised this century made from chicle gum of the sapodilla plum tree

☐ See **CAREERS, CULTURE.**

CHICAGO

City of Illinois, USA. In a sixty-year period in Chicago, over 1,000 murders were committed. Prosecutions secured only thirteen convictions. During the first television interview given by the Beatles in the United States, practically no major crime was committed by a teenager anywhere in the country.

☐ See also: *acronym.*

CHICKEN

The average British hen lays 230 eggs year. This is a more efficient utilisation of food production methods than eating the bird itself since 2½ lb of grain need to b invested for every pound of chicken meat.

☐ See also: ***cuckoo, envy, knowledge, Melbourne, shoplifting, umbrella.***

CHIENS

The all-American wonder dog, Rin-Tin-Tin, was born in France. Every year in France 3,500 postmen are bitten by dogs, causing a loss of 65,500 days off work. There are eighty flushing lavatories for dogs in Paris.

CHILBLAINS

According to a Derbyshire remedy, chilblains should be thrashed with holly. According to Noel Coward, certain women should be struck regularly, like gongs (*Private Lives*).

CHILDREN

The ancient Greeks believed that the womb had two compartments: one on the right from which girls emerged and one on the left for boy babies. Hippocrates completed this symmetrical picture with a belief that the testes were similarly programmed one to produce girls, the other for boys.

A survey was conducted in 1981 to discover what most annoyed British children. The most popular reply was 'my brother', followed closely by 'my sister'.

CHILE

Republic of South America, 2,650 miles long, 120 miles wide, having no public lavatories.

☐ See also: ***cowboy, Sahara.***

CHIMPANZEE

(*Anthropopithecus troglodytes*)

☐ See **ART, ETIQUETTE.**

CHINA

China is the world's greatest place for disasters. Nineteenth-century rebellions accounted for the deaths of approximately 30 million people; the general famine between 1969 and 1971 killed about another

French postmen also have trouble with cats sometimes

20 million; 3½ million succumbed to the floods of 1931. Compared with these figures, the 830,000 engulfed in the 1556 earthquake hardly merits a mention on an inside page. Despite all these accidents, about one in seven of the world's population persist in speaking Mandarin Chinese.

☐ See also: **demography, Ford, India, Kipling, misogyny, money, orange, panda, peanut, prudery, relativity, Saudi Arabia, sausage, suicide, wind.**

CHLOROFORM

(Trichloromethane, $CHCl_3$.) The use of chloroform in childbirth was opposed by the clergy, citing the text: 'in sorrow thou shalt bring forth children'. In 1853, however, Queen Victoria sanctioned the use of chloroform for the birth of her second child, having had quite enough sorrow with the first. Thereafter the clergy were silent on the matter.

In the Middle Ages, it was generally believed that men were born with one less rib than women because of the account of Eve's creation in the Book of Genesis.

CHOCOLATE

Beverage and confectionery prepared from the bean of the Cacao Theobroma. In Central America in the eighteenth century, chocolate was considered a temptation of the devil, with the penalty of excommunication for anyone caught drinking it. Puritans in Europe concurred with these views, denouncing it for 'inflaming the lusts of the flesh'. The chocolate bar, doubtless less inflammatory than the drink, was not invented until 1847; milk chocolate followed in 1876. In fact the Spanish had been the first to drink chocolate in Europe, when it was imported from Mexico in 1520. The first nice cup of cocoa in England was drunk around 1656.

Inflammation of the lusts caused by chocolate must be a common inconvenience in Switzerland where enough of the stuff is sold every day to provide two large bars for every member of the population.

☐ See also: **acne, aphrodisiac, cat, gramophone, toothache.**

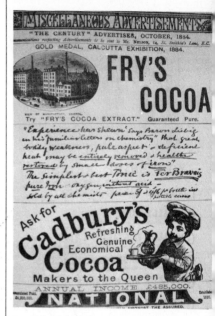

CHOLESTEROL

(From the Greek: *chole*, bile; *stereos*, firm.)

☐ See **KANGAROO, POSSUM.**

CHOPIN, Frédéric François (1810–49)

Polish composer whose first composition, the G-minor Polonaise, was written at the age of seven. He died thirty-two years later. Chopin's heart was buried in Poland, the remainder of him rests in Paris. Henry I of England enjoys a similar posthumous bisection, with most of him in England but his bowels are buried in France.

A portion of Napoleon's intestines used to be kept at the Royal College of Surgeons in London, but they were destroyed in an air raid sometime in 1940.

☐ See also: ***musical composition.***

HOWDER

(From the French: *chaudière*, a pot.) Fish dish with meat and veg (optional).

☐ See **KENNEDY.**

HRISTENING

Until 1970 names of French children had to be chosen from an approved list at the Ministry of the Interior. Just the sort of restriction to nomenclature one might expect from the country which gave car number plates to the world in 1893. But such an idea may also restrain parents from wild folly; a retired United States paratrooper recently named his children Ripcord and Canopy. The parachute, incidentally, was invented about a century before the aeroplane. The first successful jump by parachute was by a dog in a basket pushed out of a balloon in 1785.

HRISTINA, Queen of Sweden (1626–89)

☐ See **BODY, DESCARTES.**

HRISTMAS

The celebration of Christmas was abolished in 1644. The Puritans also banned the singing of Christmas carols and illegalised the eating of mince pies and plum pudding, both denounced as heathen practices. It is still against the law to eat these substances on Christmas Day. In California, however, the Christmas spirit evidently lives on. On 25 December 1983, in Oakland, California, a 70-year-old woman shot and killed her husband, aged 72, because he was having an affair with another woman.

☐ See also: ***Denmark.***

HRYSIPPUS (287–207 BC)

A stoic philosopher of Tarsus who thought it good that parents should marry their children, and advised that dead bodies should be eaten rather than buried.

☐ See **HUMOUR.**

CHRONOMETRY

(From the Greek: *chronos*, time; *metron*, measure.) Travelling from Washington to San Francisco in 1870, one would have had to set one's watch more than two hundred times if it was to give correct local time at all places. Only with the Prime Meridian Conference in Washington in 1884 was the world divided into time zones and Greenwich selected as the central point from which all times were calculated. Before the great clock-setting of 1884, St Petersburg was exactly 2 hr 1 min 18.7 sec ahead of Greenwich.

CHURCHILL, John, 1st Duke of Marlborough (1650–1722)

John Churchill, 1st Duke of Marlborough, was allergic to cabbage.

CHURCHILL, Lord Randolph (1849–95)

British politician and third son of the 7th Duke of Marlborough. He died on 24 January 1895, but not before he had become the father of Winston Churchill, who was also to die on 24 January in 1965. The other important date to remember is 5 April, date of the resignations of both Winston Churchill and Harold Wilson. Winston Churchill, incidentally, had the same governess when a child as Clement Attlee.

CHURCHILL, Sir Winston Leonard Spencer (1874–1965)

Winston Churchill was born in a ladies' cloakroom at Blenheim Castle. Perhaps this accident influenced his parents' choice of his initials. He often took his cat with him to cabinet meetings and had a lucky walking stick which he always carried with him on Fridays.

An elegant walking stick with a monkey on the handle

Benjamin Franklin had a crabtree walking stick with a gold head, which he left in his will to George Washington.

☐ See also: *insomnia, last words, Manhattan.*

CICADA

Group of large, four-winged insects. The cicada spends seventeen years developing as a larva then enjoys a brief four-week life as an adult. But all those years in the larval stage have not been totally wasted, a female cicada can hear the call of her mate a mile away.

CICERO (104–43 BC)

Roman poet, orator and statesman Marcus Tullius was called Cicero because he had a wart on the end of his nose. *Cicer* is the Latin for wart.

☐ See also: *beans.*

CIGARETTE

(Diminutive of the word cigar, from the Spanish *cigarro*.) The cigarette owes its invention to Turkish troops who were forced to improvise at the Battle of Acre in 1799 when their hookah was destroyed by French cannon fire. In those early days every cannon ball should have come with a government health warning.

☐ See also: *Albania, Cuba, productivity, Stalin.*

CIRCUMCISION
☐ See **HAIRCUT.**

CIRCUMNAVIGATION

If all the corks from all the wine bottled in France in a single year were stuck together they would go round the world three times. If all the roads in the USA were joined up they would go round the world 153 times. Or, if you preferred, you could wrap them fifty-one times round the French corks.

☐ See also: *Australia.*

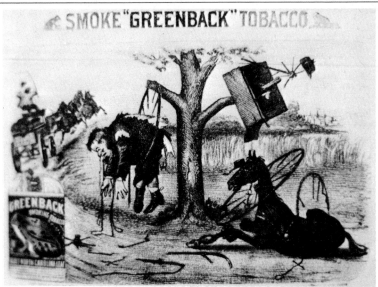

CIRRHOSIS

(From the Greek: *kirrhos*, a reddish-yellow colour.)

☐ See **GEORGE IV, PITT.**

CIVILISATION

There are 170 million telephones in the United States and 350 million phone calls are made every day. Photocopying comes close behind with the Americans indulging their reproductive urges in this manner 300 million times a day (half the world's total daily production of photocopies). Nevertheless, Monaco has the highest number of telephones for its size of population, with almost one phone per person. The Cayman Islands lead the Telex race with about one Telex machine per 100 people.

CIVIL SERVICE

Mandarins in ancient China always faced south when called upon to act in authority. Their Civil Service entrance exams were taken over a period of three days spent in solitary confinement. Any candidate who died during this time was liable to be lifted out through the roof, since the gates to the examination halls would not be unlocked under any circumstances.

Emperors of China always faced south when ascending their thrones. No corpse was permitted to enter a Chinese city by the southern gate.

CLAM

A bivalve mollusc.

☐ See **LONGEVITY.**

CLARENCE, George, Duke of (1449–78)

☐ See **EDWARD IV.**

CLARKE, Jeremiah (*c.* 1674–1707)

Composer and organist.

☐ See **PURCELL.**

CLEANLINESS

Two tramps, Pat Burke and Billy O'Rourke, were given a bath in a St Louis hostel in 1903. It was their first bath for twenty years. They both died shortly afterwards.

☐ See also: *soap.*

CLEMENCEAU, Georges Eugène Benjamin (1841–1929)

French statesman, writer and pigeon-keeper.

☐ See **BURIAL.**

CLEOPATRA (69–30 BC)

Whatever may be said against Cleopatra, it cannot be denied that she loved her brothers. At the age of 18, she married one of her brothers, Ptolemy XIII, who was then aged 12. When she was 24, she married her other brother Ptolemy XIV, also aged 12. After running out of Ptolemies she moved on to dalliances with Julius Caesar and Mark Antony.

She gave her name to Cleopatra's needles. A remarkable donation, since the obelisks were originally erected at Heliopolis by Thothmes III around 1475 BC over 1400 years before Cleopatra was born. When the London needle was en route to its destination on the Embankment in 1877, it was encased in a raft for towing by sea. It had to be abandoned in a storm in the Bay of Biscay and was only recovered thanks to the generosity of Sir Erasmus Wilson who defrayed the expenses of the salvation trip.

Both Cleopatra and Margaret Thatcher gave birth to twins.

CLOCK

In Shakespeare's Julius Caesar, Act II, Scene i, a clock strikes three. 'Peace! count the clock,' says Brutus. 'The clock hath stricken three,' replies Trebonius. Neither is at all surprised, despite the fact that the chiming clock was not to be invented for another fourteen centuries.

☐ See also: *Malta, Salisbury, starling.*

CLOTHES

In fourteenth-century France, King Philip the Fair decreed restrictions on the number of items of clothing owned by his subjects. Dukes, counts, barons and their wives were permitted to possess not more than four garments; unmarried women were restricted to a single dress, unless they were heiresses with castles. However, there was no limit on the number of shoes allowed to lurk on wardrobe floors.

CLOTHES PEG

Since 1979 there has been a quota imposed on the import of clothes pegs into the United States. Originally made for three years, this important order was renewed for a further two years in 1982.

CLOWN

Each clown performing in any circus has his own individual face which is registered and copyrighted by being painted on an eggshell.

COAL

Colombia has more coal reserves than the rest of South America combined. Colombians wishing to give thanks for this amazing natural gift may find it appropriate to worship in the underground cathedral in the city of Zipaquira.

☐ See also: *productivity.*

COCA-COLA

Coca-Cola is a registered trade mark.

☐ See **BIBLE, HEADACHE.**

COCK

A cock (or rooster if you prefer) was tried in Basle, Switzerland, in 1474 on the charge of laying an egg. The case was long and well argued. The prosecution satisfactorily proved its case concerning the magical value of a cock's egg. Counsel for the cock, however, claimed that laying an egg was an involuntary act and therefore not punish able in law. Despite his efforts, the cock was found guilty and, together with its egg, was burnt at the stake 'not as a cock but as a sorcerer or devil in the form of a cock'.

☐ See also: *alectryomancy.*

OCKROACH

(From the Spanish: *cucaracha*, a cockroach.) The brain of the cockroach is not essential for its survival. If its head is cut off carefully, the cockroach can still live for some weeks. Properly looked after it will then die eventually of starvation.

An old English folk cure for earache involves stuffing into the affected ear a cockroach boiled in oil. Boiling in oil may generally be recommended as a more reliable way of killing the pest than cutting its head off. As many restaurant customers have discovered, baking them into a meal generally finishes them off too.

☐ See also: *bounty hunters, electricity, evolution.*

OCKTAIL PARTY

The expression 'Cocktail Party' dates back all the way to 1929.

☐ See SEX.

OCOA

(More correctly, cacao.)
☐ See APHRODISIAC.

OCONUT

Fruit of the coconut palm (*Cocos nucifera*). In the Solomon Islands, there are nine different words for the various stages of maturation of the coconut. In the Eskimo language there are more than twenty words for snow. In the Nigerian Navy, however, there are twenty ships all of whose names mean 'hippopotamus' in various dialects of the country.

OD

An edible fish (*Gadus morrhua*).
☐ See FRECKLES.

CODPIECE

(From the Old English: *codd*, a small bag.)
☐ See ETIQUETTE, FASHION.

COFFEE

(From the Arab: *qahwah*; or the Turkish: *qahveh*.) Genus of trees and shrubs of the order Rubiaceae. They drink more coffee in Sweden (eleven cups each every day on average) than anywhere else on earth. Gambling, however, is illegal in Sweden. The Irish drink more tea (eight cups a day each) than any other nation. The British manage to indulge their love of tea only five times a day, while it takes the average American two days to drain each teacup. In Cornwallis, Oregon, it is illegal for a young girl to buy coffee after 6 pm.

☐ See also: *Ceylon, Frederick the Great, Gustav III, Voltaire.*

COFFIN

Until recently the most common method of execution in Mongolia was to nail the victim into a wooden coffin and leave him to die. Mongolia is the largest inland country in the world.

☐ See also: *Bernhardt, Nelson.*

COINCIDENCE

The north German liner *Grosser Kurfurst* sailed from Bremen to New York in 1906. On the voyage three mothers gave birth. The woman in third class had triplets, the one travelling second class had twins, and the lady in first class produced just a single baby.

☐ See also: *shipwreck.*

COLERIDGE, Samuel Taylor (1772–1834)

British poet whose original intention had been to apprentice himself to a shoemaker.

☐ See BAUDELAIRE.

COLIC

(From the Greek: *kolikos*, pertaining to the

colon.) Disease bringing acute abdominal pains.

□ See **APOPLEXY, WIND.**

COLOGNE

German city and state of the Holy Roman Empire. In 1956 the manufacturers of the brand of Eau de Cologne known as 4711 brought an action against Herr Koelsch of Siegen in northern Germany. Their objection was that Herr Koelsch, by profession an emptier of cess-pits, was plying his trade by displaying his phone number prominently on the side of his business van. His phone number was 4711.

□ See also: *germ warfare.*

COLOMBIA

A republic of the Andes.

□ See **BOLIVIA, COAL, GOLDFISH.**

COLORADO BEETLE

(Or Potato Bug, Chrysomela or Doryphora decemlineata.)

□ See **ASTHMA.**

COLOUR-BLINDNESS

(Also known as Daltonism or achromatopsia.) Waving a red rag at a bull has precisely the same effect as waving any other colour of rag, since bulls cannot distinguish red from other hues. Men are ten times more likely to be colour-blind than women. The gene responsible is on the sex-linked chromosome; the daughter of a colour-blind mother will probably be normal, but the son will be colour-blind.

Giraffes cannot distinguish between green, yellow and orange. Neither can they sleep lying down for more than five minutes at a time.

□ See also: *hamster, medicine.*

COLUMBUS, Christopher (c. 1451–1506)

Before Christopher Columbus set foot in the Americas, no native American Indian had blood type B. If all the blood vessels in the human body were laid end to end, they would stretch 100,000 miles.

□ See also: *Antigua.*

COMA

(From the Greek: *koma*, lethargy.) A condition of profound unconsciousness. Ringo Starr of the Beatles (or Richard Starkey as he was then known) was in a coma for ten days after an attack of appendicitis at the age of 6. Edward VII is the only English king whose coronation had to be postponed to allow an emergency appendectomy to be performed.

COMMITTEES

According to a study published in the Harvard Business Review, the average American committee comprises eight executives, each of whom wishes at least three of the other seven were not on the committee.

COMMON COLD

Whisky is widely regarded as one of the few effective remedies for this ailment, but only an old Canadian cure specifies precisely how to determine the correct dosage: remove your hat and place it on a table; continue drinking the whisky until two hats are visible, then go to bed and stay there.

There is an equally simple old English cure, starting at the other end of the body: remove shoes and stockings, run a finger between your toes, then sniff the finger.

More modern research into the common cold, at the University of Michigan, shows that the incidence of colds is higher among the better educated. It is generally believed that the incidence of smelly feet is higher among the less well educated, so this finding would tally with the view that odorous toes are good for a cold.

☐ See also: *ferret, shark, sneezing, Sri Lanka.*

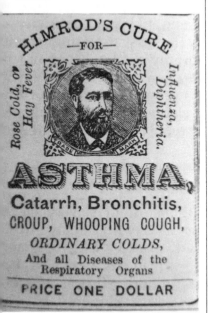

COMMUNICATION

The Karaja Indians of the Amazon valley speak through their noses with their mouths closed. Males and females have a different dialect and can barely understand one another. Analogous phenomena have been reported in London's Thames valley.

COMMUNISM

J. Edgar Hoover was director of the FBI from 1924 until his death in 1972. He was so anti-communist that he would never let his chauffeur take a left turn in the car. This necessitated lengthy detours and ingenious route planning, but it kept them free from sinister influences. In Japan only the Imperial family may use a maroon-coloured car.

COMPASSION

Gary Smart of Smart's Circus was once given two weeks compassionate leave from his army service because a killer whale was pining for him back home.

COMPENSATION

In 1972, Bimbo the elephant lost interest in dancing and water-skiing after a road accident involving the trailer in which he was travelling. The California Supreme Court awarded 7-year-old Bimbo accident damages of $4,500. The name of the judge was Turtle.

In 1974 spoon-bender Uri Geller had a paternity suit filed against him by a young mother in Sweden. She did not allege any amorous liaison, but claimed that his powers over metal objects had rendered her contraceptive coil inoperative.

☐ See also: *lip.*

COMPUTER

The first computer ever to be designed was Charles Babbage's 'analytical engine', a steam-powered calculating machine. Owing to lack of finance it was never built. Babbage's assistant was Byron's daughter, Augusta Ada, Countess Lovelace, the

Re-training for basketball after his water-skiing career is over (see Compensation*)*

spiritual mother of computer programming.

CONAN DOYLE, Sir Arthur (1859–1930)

Like his creation Sherlock Holmes, Sir Arthur Conan Doyle found cocaine a stimulant to his thinking processes. On his only known innings at Lords in a cricket match between Authors and Publishers, he only scored fourteen runs, batting at number five in the order, but he did take the wickets of both Publishers' opening batsmen, each of whom was out for a duck.

There is a statue of a duck erected at Freiburg, West Germany, in memory of its alerting the population to an impending air raid on 17 November 1944.

☐ See also: *hobbies, Holmes.*

CONDUCTORS

Anyone who wants to become a great British conductor would be well advised t be born on 29 April. Sir Thomas Beecha and Sir Malcolm Sargent shared that birt day.

CONFIDENCE TRICKSTERS

Arthur Ferguson made a practice of sellin British monuments to unsuspecting an highly gullible tourists. In 1924 he sold B Ben for £1,000, accepted an offer of £6,0C for Nelson's column and even took a dow payment on Buckingham Palace. He di not, however, fool as many people as di Eric the Red, who, in 982, named a hug and barren land 'Greenland' in order t encourage Norsemen to emigrate ther His implied promise of greenery succeede in tricking twenty-five boatloads to mak the long journey.

CONGO

In some tribal villages in the Congo a mother giving birth to twins is put to deat It is considered to be proof that she h been unfaithful. Little surprise then th there are no armadillos in the Congo, sin the armadillo always produces identic twins.

CONJUNCTION

A part of speech joining together (from th Latin: *conjunctio*, a joining together) par of a sentence. 'And' is a copulative co junction (from the Latin: *copula*, a joinir together). A conjunction of Saturn, Jupit and Mars was held to be responsible f bringing the Great Plague of 1348 t Europe.

On 2 February 1962 a conjunction c eight planets, the first such event for fo centuries, was predicted to portend the en of the world. Indian astrologers led millio in a massive pray-in, burning marigolds an tons of butter and chanting the liturgy 4 million times. The Burmese Prime Minist set free an assortment of bulls, pigs, goat doves and crabs to placate the deities. worked and the world rolls on.

'Notwithstanding' is the longest conjunction in English in common use.

☐ See also: *flood.*

CONSOLATION

Giving solace to someone in distress. In 1613 the Archbishop of Canterbury was in distress after shooting a gamekeeper while out hunting. King James I offered suitable words of consolation by telling him that the Queen had recently killed his favourite dog in just the same manner.

CONSTANTINE V, East Roman Emperor 719–75)

☐ See **GREECE.**

CONSTANTINOPLE

(Now Istanbul, on the site of the old Byzantium.) The history of Constantinople betrays a certain repetitiveness: in 695, Leontius overthrew the Emperor Justinian II and cut off his nose; in 698, General Tiberius III overthrew Leontius and cut off his nose; in 705, the noseless Justinian overthrew Tiberius to reclaim his throne. He also put an end to the saga of proboscectomies by executing both Tiberius and Leontius.

CONSTIPATION

The world record duration for an attack of constipation is 102 days. It must have happened in a land devoid of pomegranates. Eating the bark of the pomegranate tree cures constipation.

CONSUMMATION

☐ See **ACCIDENTS.**

CONTACT LENS

☐ See **DOG.**

CONTRACEPTION

The earliest recorded contraceptive concoction comes from an Egyptian papyrus of around 1850 BC. Honey, soda, crocodile excrement and a gummy substance had to be combined and introduced into the vagina. The first contraceptive sheaths, used by the Romans, were made of sheep's intestines; the earliest diaphragms were the peel of half an orange. By the seventeenth century AD science had progressed and it was commonly believed that bare-footed sex prevented pregnancy because the vital fluids would rush to warm the cold feet. It was more fun than crocodile dung anyway.

☐ See also: *Casanova, demography, euphemism, pigeon.*

The barrier method of contraception is 100 per cent effective

CONVERSATION

Three-quarters of the world's population speak one of the twenty-five major languages. The top one hundred languages account for about 95 per cent of all human speech. The remaining 5 per cent is spread among 8,000 different tongues. In normal conversational English more than a quarter of all the words spoken will be found in this list of eleven: I, the, of, and, a, to, in, that, is, it, you.

☐ See also: *flax.*

CONVEYANCING

The oldest conveyance of which there is record is that of the cave of Macpelah from the sons of Heth to Abraham. The language of conveyancing has altered but little in the interim:

'And the field of Ephron which was in Macpelah, which was before Mamre, the field, and the cave which was therein, and all the trees that were in the field, that were in all the borders round about, were made sure unto Abraham.' We do not know whether Abraham also had a survey done of the property. The illustration shows a surveyor testing for dry rot.

COOK, James (1728–79)

British navigator.

☐ See **ANTIGUA, MISUNDERSTANDING.**

COOKERY

It is of prime importance to cook your roa for the correct length of time. In 1973 Frenchman, M. Noel Carriou, aged 54, wa sentenced to eight years imprisonment fo killing his second wife after she overdid h roast. Seventeen years earlier he had bee found to be responsible for the death of h first wife, after throwing her out of bed an breaking her neck during an argument. Th dispute had been caused by her serving hi underdone meat.

The sufferings of M. Carriou might b compared with those of Frau Irmgar Brens, who lived in Berlin in the nineteent century. Frau Brens was widowed six time Each of her husbands committed suicide.

☐ See also: *Sauce Béarnaise.*

COOLIDGE, John Calvin (1872–1933)

American president whose last words were 'Good morning, Robert.'

☐ See **INDEPENDENCE.**

COOPERPERSON, Ellen

☐ See **NAMES.**

COPULATION

☐ See **BOREDOM, MATING, MYXOMATOSIS, WHALE.**

CORMORANT

(From the Latin: *corvus marinus*, se crow.) In Yugoslavia, trained cormoran are used to catch fish. The bird has a bar tied round its neck to prevent it fro swallowing and the catch may easily b removed from its mouth. Emperor Hir hito of Japan was one of his country's lea ing authorities on fish.

CORNEAL TRANSPLANT
☐ See **DRAGONFLY, JAUNDICE.**

CORONATION
The coronation of William III posed a great constitutional problem. James II had fled with parliament already dissolved, but only parliament had the power to declare William king, and only the King could summon a new parliament. The dilemma was resolved by simultaneously declaring the new King and summoning the parliament which made the declaration. William III thus became the first English monarch to have been baptised with more than one name, but Henry VIII was the first to be called 'Your Majesty'.

☐ See also: *coma, Edward VII.*

CORPSE
☐ See **AMUSEMENT, BIRTHMARK, CRUELTY, SOMALIA.**

CORSICA
Mediterranean island and birthplace of Napoleon I.

☐ See **COUVADE.**

COSMETICS
(From the Greek: *kosmein*, to beautify.) The largest make-up job in the history of the cinema may have been that which had to be performed on Anna May in the film *The Great Barnum*. She played the part of Jumbo the elephant and needed artificial ears and dummy tusks to conceal the fact that she was really an Indian elephant. Nero's wife, Poppaea, did not, as far as is known, wear artificial ears, but she did preserve her good looks with a nightly face mask of breadcrumbs and asses' milk.

☐ See also: *Coventry, Japan.*

COUVADE
(From the French: *couvade*, hatching.) Couvade is a custom shared by many primitive tribes whereby the husband shares his wife's labour pains during childbirth. It dates back to Corsica in the first century, out has been observed in modern times among the Witoto tribe of the Amazon. While no doubt appreciating the husband's suffering on her behalf, the wife may maintain some reservations about the full couvade ritual, which demands her returning to work as soon as possible, often on the day of the birth itself, and continuing to minister to her still ailing spouse.

COVENTRY
Lady Coventry died on 1 October 1760 from the effects of painting her face with white lead. She thus became the first martyr to modern cosmetics. Isabel of Bavaria, a fourth-century queen of France, used the far safer concoction of boars' brains, wolf's blood and crocodile glands.

COW
The cow has four stomachs. There is no concrete evidence that cows ever sleep, but in Moscow circuses they have been trained to play football. An Austrian animal trainer once spent fifteen years before he finally succeeded in training a trout to jump into a beer mug.

☐ See also: *acronym, boils, crime, defection, dentistry, fright, hospital, lactation, rabies, road safety, sorcery, Switzerland, yak.*

COWARD, Noel (1899–1976)
☐ See **CHILBLAINS.**

COWARDICE
☐ See **ELEGANCE.**

COWBOY
An aid to identifying cowboys in South America is the knowledge that Chilean cowboys (called *huasos*) use stirrups made of wood. The gauchos in Argentina wear boots made of pony hide with a hole in the front to give their big toes freedom to move. Despite this advantage, it can still be

quicker to travel by rail in Argentina, especially since that country has more miles of railway than road.

☐ See also: ***Bentham, manure.***

CRAB

The nobody crab has no body.

☐ See also: ***speed.***

CRAMP

According to an old English remedy, this painful condition can be avoided by wearing an eel garter. In Lincolnshire, where eels were perhaps in short supply, a layer of cork between the bedsheets, or between bed and mattress, was preferred as a cramp prophylactic. If these preventive measures fail, cramp may be cured by carrying the foot of a mole in your pocket. The forefoot of the mole is appropriate for cramp in the arms, the hind foot for leg cramps. But do be careful, because pocketing the wrong mole foot will cause the cramp to spread.

☐ See also: ***hare, wind.***

CRANE

(From the Greek: *geranos*.) Family of birds of the order Grallatores (Latin, going on stilts).

☐ See **TERRAPIN.**

CRAP

(Originally from the Old Dutch: *krappe*, but usage of the word was considerably enhanced by Thomas Crapper, English sanitary engineer, whose name appeared on his porcelain devices.)

☐ See **ACRONYM, RUMANIA.**

CREAM

Cream made from camel's milk is the best way yet discovered to rid oneself of fleas. Just smear the cream over a passing friend or stranger and the fleas will instantly desert you for him. There is nothing fleas like better than camel's cream. A camel can drink 35 gallons of water in ten minutes.

CREATION

James Usher (1581–1656), Bishop of Meath, calculated the date of the creation to have been 23 October 4004 BC. John Lightfoot (1602–75), Vice-Chancellor of Cambridge University, agreed with him and pointed out that it happened at 9 am. Their logic was based upon Biblical sources. Genesis identifies the day of the creation as the autumnal equinox (when periods of light and dark will be equal) and the rest follows impeccably.

On less theological and more observational grounds, the Greek philosopher Heraclitus believed that a new sun was created every morning.

CREMATION

Dr William Price, a Victorian advocate of cremation (from the Latin: *cremare*, to burn) stated in his will that he desired his

Escape from the crematorium

body to be burned in public, on the top of a hill. His request was carried out, and a crowd of 20,000 turned up, and indeed paid a small sum each, for the privilege of watching the ceremony.

☐ See also: *lost property, reincarnation.*

CREOSOTE

An oily tarry liquid, or an American bush (*Larrea mexicana* of the family Zygophyllaceae) which smells like an oily, tarry liquid.

☐ See **LONGEVITY.**

RETE

Mediterranean island.

☐ See **BUMPH.**

CRICKET

The summer game in England; the winter game in India. In 1933 in Mysore a 17-year-old wicket-keeper named Nurayana was killed by the metal shoe of a cricket stump which had been shattered by a fast bowler. The fragment pierced his heart killing him instantly. No such tragedy ever befell the East Ham Corinthians cricket team in 1923, though they regularly took to the field with a one-legged wicket-keeper, Mr S. J. H. Corner. The mating call of the cricket is pitched at the third D above high C.

☐ See also: *amputees, Charles VIII, Conan Doyle, missionary, temperature, umpiring, Wodehouse.*

CRIME

The punishment for the crime of insulting the King's bard in ancient Britain was a fine of six cows and eight pence. Evidently this was considered to be a less serious offence than picking the branch of a sacred tree in old Scandinavia. The culprit, when apprehended, would have his navel cut out and nailed to the tree. He would then be chased round the tree until his intestines had fully unwound. An imaginative punishment for a relatively mundane crime. There follow some examples of creative criminality: First, the unknown burglar who robbed Mrs Janet Winn of Paddington, London.

The first the poor lady knew of the theft was when she opened her diary to read, written in an unidentifiable hand: 'House burgled – 5 am'. She then looked in her handbag and discovered that £24 had been removed as she slept.

Unusual weapons have also featured in some recent crimes. An American in 1975 was arrested and charged with attempting to drown his wife in a water bed. Clearly a more violent man than 59-year-old Harry Fitchett, the Australian who walked into a bank in Wollongong in 1980, brandishing a knife and fork and demanding money. He was found not guilty of demanding money with menaces.

Less fortunate were the seven horned beetles, held in custody in Belo Horizonte in Brazil, charged with being accomplices in pilfering. They had been trained by bus drivers to crawl into the fare boxes and steal the plastic tokens. The beetles died of starvation in their cells. It all happened in 1969, when the life of a beetle was held cheaply in the tough world of Latin America.

Equally unlucky was the Nigerian witch doctor sentenced to death for shooting and killing a client. He had only been testing a charm which was claimed to provide protection from bullets. Professional incompetence seems endemic to the continent of Africa. Another example was the young Zimbabwe burglar caught in October 1983 after leaving his trousers at the scene of the crime. He had removed them and other items of clothing in order to enable himself to squeeze through the 'burglar-proof' bars over a window. Disturbed by noises in the house, he made a hurried exit, leaving his garments behind. The police tracked him down with little difficulty, aided by the identity card which he had left in his trouser pocket.

The punishment imposed on the young Zimbabwean may well have been more severe than the three years imprisonment imposed upon Oskar Zaettel of Munich in 1936 for one of the rarest crimes of all. He had bitten another man to death. His victim had been an innkeeper named Derel. When 24-year-old Zaettel was presented with his bill for 6 quarts of beer, he argued about the price. In the quarrel, Derel was bitten in the neck and died of infection five days later.

CROCKERY

Marie Antoinette commissioned a cup from the Sèvres porcelain factory to be modelled to the exact shape of her left breast. In order not to discomfort the good lady, the modelling clay used for the fittings was specially warmed beforehand.

CROCODILE

(From the Greek: *krokodeilos*.) A large reptile of the Nile, of the genus *Crocodil* and order Crocodilia. Ten per cent of the weight of an adult crocodile is account for by pebbles which it has swallowed in t course of its life. The mature crocodile is better swimmer than a young croc, becau its greater pebble intake acts as a balla and causes it to lie lower in the water.

☐ See also: **contraception, eyelid, massacre, musical appreciation.**

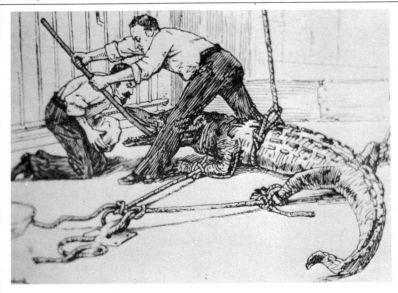

Force-feeding a crocodile

CROMWELL, Oliver (1599–1658)

Within two years of Cromwell's state funeral, official opinion of him had fallen somewhat, and his body was dug up and decapitated. His head was then impaled on a spike and mounted aloft the roof of Westminster Abbey. There it remained for a quarter of a century before being blown off in a bad storm in 1685 (the year of birth of Bach, Handel and Domenico Scarlatti). The fallen head was retrieved by a captain of the guard who took it home secretly and hid it in his chimney, telling no one of its existence there. On his deathbed, the captain bequeathed the secret head to his only daughter. In 1775, Cromwell's head was offered to his old Cambridge College, Sidney Sussex. The college refused, but given a second chance in 1960, they accepted and buried the head in a private ceremony.

Oliver Cromwell was almost Oliver Williams, for Williams was his family name until his grandfather chose to adopt his mother's maiden name of Cromwell.

☐ See also: *pragmatism.*

CROSSWORD

Although the crossword is a typically English institution, it was first published in the *New York World* in America, in December 1913. The craze hit England only in 1924.

Anyone who claims to time his soft-boiled eggs by the time it takes him to complete *The Times* crossword is either lying, eating ostrich eggs, or committing the gastronomic sin of putting the eggs in cold water. Trials have shown that it is physically impossible to read all the clues and fill in the answers in less than four or five minutes.

CROW

Name given to the Corvidae family of birds, most of which are black or black and white.

☐ See **DANCING.**

CROWLEY, Aleister (1875–1947)

Known as 'The Beast' or 'The Wickedest Man in the World', Aleister Crowley once sued a publisher for claiming that he practised black magic. Crowley testified that he practised only white magic. He lost the case.

☐ See **PERFUME**.

CRUDEN, Alexander (1701–70)

Scottish moralist and eccentric.

☐ See **MORALITY**.

CRUELTY

Mrs Margaret E. Dayton was awarded a divorce on the grounds of cruelty in San Francisco in 1943. Her complaint was that her husband constantly forced her to eat venison. In the same year in Chicago, Mrs Josephine Skrodenis won a divorce after complaining that her husband, a murder story fan, took up most of her evenings by making her lie on the floor as the corpse while he tried to reconstruct the crime.

CRUELTY TO ANIMALS

☐ See **PIGTAIL**.

CRUSADES

The first Crusade was led by Peter the Hermit and Walter the Penniless in 1069. Hordes marched with them across Europe, thousands perishing on the journey, the remainder being destroyed by the Turks at Nicaea. Later Crusades were less disastrous.

☐ See **EMBALMING, RICHARD I**.

CUBA

The island of Cuba produces 15.8 billion cigars each year. Belgium produces 45 billion matches each year, enough to light each cigar almost three times if they all work. The lucifer match was invented in 1827 by the chemist John Walker who omitted to take out a patent on his idea. Curiously, the invention of the cigarette lighter predates that of the match, thank to a moment of inspiration for J. W Dobereiner in 1816.

☐ See also: *speed.*

CUCKOLDRY

The deception of a man whose wife ha taken a lover. But there can be benefici side effects to this otherwise undesirabl state. La Marquise de Brinvillers wa executed in Paris in 1676 for poisoning he father and two brothers. She had als repeatedly tried to poison her husband, b her lover kept administering antidotes t save himself from the fate of having t marry such a wicked woman.

CUCKOO

A churkey was successfully bred in 1937 a Southfleet in Kent. Its father was a turkey its mother was a chicken. The triumphan breeder was a woman named Mrs Cuckoo Tigons, ligers and a zeedonk have also bee created by miscegenating mammals. Th zeedonk has the legs of a zebra and th body of a donkey.

CUCUMBER

Fruiting plant used as a vegetable, of th natural order Cucurbitaceae and genu *Cucumis*.

☐ See **MERMAID**.

CULTURE

According to a statement in 1983 by th Singapore Minister of Culture, an amoun equivalent to £50,000 had been spent in th previous twelve months on the costs removing chewing gum from official floo and walls.

CURIE, Pierre (1859–1906)

Despite his being married to a woman wh won two Nobel prizes (Marie Curie, 1867 1934) and sharing with her the discovery **RADIUM**, Pierre Curie was run over an killed by a horse and cart. The old tech nology strikes back.

CUSTER, General George (1839–76)

Killed with his men at the battle of the Little Big Horn.

□ See **INSURANCE.**

CUSTOMS

Duties on imports and exports.

□ See **ART.**

CYPRUS

Third largest island in the east Mediterranean. In Cyprus many large cats are kept in order to keep down the viper population. Snakes are more popular in Florida, USA, where rattlesnake meat is quite a delicacy as an appetiser. In Hong Kong they are even more sophisticated and drink snake wine, made by fermenting a snake in alcohol for up to twenty years.

CZECHOSLOVAKIA

There is a church in the town of Sedlec in Bohemia which is decorated with human bones. A pile of skulls forms an attractive centrepiece in the shape of the crest of a noble family of the town. The chapel at the monastery of St Francis in Evora, Portugal, exhibits a similar style in interior design.

After the battle of Waterloo in 1815, the Duke of York had a corridor of his home lined with the teeth of horses killed in the battle.

D

DACHSHUND

(From the German: *Dachs*, badger; *Hund*, dog.) The poor dachshund fell foul of anti-German feeling in the United States during the First World War. There were even organised kick-a-dog campaigns to make these hunnish hounds aware of their origins.

DANCING

The most dangerous dance in the world is probably the zbojnicki in Poland. The male partner swings an axe in circles just above the ground, while the girl jumps over it each time it passes. It should not be performed in the presence of crows, wolves or pigeons, all considered signs of bad luck in Poland.

Possibly the second most dangerous dance in the world

A goat, however, is a sign of good fortune.

At Waterloo there is a tomb dedicated to the leg of Lord Uxbridge. The unfortunate limb had to be amputated after wounds sustained in the 1815 battle. As far as is known, Lord Uxbridge never danced the zbojnicki.

DA PONTE, Lorenzo (1749–1838)

After writing the libretti for Mozart's operas, *The Marriage of Figaro, Cosí Fan Tutti* and *Don Giovanni*, Lorenzo da Ponte fell so much into debt that he had to leave Europe in 1808. After failing as a grocer in Philadelphia, he became professor of Italian at Columbia University, New York.

Research shows that newborn babies enjoy Mozart and Vivaldi but tend to sleep through any Beethoven which may be played at them.

DARWIN, Charles Robert (1809–82)

Darwin's nose almost lost him the job as ship's naturalist on board the *Beagle*. The ship's captain, Robert Fitzroy, was a keen physiognomist and saw Darwin's broad, squat nose as an indication that he lacked the stamina and application necessary for the long voyage.

Darwin's cousin, Sir Francis Galton, was responsible for much of the work which led Scotland Yard to adopt fingerprinting as a means of identification. The Chinese, however, had known about fingerprints for two thousand years and had used them for legal purposes since around AD 700.

The telegraphic address of Old Scotland Yard was 'Handcuffs'.

DATE

Fruit of the date palm (Phoenix dactylifera).

☐ See **IRAQ.**

DA VINCI, Leonardo

☐ See **LEONARDO.**

DEAFNESS

The German for a pigeon (eine Taube) also means a deaf woman.

☐ See **EDISON, LIP-READING.**

DEATH

Some of the more remarkable deaths in history are the following:
King George II of England, who fell to his death from a toilet seat;
King Haakon VII of Norway, who died from complications resulting from falling into a bath in 1957;
King Alexander of Greece, who died in 1920 from blood poisoning which he contracted when bitten by his pet monkey;
King Henry I of England, who died in 1135 from a surfeit of lampreys (eel-like fish to which the king was evidently partial).

But royalty by no means have a monopoly on odd deaths:
Francis Bacon died in 1626 from a severe cold caught while trying to stuff a chicken with snow in an early attempt to invent frozen food;
Aeschylus was killed in 456 BC when a tortoise dropped on his head. An eagle carrying the tortoise is supposed to have mistaken his glabrous dome for a rock and tried to crack the tortoise's shell on it. The fate of the tortoise is not recorded;
Arnold Bennett, the novelist, died of typhoid in an unsuccessful attempt to demonstrate that it was safe to drink a glass of Parisian water in 1931;
Marc Quinquadon, the world snail-eating champion, looked set

to topple his own record of 144 snails in 11 min. 30 sec.; he had gobbled his way through 72 snails in three minutes in November 1979 before he collapsed and died;

Endre Bascany, a Hungarian hunter, was another who died for his art. His imitation of a stag's mating call was so accurate that another hunter shot him.

It was pride as much as the assassin's bullet which killed **Ferdinand, Archduke of Austria**. He liked to be sewn into his uniform to eliminate any possible creasing. When he was shot in 1914 it was impossible to cut him out in time to staunch the bleeding and he bled to death.

Another proud man was **Colonel Pierrepoint**, the man responsible for erecting the first traffic island in Piccadilly to provide safe crossing for pedestrians. Stepping back to admire his work, he was knocked down by a Hansom cab.

In 1811, the blacksmith of Stroud in Gloucestershire ate a pint of periwinkles with their shells still on. He did it for a bet. Having collected his winnings, he repeated the feat on request, then dropped dead.

Jean-Baptiste Lully, French composer and conductor, used to conduct with a long staff with which he banged the floor. One day he stabbed his foot with it and later died of blood poisoning. The smaller baton then came rapidly into fashion.

At least three Popes met strange ends:

Pope Adrian IV choked on a fly which had flown into his drinking water. His last act had been to threaten the Emperor Frederick I with excommunication. **Pope Clement VII** met his end after eating a poison toadstool. Probably **Pope Leo VIII** had the happiest end: a heart attack while committing adultery.

The Greeks tended to meet more violent ends:

Euripides, torn to pieces by a pack of hunting dogs while he was out taking a stroll;

Anaxarchus, pounded to death with pestles, after making the mistake of criticising the King of Cyprus.

And finally, to end on a modern note, **Louise Ramon** was arrested for shoplifting in San Diego in October 1983. So incensed was she that she threatened to hold her breath 'until I turn blue', unless she was released. When she was not immediately set free, she carried out her threat, and died.

DEBT

(Pronounced *det*. From the Latin: *debitum*, that which is owed.) Marco Polo reported a nice way of dealing with debtors in India: If repayment of the debt was not forthcoming, the creditor drew a circle round his debtor. If the debtor stepped outside the circle he was liable to punishment by death. Sounds a little harsh if he just happens to have left his wallet and cheque book outside the circle.

DECENCY

In 1971 a nun was assigned to St Peter's Basilica in Rome with the task of refusing entry to ladies considered to be improperly clad in mini-skirts, see-through blouses, low necklines or midriff-exposing trouser suits. The strains of upholding moral standards in this manner led to the nun having to be relieved of her duties after suffering a nervous breakdown. Later the policy was changed to provide visitors with simple garments to cover any bits thought to be indecorously exposed (cf. **INDECENCY**).

DEER

Name given to all members of the family Cervidae of even-toed hoofed mammals.

□ See **FIREFLY, SPEED.**

DEFECTION

One of the very few known cases of defection from the West to East Germany was that of a cow which swam 150 yards across the river Elbe from Luchow to escape mating. The East Germans considered the merits of her case and decided not to return her to the loose bovine morality of the West.

DEMOGRAPHY

One quarter of the world's people and 21 per cent of the world's chickens live in **CHINA**. Another quarter of the people live in India, the USSR and the USA put together. Almost 40 per cent of the world's population are under 15. So Chinese children must account for a tenth of the people on earth.

Albania, with less than 0.1 per cent of the world's population, has banned the use of contraceptives until it has as many people as the Soviet Union.

DEMOLITION

□ See **DOORKNOB.**

DEMOSTHENES (*c.* 383–322 BC)

Athenian orator and statesman who shaved one half of his head and ended his life by taking poison which he always carried in a quill.

□ See **STAMMERING.**

DENMARK

The Danish flag of a white cross on red background dates back to 1209 and is the oldest national flag in continuous use. For a long time, Danish names had the same problem as those in Iceland (*qv*), having no surnames. In 1828 it was decreed that all families should henceforth stick to their family name and dispense with the old patronymics. This led to a national surname shortage, since all the names in existence were simply the first names of the previous generation. To make matters easier for all, telephone directories list people by their occupation.

Anyone liking these quaint customs and thinking of emigrating should be warned that Danes begin Christmas dinner with rice pudding. But Midsummer Eve, 23 June, is a cause for great celebration.

□ See also: *geography.*

DENTISTRY

Experiments have shown that milk production among Spanish cows can be improved

by up to 60 per cent by fitting them with steel teeth to enable them to digest grass more easily. In Argentina, cattle fitted with chromium–cobalt dentures are 25 per cent more fertile than those with their own teeth.

A traffic jam was caused in Brazil in 1964 when a human couple kissed in a car and their dentures become inextricably interlocked.

☐ See also: ***anaesthetics, doorknob, Washington.***

DEODORANT

(From the Latin: *de*, away; *odor*, smell.)

☐ See **VINEGAR.**

DESCARTES, René (1596–1650)

Early to bed; early to rise;
Descartes gets pneumonia, later he dies.

In 1649, Descartes, after much persuasion, agreed to come to Sweden at the behest of Queen Christina, in order to instruct her and to set up an academy. The rigorous schedule involved classes beginning at five in the morning. The cold air and punishing discipline of this timetable have been blamed for causing the pneumonia which finished off the old philosopher.

DESCHANEL, Paul Eugène Louis (1856–1922)

French statesman, born near Brussels where his father was in exile. His godfather was Victor Hugo.

☐ See **PYJAMAS.**

DEVIL

Name given generally to evil spirits, especially Satan, prince of the powers of darkness.

☐ See **CHOCOLATE, COCK, FILMS, MALTA.**

DIARISTS

The entry in the diary of George III, King of England, on 4 July 1776 read: 'Nothing of importance happened today.' News from America travelled slowly in those days. King Louis XVI of France was even more succinct on the day of the storming of the Bastille. His diary entry for 14 July 1789, written after returning from a hunting trip, read simply: 'nothing'.

DICKENS, Charles John Huffham (1812–70)

Charles Dickens believed that magnetic currents could affect one's bodily energies. He always slept with his bed aligned north–south, and always faced north when writing. Itinerant Arabs whose knees may have lost their sense of direction have had their prayers answered by British ingenuity. A Swiss company has ordered one million British-made Muslim prayer compasses, which are to be sewn into the corners of their prayer mats. Kneel in the direction indicated by the arrow and you will be facing Mecca.

☐ See also: ***Niagara Falls.***

DIET

The simplest diet on which one can live healthily is bread, bananas and orange juice according to one dietician. Unclassified US Government data include the information that nearly 2,800 different ways have been tried by people wanting to lose weight.

☐ See also: ***Slimming.***

DIFFERENTIALS

Henry V had a policy of equality in paying his servants: the minstrels and the master surgeon received the same rate of one shilling a day. By 1837, differentials had crept into the royal wage bill. The chimney sweep was paid £111 a year, compared with £100 for the dentist and £80 for the rat catcher. The Poet Laureate was considered to be worth only £72.

DILLINGER, John (1903–34)

American gangster rated 'Public Enemy Number One' by the FBI. In one year he robbed more banks than Jesse James had managed in sixteen.

□ See **ENTREPRENEURS.**

INGO

(*Canis dingo*) The wild dog of Australia.

□ See **INDIVIDUALITY.**

ISCIPLINE

Beating or smacking children is illegal in Sweden. It is permitted in Switzerland, but you are not allowed to hunt snails in the Swiss canton of Valais.

DISCOVERY

For every new industrial chemical substance produced for use in commercial laboratories, one new species of insect is discovered. The current rate of discovery in each field is running at three additions to the taxonomy every day. There are already over 30,000 chemicals in commercial use.

DISCRIMINATION

□ See **AIRCRAFT.**

DISEASE

Throughout the world, 180 medical journals are published every hour. With all this activity, it is hardly surprising that many more diseases are being discovered so that doctors can write about them. Here are some of the ailments afflicting modern society:

Jogger's Kidney is a potentially highly dangerous complaint, caused by the kidney being shaken loose while its owner is out jogging. Compared with this, the problem of *Jogger's Nipple*, caused by friction of the T-shirt, is but a minor irritation.

Jeans Folliculitis, an inflammation of the hair follicles of the upper thigh, is caused by wearing jeans which are too tight. The same fashionable habit has been credited with responsibility for a decrease in unwanted pregnancies thanks to its contraceptive effect on male wearers.

Space Invaders Wrist can set in as the hand used to control the laser gun seizes up through performing a limited repertoire of actions too repetitively. It is closely related to *Slot Machine Tendonitis*.

Another disease caused by the relentless pace of modern living is *Disco Felon*, a skin infection caused by too much finger-snapping. Drivers of Alaskan dog sleds might occasionally snap their fingers at the dogs, but their real problem is *Musher's Knee*.

The University of Chicago was first to identify *Hunan Hand*, an inflammation associated with using red peppers in Chinese cookery. That is but one of an ever-increasing number of medical problems traced to Oriental food. In 1967 a girl from Darlington ate a curry. Nothing unusual in that, except that shortly after, she discovered that everything she touched turned pink. Four days of laboratory tests finally isolated a spice which was responsible for reacting with something in her system to produce a pink dye which seeped out through her pores.

The most common Oriental food malady is *Kwok's Disease*, also known as *Chinese Restaurant Syndrome*, which is caused by an overdose of monosodium glutamate. The symptoms are sleepiness, headache, sweating or depression. The *New England Journal of Medicine* in 1978 reported a case in which a relapse was caused by a bowl of wonton soup. Further research on this condition has shown that monosodium glutamate can cause brain damage in infant mice.

There is only one thing which may be medically more damaging than Chinese food, and that is Rubik's Cube. The principal side effect is *Rubik's Thumb*, a painful condition of swollen fingers, but the cube has also been held responsible for other, less direct, effects. It has been accused of causing marital breakdown by so exhausting husbands that they are too tired to make love. And the *People's Daily* in China published in 1982 a warning of the time-wasting temptations of the Cube. They also blamed it for distracting a baker and causing him to burn a batch of loaves. More scientific evidence was sought by Southwark Council in London. They studied a batch of Cubes and discovered that the colouring in the squares had an alarmingly high lead content. The yellow squares were most dangerous, with more than ten times the permitted level of lead.

DISINFECTANT

□ See **SOUTH AFRICA**.

DISNEY, Walter Elias (1901–66)

Probably the only Hollywood producer to have had a postage stamp issued in his honour (in the USA in 1968).

□ See **INDIVIDUALITY**.

DISORDERLY CONDUCT

□ See **UKELELE**.

DISRAELI, Benjamin, Earl of Beaconsfield (1804–81)

On the death of Mary Anne Disraeli, wife of the Prime Minister, it was discovered that for thirty-three years she had been saving the hairs which were shorn off when she gave her husband haircuts.

□ See also: *accidents, hobbies.*

DIVORCE

(From the Latin: *divertere*, or *divortere*, to separate.) In 1832 a Carlisle farmer named Joseph Thompson sold his wife for twenty shillings and a Newfoundland dog. Divorce by legalised sale was still practised in Britain at that time (though a man was not allowed to sell his wife for less than one shilling). In Morocco, it is not necessary to go to all that trouble. It is sufficient for a man to say 'I divorce you' three times, and the marriage is over. He has to make it clear to whom he is speaking, though; a Moroccan may have up to four wives, provided he can afford them and they all agree to the arrangement.

□ See also: *cruelty, Palmerston, rape.*

DODO

(From the Portuguese: *doudo*, stupid.) The only artist to have had the opportunity to sketch a live dodo (*Didus ineptus*) was the Belgian Roelandt Savery. Later dodo drawers have copied Savery's original model, including a rather elementary mistake in reconstructing the bits of the bird which were out of sight. That is why in most pictures of the dodo, the bird is portrayed as having two right legs.

It has been estimated that of all forms of life ever to have been on earth, 99 per cent are now extinct.

DOG

Dogs are digitigrade (they walk on their

toes). They have four toes on the hind feet and five on the fore feet (except for the Cape hunting dog). The first dog in Spain to be fitted with contact lenses was knocked down and killed by a car the following day. The accident happened in Bilbao. The dog's name was Stan.

If all the hot-dogs made each year in the United States were joined end to end, they would stretch from the earth to the moon and back two and a half times. That would, however, create yet another hazard for cosmonauts, already rated America's number one insurance risk, ahead of test pilots, stuntmen, toreadors, hot-air balloonists, lion tamers and trapeze artists who perform without nets.

☐ See also: *Angola, banana, Byron, divorce, etiquette, Ford, Iceland, indecency, Libya, llama, oil, pampered pets, pets, potoroo, rabies, Satie, sedative, shock, terrapin, Victoria, wealth.*

DOG SHOW

The first official dog show was held in Newcastle, England, in 1859, twenty-nine years before the first official human beauty contest which took place in Belgium in 1888. Sixty pointers and setters took part in the dog show. Leonardo da Vinci did not participate in the beauty contest, but his friends described him as the most beautiful man who ever lived.

DOLPHIN

Cetacean of the genus *Delphinus*. The bottle-nosed dolphin has extra-ordinary powers of hearing and can detect sounds at a higher frequency than even a bat's radar can pick up. In 1978 Californian vets had a great problem in removing a piece of metal from a dolphin's stomach. It had been inadvertently swallowed and was in danger of severely damaging the animal's insides. They solved their problem (and the dolphin's) by enlisting the help of a baseball

player, Clifford Ray, to reach into the animal's mouth deep into its stomach to retrieve the lump of metal. Mr Ray's specialist qualification was an arm length of 3ft 9in. The first recorded use of the word 'baseball' was by Jane Austen in North-anger Abbey (1803). Haiti is the world's major producer of baseballs.

☐ See also: *otter.*

DOMINICA

Although there is only one chemist's shop in Dominica, it still has more chemist's shops per head of population than Zaire. There is a chemist's shop in Miami which is run by the sister of Fidel Castro.

DOMINOES

According to a calculation made by a German arithmetician in 1882, if two players sat down and played four games of dominoes a minute, they could exhaust all possible combinations of the game in just 118 million years.

DONKEY

Division of the genus *Equus* also known as **ASS**. The largest donkey is the Tibetan kiang, standing about thirteen hands high

at the withers. More people are kicked t death by donkeys than die in flying acc dents. Donkeys are allergic to buttercups.

☐ See also: ***cuckoo, humour, whooping cough.***

DOODLING

In a paper entitled: 'Personality Functior of Graphic Constrictedness and Expansive ness', written in 1960, Wallach and Gahn reported that extroverts draw more expar sive doodles than introverts. Stalin ofte doodled at meetings, but he always drev heads of wolves.

DOORKNOB

The traditional method of tooth extractio was to tie a string to the defective tooth with the other end attached to the door knob of an open door. The door would the be slammed shut, preferably by a maide aunt. This method faded from popularit with the mass production of shoddy door knobs. In Nantwich, Cheshire, there was case reported in the early 1950s, of a whol new council house being caused to collaps by an attempt at this primitive denta technique. The patient emerged from th wreckage with his tooth still intact. Ther are strong grounds for suspecting that h did not employ the services of a maide aunt to slam the door.

DORMOUSE

The dormouse (Myoxidae) spends abo six months a year in hibernation. Th ancient Romans were fond of dormice preferably roast. Before being sent to th abattoir, the dormouse would be fed o nuts to improve its flavour. The name of th dormouse probably has some connectio with the Latin *dormire*, to sleep. Cats slee for fourteen hours a day. The ancier Egyptians used to sleep on pillows of stone

DORS, Diana (1931–84)
☐ See **BEAUTY.**

DOSTOYEVSKY, Fiodor Mikhailovich (1822–81)

Dostoyevsky was a sickly child who suffered from hallucinations and attacks of epilepsy. In 1849 he was arrested for his political affiliations and put in front of a firing squad. This turned out to be just a little harmless Czarist joke and when the giggles had died down Dostoyevsky was sent to Siberia where he languished for four years.

DOVE

Doves' brains were considered an aphrodisiac in Georgian England. Elephants' brains were not so highly regarded though presumably in more plentiful supply since an elephant has one ounce of brain for each pound of body weight. The first elephant twins to be born in captivity were in Tanzania in 1976.

DOWNING STREET, SW1

□ See **SECURITY, THEFT.**

DRACO (seventh century BC)

Draco was an Athenian magistrate who flourished around 620 BC. He produced the first written code of laws for Athens, said to be written in letters of blood on account of their severity. Almost all crimes, including idleness, were punishable by death. Draco did, however, have moments of great popularity and is one of the few politicians to have been mobbed to death by his fans. It happened in a theatre in Aegina when the Athenians, as was their custom, showed their respect for the lawgiver by throwing their garments on him. When the pile of caps and cloaks was removed, Draco was found to have suffocated to death beneath them. The word 'Draconian' (meaning severe) derives from Draco and has nothing whatever to do with dragons. The word 'draconian' (with a small 'd') means 'pertaining to dragons'.

DRACULA

Transylvanian vampire created by Bram Stoker.

□ See **TANZANIA.**

DRAGONFLY

(*Odonata*) The dragonfly's eyes are compound structures of more than 28,000 lenses. Despite this obvious challenge, no corneal transplant has ever been performed on a dragonfly. The first successful corneal transplant was in fact performed in 1835 by a British army surgeon in India. The lucky patient was his pet antelope.

DRAMA

Best acting performances by animals in films are awarded 'Patsies' by the American Humane Association (cf. **FORD, G.**).

DREAM

Queen Ranavalona of Madagascar thought it so unbefitting her royal status that she made it illegal for her subjects to dream about her. She also outlawed Christianity in 1835 and died in 1861.

DROPSY

(Originally hydropsy, but the hy dropped off.) Morbid accumulation of water in any part of the body.

□ See **GEORGE IV, WIND.**

DROWNING

'There are not many people who know that a fish could drown if it swallows too much water.' The wise words of a modest RSPCA inspector, commended after saving the life of a goldfish. The fish had been found drowning after a pebble had become stuck in its mouth and interfered with its breathing.

□ See also: *Edward IV.*

Friendly RSPCA men give mouth-to-mouth resuscitation to a passing fish

DRUGS

☐ See **CANNABIS, GERBIL.**

DRUM

Instrument of percussion consisting of a membrane stretched over a hollow body.

☐ See **OMAN.**

DRUNKEN DRIVING

In 1970 an intoxicated Japanese driver continued his journey for more than a mile before he noticed that his arm, which he had last seen hanging out of the window, had been torn off when it collided with an oncoming lorry. A passing pedestrian found the arm and told the police. Later the driver reported the loss of his arm to another police station. Fortunately only one such limb had been handed in that day in the area, so there was little delay in re-uniting man and arm.

☐ See also: *party spirit.*

DUBLIN

Capital city of the republic of Ireland.

☐ See **NEW YORK, OHIO, QUIZ.**

DUCK

The duck lays eggs only in the ear* morning. When swimming it is six times le* efficient than a ship at converting energ* into work.

☐ See also: *avalanche, bath, Conan Doyle* *flea, gluttony, interment, Mexico,* *potato, reindeer, yak.*

DUELLING

In the space of eight years at the beginnin* of the eighteenth century, over 2,00* French aristocrats died in duels. Duelling still permitted in Uruguay, but only if bot* participants are registered blood donors.

☐ See also: *marksmanship, peanut.*

Irate French aristocrats

DUGONG

Herbivorous marine creature sometimes mistaken for a mermaid.

☐ See **ALBANIA.**

DUMAS, Alexandre, Fils (1824–95)

Son of Dumas, Alexandre, Père.

☐ See **INSOMNIA.**

DUMAS, Alexandre, Père (1802–70)

Father of Dumas, Alexandre, Fils. His full name was Alexandre Dumas-Davy de la Pailleterie and his father was the illegitimate son of a French noble.

☐ See **MONTEZ.**

DUNCAN, Isadora (1878–1927)

Isadora Duncan attributed some of her taste and temperament to her mother's diet while she was pregnant: she would for some time eat nothing but iced oysters and iced champagne. Finally Miss Duncan fell victim to fashion: she was strangled and her neck was broken when her scarf was caught in the wheels of a car. The illustration is of Giuseppe Verdi apparently also having trouble with a tight scarf.

DUNG BEETLE

(*Geotrupes stercorarius*) A horde of dung beetles can dispose of a pile of elephant droppings in an hour.

☐ See **FUSSINESS.**

DUNG-THROWING

Top people's sport of Oklahoma, USA.

☐ See **ELITISM.**

DWARF

Only two dwarfs have ever reached the age of 100. Only two British hereditary peer have ever reached the age of 100. Neither o the centenarian peers was a dwarf.

☐ See also: ***Henry I, trees, William the Conqueror.***

E

EADRED, King of England (reigned 946–55)

Little is known of King Eadred save that he died of a fatal quinsy in AD 955. King Athelstan died in AD 940.

EAGLE

In 1946 an eagle, which had been rescued from a trap in Inverness, was taken to London Zoo for treatment. When the injuries had healed, the eagle had to be taken back to Inverness to be set free. It travelled by train from Euston, riding in the luggage compartment, and was charged at the parcels rate of ten shillings.

Between 1946 and 1969, former Italian member of parliament Dr Francesco Saverio d'Ayla lived day and night on trains and it cost him nothing. One of the few negotiable assets he had managed to cling onto after his parliamentary career had been his permanent free pass on the railways. He was a well-known figure on the trains and any letters addressed to him usually found him within a day or two.

EAR

By a 1552–3 Act of Edward VI the penalty for brawling in a church or churchyard was to have an ear cut off. For a second offence, the other ear would also be removed. When the brawler had run out of ears, he would be branded with the letter F for fraymaker.

☐ See also: *adultery, cockroach, Edison, llama, violence.*

EARACHE
☐ See **FINGERPRINTS.**

EARTHQUAKE

The general mechanical principles which cause earthquakes to happen are broadly agreed, but the precise manner of operation of those mechanics is still a matter for high-level dispute. Indian mythology, for example, maintains that the earth rests on the head of a great elephant named Muha-Pudma. When the elephant moves its head to change posture, it causes earth tremors. Other Eastern mystics pour scorn on the elephant theory, saying instead that it is the back of a tortoise which carries the earth and causes it to quake. Tibetan lamas, however, maintain that the carrier is a frog. (There is, however, no reciprocal agreement whereby the French believe a llama to be doing the work.)

☐ See also: *China, panda.*

EATING

An average Aborigine will not be at all put out to be seen naked, or even defecating, but he will be terribly ashamed and embarrassed if a stranger catches a glimpse of him eating.

ECHIDNA

The spiny ant-eater of Australia. There are two species, the five-toed and the three-toed. The echidna and the ornithorhynchus are the only mammals with a cloaca (a single orifice which serves as alimentary, urinary and genital excretory device – from the Latin: *cloaca*, a main drain).

☐ See also: *proposal.*

ECLIPSE

In 1628 an eclipse of the sun had been foretold which was expected to signal the death of Pope Urban VIII. The Pope employed the services of magician Tommaso Campanella to ward off the ill omen. In a sealed room, an artificial sky was created with lamps and torches; jewels took the places of stars and various plants added to the confusion. The fates were utterly fooled and the Urban terror subsided. He lived until 1644.

☐ See also: *frog.*

ECONOMICS

Monetarist Milton Friedman declared: 'There is no such thing as a free lunch.' Was he aware, we must wonder, that Elizabethan brothels used to serve free prunes at lunch? Guzzler extraordinary, Alan Newbold, ate 150 prunes in eleven seconds (though not in a brothel) when setting his world prune-eating record, and he suffered no ill effects. But he did get food poisoning when, in 1983, he tried to consume 250 oysters in less than 2 min. 53 sec.

When eating sheep's eyes for charity, Mr Newbold stated a preference for them to be blue.

☐ See also: *building.*

ECUADOR

The city of Guayaquil in Ecuador proudly displays a statue of Lord Byron. The townsfolk actually wanted to erect a statue of local poet José Olmedo, but the estimate for sculpting one was more than they were prepared to pay, so they bought a second hand statue of Byron instead. Byron died o a fever caught in the Missolonghi marche Had he lived long enough to see his statu in Ecuador, he might well have died influenza instead. Ecuador boasts th second highest influenza death rate in th world.

☐ See also: *headgear.*

EDGAR, King of England (944–75)

The younger son of King Edmund an great-grandson of Alfred the Great, Kir Edgar was reprimanded by Archbishe Dunstan for seducing a nun. Anothe nun-fancier was the painter Fra Filipp Lippi, a Carmelite monk, who painted h 'Madonna and Child', then ran off with th nun who had posed as the Madonna.

EDISON, Thomas Alva (1847–1931)

Although there was nothing wrong with h eyesight, Edison preferred to read Braille. He was, however, a bit deaf an proposed to his future wife using Mor code. It is not known whether he had fir tried an old Scottish remedy for deafnes mixing ants' eggs with onion juice ar dropping the resulting concoction into th affected ear.

☐ See also: *Gilbert, gramophone, vision.*

EDWARD THE CONFESSOR,
King of England (*c.* 1005–66)

Son of **ETHELRED** the Unready ar brother of Hardicanute, who invited him England in 1041.

☐ See **GLOUCESTER, SCROFULA.**

EDWARD I, King of England (1239–1307)

One of the greatest of English Kings. F conquered Wales and was invading Sco land when he died.

☐ See **LAST WORDS, SCROFULA.**

EDWARD III, King of England (1312–77)
☐ See **ARCHERY, GANNET, LEPROS**

Edward the Confessor

Edward, Duke of York (1739–67), brother of George III, was born exactly 500 years after Edward I

EDWARD IV, King of England (1442–83)

It is well known that George, Duke of Clarence, met his end by drowning in a butt of malmsey wine in 1478. Less publicity has been given to the fact that the malmsey had been a gift from his brother, Edward IV. Malmsey is the sweetest form of madeira. If its dark yet tangy insouciance is not to your taste, try drowning in a dry sercial, or take a 1955 port for those special submergings.

EDWARD VI, King of England (1537–53)

Edward VI came to the throne at the age of 9. He showed little respect for his father Henry VIII when, in the first year of his reign (1547), he repealed an act which Henry had passed sixteen years previously. The old act specified a punishment of boiling to death for those convicted of murdering by poisoning.

☐ See also: *ear, hanging, puberty.*

EDWARD VII, King of England (1841–1910)

At the coronation of Edward VII in 1901, the aged and infirm Archbishop of Canterbury was handed the crown by the equally aged and infirm Dean of Westminster. So relieved were the congregation that the crown was not dropped during the ceremony that nobody really minded when it was noticed that it had been placed back-to-front on the new King's head.

King Edward VII was the owner of three Derby winners and was such a concerned host at Sandringham weekends that he would weigh guests on arrival and departure to ensure that they had eaten well. The larva of the polyphemus moth can eat 86,000 times its own weight in fifty-six days.

☐ See also: *coma.*

EDWARD VIII, briefly King of England (1894–1972)

After twenty years unpaid and loyal service to Edward VIII and, as he became after his abdication, the Duke of Windsor, Walter Monckton was presented with a cigarette case with his name engraved upon it. The name was misspelt.

EEL

Any fish of the Anguillidae, Muraenidae or other family of Apodes.

☐ See **CRAMP, SMELL, TABOO.**

EGG

The largest recorded hen's egg had nine yolks and weighed 14 oz. It was laid in Russia and was 5½ inches long.

☐ See also: *Barbados, children, clown, crossword, duck, envy, fatalities, Israel, mayfly, New Zealand, ostrich, pigeon, reincarnation, yak.*

EGYPT

The television series *Dallas* was banned in Egypt on grounds of morality.

☐ See **PRUDERY, WELLINGTON.**

EIFFEL, Alexandre Gustave (1832–1923)

The Statue of Liberty in New York harbour had its framework designed by M. Eiffel. The statue itself was carved by Frederic Auguste Bartholdi (1834–1904) of Paris. The lady with the torch is M. Bartholdi's mother. The statue was presented to the United States as a centenary present from the French people in 1876. The Eiffel Tower in Paris is held together by 2½ million rivets.

☐ See also: *temperature.*

EINSTEIN, Albert (1879–1955)

The young Einstein was a late developer who did not speak until he was 4 years old and was still not fluent by the age of 9. He failed the entrance examinations for the Federal Polytechnic of Zurich and never used shaving soap. His final mistake in life was to utter his last words in German, a language his nurse did not understand.

☐ See also: *socks.*

EISENHOWER, Dwight David (1890–1969)

Dwight D. Eisenhower attained the rank o five-star general and became President o the United States despite being brought up by parents who were pacifists. He hated cats so much that he ordered them sho on sight within the grounds of the White House. The correct collective noun fo young cats is a kindle of kittens.

☐ See also: *uniqueness.*

ELECTRIC CHAIR

The only emperor in history to have had a electric chair for his throne was Menelik I of Abyssinia. Wanting to modernise hi country, ready for its entry into the twen tieth century, he ordered three of the new electric chairs from the United States having been suitably impressed when read ing of their first use in that country in 1890 When they arrived it was discovered tha they did not work, because at that tim Abyssinia had no electricity. Not wishing to waste the consignment, Menelik had on of the chairs converted into an imperia throne.

☐ See also: *guillotine.*

ELECTRICITY

Not only can a cockroach survive with it head cut off, but experiments have show that such decapitated cockroaches lear more quickly than normal cockroaches to avoid electric shocks by holding their leg above a live wire. (Of course only mil shocks are administered to the ex perimental insects; one would not wish to cause them any undue distress.) 'When a man knows he is to be hanged in a fortnight,' said Dr Johnson, 'it concentrate his mind wonderfully.' Perhaps in the cas of the cockroach the increased concentra tion only takes place after the execution.

Electric catfish have never been used i the cockroach experiment. Probably be cause they can fight back by discharging u to 650 volts.

☐ See also: *shock.*

ELEGANCE

In fourteenth-century France, shoes were a symbol of elegance. The Poulaine was a shoe which doubled as a status symbol with the length of the tip being the most important feature. The longest such item of footwear measured up to two feet in length and was worn only by princes and noblemen. At the battle of Nicopolis in 1396 French Crusaders had to submit to the ultimate indignity of hacking off the ends of their shoes so that they could run away quickly enough.

☐ See also: ***Mata Hari.***

ELEPHANT

A proboscidean (*Elephas*) of which two species survive. Its tusks are different from those of any other animal, being overgrown incisor teeth growing from the upper jaw. The elephant may also be distinguished from other animals by its knee joints which are much lower down than in most hoofed creatures. It is thus able to bend its hind legs in the fashion of a kneeling man, which accounts for the (somewhat inaccurate) description of the elephant as the only animal with four knees. In addition to this proliferation of knees, the elephant has 40,000 muscles and no bones in its trunk, which can hold 1½ gallons of water. It cannot jump, but is the only animal apart from man which has been taught to stand on its head. Bears, however, have been taught to play basketball. Dr Leon Smith, their basketball coach, commented: 'Food is now secondary to the thrill of making a score.'

☐ See also: ***aircraft, beans (baked), Burma, compensation, cosmetics, dove, earthquake, food, fussiness, Mahomet, maternity, party spirit, pregnancy, Ritz, sleep, sloth, sperm, swimming, Syria, toothache.***

ELITISM

Judging by a list of the winners, the most élitist sport in America in the early 1970s

was dung-throwing. The 1972 world championship was won by ex-Governor Dewy Bartlett of Oklahoma, who propelled his cow pat 138 feet, thereby shattering the world record. In the final throw he beat the Republican Governor, David Hall, who had been the champion dung-thrower the previous year.

ELIZABETH OF YORK (1465–1503)

Daughter and heiress of Edward IV, Elizabeth of York narrowly avoided arranged marriages with the dauphin of France (later Charles VIII) and with Richard III before finally marrying **HENRY VII**.

ELIZABETH I, Queen of England (1533–1603)

Daughter of Henry VIII and Anne Boleyn. Despite possessing 150 wigs herself, Queen Elizabeth I signed an act early in her reign taxing all who wore whiskers. Later she lost all her teeth and used to stuff her mouth with cloth in order to counteract the sunken look in her cheeks.

☐ See also: ***annulment, farting.***

ELIZABETH I, Empress of Russia (1709–6.

Daughter of Peter the Great, Elizabet Petrovna to her friends, Elizabeth I o Russia changed clothes on average twelv times a day. She had 15,000 dresses and wa the only one in the land permitted to wea pink. The penalty for anyone else wh dared dress in that colour was mutilatior She founded Moscow University in 1755.

ELIZABETH II, Queen of England (*b.* 1926.

☐ See **OBSCENITY, WEATHER.**

EMBALMING

(From the French: *em-*, in; *baume*, baln *Baume* comes from the Greek: *balsamor* balsam.) Families of soldiers killed in th American Civil War would sometimes pa to have the bodies of their loved on embalmed and sent home. One 'D Thomas Holmes charged $100 a time f this service. One of the great entrepreneu of that era, he embalmed 4,028 dea soldiers during the course of the war.

When English soldiers were killed durir the Crusades, it was customary to boil dow their bodies and send the bones back for decent Christian burial. Probably made decent stock too, if you got the seasonir right.

EMERGENCY

(From the Latin: *e*, out of; *mergere*, plunge.) Police in Winchester, Englan once received a 999 emergency call from man whose wife had hidden his wooden le

EMMA OF NORMANDY (*d.* 1052)

Daughter of Richard of Normandy, wife ETHELRED II, mother of Edward t Confessor, great-aunt of William the Co queror, just good friends with the Bishop Winchester.

EMU

(From the Portuguese: *ema*, an ostrich Large bird (*Dromaeus novae-hollandia* belonging to the division Ratitae. In 19:

the Australian army was called out to do battle with a huge migrating horde of emus which were creating havoc in their path. The army managed to kill a few hundred, but the whole operation was not considered a success. The emu can run at 30 mph. The average length of its stride is between three and four feet, just a little longer than the average bull's penis.

☐ See also: *flying.*

EMULSION

The 1974 Golden Pillow Award for the most boring lecturer in the world was won by Dr Ashley Clarke for his account of 'Mechanical Formalism of Emulsion in an Infinite Viscous Medium'. The crucially dull part of the lecture came with Dr Clarke's closing drone: 'This only applies in an infinite viscous medium, so in practice it doesn't work.'

ENGLISH

George I (reigned 1714–27) could not speak English. The language has about 800,000 words, but a mere 2,000 of them account for 99 per cent of all speech. An English animal lover, Miss Farff, trained a seal to recognise 35 different words. Two otters (one evidently a little brighter than the other) recognised 18 and 16 words respectively. Her rat had a vocabulary sufficient to comprehend six words, and some squirrels could cope with five. The Mexican tree squirrel does not speak English but can survive a fall of 600 feet.

☐ See also: *conversation, science, segregation, tattoo, words.*

ENTREPRENEURS

Admirable opportunism was shown in 1910 when a brisk trade was done in selling anti-comet pills at $1 a box in America, guaranteed to protect against the ill effects of Halley's comet. In 1934 there was a similar demand for bottles of Dillinger Blood (mostly fake, to judge from the amounts sold) after the arch criminal had

been betrayed by his girlfriend and shot by the FBI. The blood of crooks is believed to protect against disease and misfortune.

Neither of those marketing coups was quite as tasteless as the vogue in Sydney, Australia, in 1982 for wallets made from kangaroo scrotums.

Nobody is quite sure how Edmund Halley pronounced his name, but informed opinion favours 'Hawley'.

☐ See also: *embalming.*

ENVY

One of the less enjoyable of the Seven Deadly Sins. Envy can create a 'pheno-menon of anguish' which may decrease the laying rate of chickens. In 1969 a French animal psychiatrist was called in to investi-gate a slump in productivity at a local battery farm. He attributed the chickens' listlessness to the effect of pigeons from a nearby dovecote whose flights above the farm were making the chickens jealous. His solution was to suspend the chickens for two hours each day from balloons so that they could enjoy the sensations of flight too. This fowl therapy worked wonders and egg production boomed.

Back home on the free range, hens generally fly better than roosters. Perhaps this explains why they also lay more eggs (cf. **COCK**).

EPILEPSY

Disease of the nervous system coming in two sizes: *petit mal* or *grand mal* (French, little sickness, big sickness).

☐ See **ALEXANDRIA, APOPLEXY, JULIUS CAESAR, WOODPECKER.**

EQUESTRIANISM

Ulysses S. Grant was fined $20 while President of the USA for exceeding the speed limit on a horse in Washington. The illustration overleaf shows the type of acci-dent which can all too easily happen when horses are speeding on a public thorough-fare.

ERIC THE RED

Tenth-century Norse leader, father of Leif Ericsson, who may have been the first European to discover mainland America.

□ See **CONFIDENCE TRICKSTERS.**

ESCALATOR

(From escalade, a method of attacking fortifications in the Middle Ages, involving the use of scaling ladders. Latin: *scala*, a ladder.)

□ See **CAREERS.**

ESCOFFIER, Georges Auguste (1846–1935)

Le Guide Culinaire by Escoffier (fourth edition 1921) includes 227 different ways of cooking chicken.

□ See **RITZ.**

ESKIMO

According to a 1920 census, less than one in forty-six Eskimos had ever seen an igloo. In 1931, it became clear that they had other ingenious solutions to their housing prob-lem. Point Hope, Alaska, was faced with such an epidemic of crime in that year that it had to order a larger jail to be built. The trouble started when word spread among the Eskimos about the warmth and good food served in the old jail and they all wanted to enjoy it.

This inversion of normal values may be more readily understood when one realises that some Eskimos use refrigerators to prevent food from freezing.

□ See also: *Arabic, coconut, food preservation, polar bear, salmon.*

ESSEX

Agricultural and maritime county of south east England.

□ See **WITCHES.**

ETHELRED II, King of England (c. 968–1016)

Son of Edgar by his second wife Aelfthryth. It gives the wrong impression to call him Ethelred the Unready. He was called Rede-less from his inability to recognise good rede, or counsel. Not so much a ditherer, perhaps more a bit of a twit. His wife Emma, mother of Edward the Confessor, was once accused of being too friendly with the Bishop of Winchester. Electing for trial by ordeal, she is said to have walked blindfolded over nine red-hot plough-shares, emerging unscathed to establish her innocence. Modern theories of juris-prudence would be less impressed by such evidence.

☐ See also: *Greece.*

THIOPIA

The name of Ethiopia comes from the

Greek: *aithein*, to burn and *ops*, face. It was originally applied to all countries populated by those of a brownish or black counte-nance. The present country of Ethiopia has some claim to being the oldest nation in continuous existence, though the name has been used for various areas of Africa. However long it has been around, Ethiopia never seems to have been in the right place when roads were being built. Although there are 22 million kilometres of roads in the world, more than half the Ethiopian population live more than ten miles from the nearest highway.

☐ See also: *exercise, saints.*

ETIQUETTE

Chimpanzees often greet one another by shaking hands. When a dog wags its tail, this should be interpreted as a welcoming gesture, but when a cat does so it must be taken as a warning. Sadly, rules for human behaviour are less precise and vary in different lands.

In Tibet, it is the height of good manners to stick your tongue out at a guest. When shaking hands, you should bump heads too.

In Siam, one's social status played an important part in determining behaviour when two men met by chance. The inferior should throw himself on the ground and wait while the superior sends an attendant to examine him and determine whether he has eaten, or carries with him, anything of an offensive smell. If so, he earns a kick from his superior and must retire at once. Otherwise the servant will pick him up and the master may deign to speak to him.

Much the same sort of thing used to happen in Ceylon, but the inferior person was obliged to throw himself to the ground and constantly repeat the name and title of his respected colleague. The latter would then pass on, usually ignoring the obsequious-ness going on at his feet.

In the Philippines matters were more dignified. To show respect in greeting, the body is bent very low, the hands are placed on the cheeks and one foot is raised in the air with the knee bent. Of course, this display loses much of its dignity if you then fall over.

When entering a house in North Korea, your shoes should be removed and left outside the front door. This might seem an imposition, but it can be considerably simpler than entering a Madagascan home. In that country it is bad manners to enter in a direction contrary to the sense of fate. The fates, or vintana, may be assumed for most purposes to travel clockwise, so if you are unlucky enough to approach the house from the wrong side, you could find yourself having to walk all the way round the building before reaching the front door.

Mealtimes are full of rules for correct behaviour. In the Middle Ages gentlemen were advised not to scratch at their codware while eating from the communal trough. Now life is even more complicated. In Nigeria it is very bad manners to touch food with one's left hand. The tyrranosaurus, however, never ate with its fingers; its forelegs were so short they could not reach its mouth.

The rules of etiquette are at their most precise in **JAPAN**, where the Ainu women always politely cover their mouth with one hand when they speak to men. Bowing is another art which must be practised. In 1979 Tokyo department stores trained their shop assistants with a bowing machine (ojigi renshuki) which instructed them by bending their bodies at the right angles. It is very important to get the right depth of bow when serving a customer in the store: 15° is sufficient inclination for a colleague or to a customer in the hallways, but 30° becomes appropriate when welcoming a customer into the store. After business has been concluded and the customer departs a farewell bow of 45° is indicated.

Gloves can be a terrible problem, but the following three rules should be remembered:

1. At balls and evening parties, appear in full dress and always wear gloves, making sure to put them on before entering the room;
2. Ladies should not remove their gloves when making an afternoon call;
3. Peers may not wear gloves in the House of Lords if the Sovereign is there.

And above all, keep your napkin on your knees; do not tuck a corner of it down your neck.

☐ See also: *visiting cards.*

EUCALYPTUS

(From the Greek: *eu*, well; *kalyptos*, covered.) Genus of trees of the natural order Myrtaceae. Baby koalas are weaned on a eucalyptus soup served direct from the mother's anus. As if somewhat ashamed at this anal fixation, the leaves of the eucalyptus tree hang vertically. Two people in the London telephone directory are named R. Sole.

EUNUCH

(From the Greek: *eune*, bed; *ekhein*, keep.) Word originally applied to men in charge o oriental ladies' bedchambers. The castra tion came later. The most useful thing eve created by a eunuch is paper, invented b Ts'ai Lun in China in AD 105. Adolescen eunuchs do not suffer from acne.

☐ See also: *burial, India.*

EUPHEMISM

The *New York Times* 'Grand Prize fo Euphemism' was awarded to the Centra Intelligence Agency for referring to a assassination unit as a 'health alteration committee'.

It is against the law to ask for contraceptives by name in a Greek chemist's shop. You must call them 'therapeutics'.

EURIPIDES (480–406 BC)

Athenian tragic poet who studied eloquence under Prodicus, ethics under Socrates and philosophy under Anaxagoras.

☐ See **DEATH.**

EUROPE

Continent to the north of Africa and to the west of Asia.

☐ See **PLAGUE, SAHARA, TURKEY.**

EUROPEAN ECONOMIC COMMUNITY

According to a statement issued in 1977 by the Bavarian Farmers' Union, there are 279 words (in German) in the ten commandments, 300 words in the American Declaration of Independence, but the EEC ordinance on the import of caramel sweets requires 25,911 words.

EUTHANASIA

(From the Greek: *eu*, well; *thanatos*, death.) Plato advocated euthanasia and this 'good death' was common under the Roman emperors. On the island of Ceos (Khios) in the Cyclades euthanasia at 60 was the rule.

☐ See **NOBEL.**

EVEREST

Highest peak in the Himalayas, named after Sir George Everest (1790–1866), surveyor-general of India. Mount Everest is one foot higher than it was a century ago and apparently still growing. No climbers have ever reached the top of Everest carrying a grand piano. The highest mountain yet conquered by a piano-carrying team is the 6,500-ft Gschollkopf peak in the Austrian Tyrol in 1975.

☐ See also: *garbage.*

EVOLUTION

According to the evidence of fossilised remains, the cockroach has remained unchanged for the last 250 million years. They had less time to enjoy themselves in those days, since the friction of the tides is constantly slowing the earth down. Four hundred million years ago, the day was two hours shorter than it is today. More important, in 1958 the Standards Department at the Board of Trade discovered that the Imperial Standard Yard was shrinking at a rate of a millionth of an inch a year.

EXCURSIONS

One of the earliest special excursions by train was a day trip to see a public hanging in Bodmin jail. After watching a public execution in Paris, Tolstoy vowed never again to work for any national government. He died in a stationmaster's office after falling fatally ill on a train.

It took 4,278 special trains to convey 2 million French soldiers to the front for the initial engagements of the First World War. All but nineteen of the trains arrived on schedule.

EXECUTION

The fifteenth-century King Scanderburg of Albania once executed two prisoners at once. They were bound together and, with a single blow of his sword, the powerful king cut them both in half at the waist.

Mary Queen of Scots could have done with the services of the good King Scanderburg at her own execution on 8 February 1587. Despite being generously tipped in advance, the executioner took fifteen blows to sever her head.

☐ See also: *coffin, Halifax, hangmen, Mata Hari, Monmouth, Raleigh, shivering, tipping.*

EXERCISE

Dancing, as a form of exercise, has been calculated to expend between 200 and 400 calories an hour. Except, of course, when one of the dancers is a traditional Ethiopian. There is a belief in that country that it is unhealthy for a woman while dancing to move her body between the waist and the knees.

☐ See also: *sex.*

EXTRACTION

Four tons of bad teeth are extracted from the mouths of children in Britain each year. The Scots do, however, have even more false teeth than the English or Welsh. The Luo tribe in Kenya is another society with a high extraction rate. They identify themselves as members of the tribe by having six of their lower front teeth removed.

EXTRA-TERRESTRIAL

(From the Latin: *extra*, outside; *terrestris* terra, the earth.) On average, just over on Californian each day claims to have had close encounter with an extra-terrestria There is a lady in South Africa who clain to spend her weekends on Alpha Centaur She has friends there. Lucky, really, be cause the hotels in these exotic places ar very expensive.

EYE

Frogs never eat with their eyes open. Whe eating, their eyeballs are used to push dow against the roof of the mouth to force foo into the stomach. Toads eat in a simila style. Butterflies' eyes are too delicate to b used in such a manner. They have abou 17,000 lenses. Bees' eyes only have 6,30 lenses.

EYELID

The crocodile has translucent eyelids. Th cobra, like all other snakes, has no eyelic at all, but the mating of cobras can la anything from two minutes to twenty-fou hours. One gram of venom from a Kin cobra can kill 150 people. For those real big jobs, though, why not consider kok frog venom? One gram of that can wipe ou 40,000 if used sparingly.

EZRA (fifth century BC)

Ezra was a Jewish scribe who lived in exi in Babylon when Artaxerxes Longiman (*qv*) was King. Verse 21 of chapter 7 of th Book of Ezra contains every letter of th alphabet except J.

F

FALCON

The falcon takes its name from its hook-like claws (Latin: *falx*, a sickle).

☐ See **SPEED.**

FALSTAFF, Sir John

Comic character in Shakespeare's *Henry IV* and *Merry Wives of Windsor*.

☐ See **POTATO.**

FAMINE

In times of famine, natives of Tierra del Fuego (Spanish: Land of Fire) say that they kill and eat the old women before the dogs come in for the same treatment. This is a very logical thing to do, since old women cannot catch seals.

☐ See also: *China.*

FARTING

Edward de Vere, Earl of Oxford (1550–1604) making his low obeisance to Queen Elizabeth, happened to let a Fart, at which he was so abashed and ashamed that he went to Travell, 7 yeares. On his returne the Queen welcomed him home, and sayd, 'My Lord, I had forgot the Fart' (Aubrey's *Brief Lives*).

Modern astronauts will not eat beans, onions or cabbage before a flight.

FASHION

Although the codpiece was a popular item of garb in the Middle Ages, and denim (from the French: *serge de Nîmes*) has been known since 1695, the first appearance in public of a denim codpiece is believed to have been on 8 September 1983 at the opening of the Stephen Oliver and Tim Rice musical *Blondel*. There are over eighty different varieties of rice in India.

☐ See also: *Catherine de Medici.*

FATALITIES

The sixth most common cause of accidental death in the USA is choking. This accounts for 2,500 fatalities each year. Bread and hard-boiled eggs are the most popular items to choke on.

FAWKES, Guy (1570–1606)

Until 1859 it was an offence in England not to celebrate Guy Fawkes day. Nowadays celebration is optional, but one would be well advised not to celebrate by riotously demolishing a hovel. Riotous demolition of a hovel is still an offence under English law.

FEAR

Mental uneasiness often caused by apprehension of something terrible.

☐ See **BOMBING, SCHOENBERG, STRING.**

FEATHER

In sixteenth- and seventeenth-century England it was generally believed that no one who lay on feathers could die in peace. A dying man would therefore be liable to have his pillow snatched away before he gave up the ghost. Eighty per cent of a swan's feathers are on its head and neck.

FERDINAND, Archduke Francis (1863–1914)

Austrian archduke assassinated at Sarajevo, bringing about the start of the First World War. His assassin's footprint is preserved in the paving stone where he stood to fire the fatal shot.

☐ See **DEATH.**

FERRARI

☐ See **BURIAL.**

FERRET

(*Putorius*) A half-tamed albino polecat. The ferret catches a cold in exactly the same way a human does. A survey has shown that humans are more likely to catch cold if they have a mother-in-law staying with them. No similar study has yet been done on mothers-in-law of ferrets.

☐ See also: *gerbil, gluttony.*

FERTILISER

Every day more than a quarter of a million tons of man-made fertiliser are used throughout the world. Of course, there is a far greater amount of natural fertiliser produced. The muck, however, is not spread at all evenly. The Netherlands use as much fertiliser as the whole of South America. Sweden uses as much as the whole of India.

Half the inhabitants of South America live in Brazil. The average age for an Indian girl to get married is 14½.

☐ See also: *auction.*

FIDELITY

Once a goose has found the right gander for her, they will remain faithful to one another for all their lives.

☐ See also: *bedtime, Congo, Thrace.*

FIELDS, Claude William Dukenfield (known as W.C.) (1880–1946)

☐ See **LAST WORDS.**

FIJI

The cannibals of Fiji used to have special forks for eating human flesh. You are not permitted to export whale teeth from Fiji without a special licence. It is an old custom among Fijian natives to mourn the passing of a friend by cutting off a joint from one little finger. There are no restrictions on the export of severed finger joints.

FILMS

The devil has been portrayed in more films than Jesus Christ. But Jesus is the only man, apart from Sir Isaac Wolfson, to have had colleges named after him at both the Universities of Oxford and Cambridge.

☐ See also: *lip.*

FINE ART

Three graduates in Fine Arts were awarded an Arts Council grant of £400 in 1976 to walk around East Anglia with a 10-foot yellow pole tied to their heads. They denied that it was a waste of money, describing their venture as 'an attempt to tread new ground in the art world'. The amount of new ground they and their pole trod was a total of 150 miles.

FINGERNAIL

The standard scientific unit of rate of growth of human nails is the nail-second, defined as the average length grown by a nail each second. One nail-second is approximately equal to .0000039 inch. Of the human fingernails, the thumbnail grows the

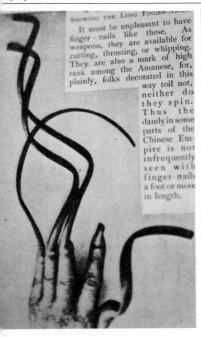

SHOWING THE LONG FINGER-NAILS

It must be unpleasant to have finger-nails like these. As weapons, they are available for cutting, thrusting, or whipping. They are also a mark of high rank among the Amanese, for, plainly, folks decorated in this way toil not, neither do they spin. Thus the dandy in some parts of the Chinese Empire is not infrequently seen with finger-nails a foot or more in length.

slowest, the middle fingernail fastest. The record length of fingernail was held by a Chinese priest in Shanghai. Uncurled they measured 58 cm (22.8 in.) and were the result of constant effort between 1883 and 1910.

Hindu babies do not have their nails cut until they are a year old.

FINGERPRINTS

Harry Jackson was the first man in Britain to be convicted on the evidence of fingerprints. The year was 1902 and his crime was the theft of some billiard balls. Mary Queen of Scots and Mozart were both keen and skilful billiard players. Haydn once tore the cloth on Mozart's billiard table. Mozart also had a slight deformity of his left ear, usually kept covered by his wig. According to Pliny the Elder, earache can be cured by the application of semen of the wild boar.

☐ See also: *Darwin, Ford.*

FINLAND

The Finnish language has over 4,000 irregular verbs. It has also been claimed that saippuakivikauppias, the Finnish word for a caustic soda dealer, is the longest palindrome in any language. This is arguable since the word seems never to have been used other than to make claims about long palindromes. The same applies to saippuakauppias (a soap-dealer), the second longest palindrome in the world. The longest English palindrome is 'redivider', one who divides again.

☐ See also: *bombing, newt.*

FIREFLY

A beetle which glows in the dark; in Europe of the family Lampyridae, in America of the genus *Pyrophorus.* The glow from a firefly is bright enough to shine through the stomach of a frog which has eaten it. The Scottish red deer can extinguish the glimmer, however, because Scottish red deer eat frogs. A deer sheds its antlers every year. If it does not do so it is probably an antelope.

☐ See also: *glow-worm.*

FIRE OF LONDON

Only six people lost their lives as a direct result of the Fire of London in 1666. It is not known how many owed their salvation to sophisticated devices such as Mr Joachim Smith's New Invented Machine for Escaping from Fire. Neither Anacreon nor Agathocles were among the six who perished, both having suffered fatal accidents sometime before the fire. Anacreon choked on a grape pip while drinking, while Agathocles choked on a toothpick at the age of 75.

Mr Joachim Smith's New Invented Machine for Escaping from Fire

A fish

ISH

The first fish in space were South American guppies which spent forty-eight days in orbit aboard Salyut 5 in 1976.

☐ See also: *angling, Barbados, capital punishment, Carter, food preservation, impotence, pets, pregnancy, productivity, Rumania, sport.*

ISHING

More than 95 per cent of all fish caught throughout the world are caught in the northern hemisphere. The codfish weighs 5,000 times as much as its brain. Although fish are not generally renowned for their intelligence it is known that goldfish remember things better in cold water than in warm water.

☐ See also: *angling, capital punishment, cormorant, Peru.*

ITZGERALD, Edward (1809–83)

Fitzgerald's celebrated translation of the Rubaiyat of Omar Khayyam was ignored until Rossetti found a copy in a second-hand shop and he and Swinburne proclaimed its genius to the world.

☐ See **BROWNING.**

LAMINGO

The flamingo (*phoenicopterus*) can eat only with its head upside down. It is not born pink but acquires that colour from its food and digestive processes. It will stay pink only if fed on a certain type of shrimp. The South American leaf-eared mouse does not eat shrimps but prefers cochineal beetles, which turn its bones pink. The lobster has blue blood.

☐ See also: *artificial limbs.*

LAX

A knowledge of flax (*linum usitatissimum*, annual herb of the natural order Linaceae) can be particularly important around the west of Poland where the legendary witch Pszepolnica roams. She is reputed to be

horse-footed and to have the habit of beheading anyone who cannot talk about flax for a whole hour.

FLEA

Family of small wingless parasitic insects. The flea can jump over two hundred times its own length. It is essential to the health of armadillos and hedgehogs, which would die if they were de-loused. Hedgehog was a delicacy in ancient Egypt, where the basic diet was bread, beer and onions. They were also quite partial to a bit of striped hyena, which was stuffed to death by force-feeding it goose and duck.

☐ See also: *beer, cream, foreplay, myxomatosis, saints, ukelele.*

FLEMING, Ian Lancaster (1908–64)

British writer and creator of James Bond.

☐ See **BEQUESTS, MUSSOLINI.**

FLIRTATION

☐ See **CAREERS.**

FLOOD

Astrologers all over Europe predicted a great flood in 1524, caused by a conjunction of all the planets in Pisces. In London 20,000 people fled for higher ground. The flood did not happen, though it did rain a lot that year.

On the day appointed for the flood, the Elector of Brandenburg took refuge on a nearby mountain. When the deluge did not come, he sent his coachman and horses back to the castle. They were struck by lightning and killed before they arrived.

☐ See also: *China, treacle.*

FLORIDA

Most south-easterly of the United States. It is forbidden to import piranha fish into Florida.

FLY

Insect of the order Diptera (from the Greek: *di-*, twice; *pteron*, a wing) with two wings.

☐ See **PAMPERED PETS, TYPHOID.**

FLYING

Of the 9,000 known species of bird, less than one per cent are flightless. The species which are grounded may possess compensatory attributes. The emu, for example, displays a remarkable skill at eating caterpillars. One emu was once found to have 2,000 caterpillars in its stomach.

FOOD

In a lifetime, the weight of food eaten by an average Western person is approximately equal to that of six large elephants. Until the fifteenth century this all had to be consumed without the benefit of plates, which were not invented before that time. Food was generally eaten on slices of stale bread, which must have been jolly good at soaking up the gravy.

FOOD PRESERVATION

When Napoleon I in 1795 felt the need for more reliable food supplies for his armies on long campaigns, he offered a prize for a means of food preservation. The winning idea came from Nicolas Appert and marked the beginning of the canned food industry.

Clarence Birdseye had the idea for frozen food in 1930 after watching Eskimos catching fish in temperatures of −50°F.

FOOTBALL

During a game of football in Argentina in 1972 a linesman was kicked to death by players. The entire team was imprisoned.

☐ See also: *cow, lip-reading, philosophy.*

FOOTWEAR

The use of socks in folk medicine has a long and pungent history. Among their uses are the following:

For a *sore throat*, prepare the sock b wearing it in boots at work for at least a week. Remove the sock and tie it round th neck (Old Appalachian remedy).

For *pneumonia*, wear woollen sock soaked in vinegar, with dry socks put o over them and finally a woollen blanket t wrap the feet. Repeat when the vinegar ha dried (Old Russian cure).

Finally another old Russian cure fo *gout*: Boil 6–8 onions in a gallon of wate for 30 minutes. Strain and use the water t wash socks. Do not rinse. Wear socks whe dry. (If the socks are very dirty, a pre-was in soapy water is recommended before th soak in onion water.)

☐ See also: *common cold, elegance, shoes, socks.*

FORD, Gerald Rudolph (*b*. 1913)

So many requests were received at th White House for the autograph of Presiden Ford's dog Patsy, that a rubber stamp wa made of its pawprint. Patsy was a retriever The Chinese were the first to appreciate th value of fingerprinting, but they never use it for dogs. Dogs are banned from cit streets in China.

FOREPLAY

In the Lundaya Murats tribe of Borneo man may be fined the sum of one pig if he i caught in the act of picking fleas from th hair of a married woman.

FORGIVENESS

In 1857 Charles Baudelaire was fined for a offence against public morals caused by th publication of *Les Fleurs du Mal*. Ninety two years later, in 1949, the authorities ha second thoughts and his conviction wa quashed by the criminal court of the Cour of Cassation in Paris.

FORSDYKE-SMITH, Ponsonby

No. 66 Fighter Squadron, RAF Ackling ton, Northumberland, had a rattlesnak named Ponsonby Forsdyke-Smith. Its ran was that of leading aircraftman. Unfortunately it died shortly after its arrival on the base, before any of its colleagues had a chance to join the Oklahoma based society, 'The Order of the White Fang' for survivors of rattlesnake bites.

FORTUNE-TELLING

Predicting the future from the sounds emanating from the stomach is called gastromancy.

□ See **ALECTRYOMANCY, MOLEOSOPHY, ONION.**

FORTY-TWO

The number forty-two had great significance in ancient Egypt. It was the number of demons believed to be present at the last judgement of each human soul. One demon represented each district of Egypt and would claim the soul if it had personal knowledge of any sins committed within its diocese. When Douglas Adams chose forty-two as the answer to the Ultimate Question of Life, the Universe and Everything in his *Hitch-hiker's Guide to the Galaxy*, he was totally unaware of the mystical significance of the number.

FOSSIL

Shrivelled up remains of once living tissue.

□ See **IMPOTENCE, PEANUT.**

FOUNTAIN

Visitors to the famous fountain at the Piazza di Trevi in Rome should be sure to acquaint themselves properly with the bye-laws. Two Italian journalists were fined in 1951 for letting their seal have a swim in the waters of the fountain. They were contravening a regulation which prohibits the throwing of anything other than money into the fountain.

FOX

Animal belonging to the genus *Vulpes*. In ancient Rome it was thought that the genitals of a fox bound to the patient's head would cure a headache. Neither was there anything wasted in the pharmacy, for the testicles of the fox were good for scrofulous tumours or mumps. Forty-two (*qv*) per cent of the United Kingdom population suffer sometimes from headaches, the highest proportion in the world. No wonder the foxes look so frightened.

The correct collective noun for foxes is a leash of foxes.

FRANCE

Country of Western Europe whose capital is Paris and language French. Charles VIII of France had six toes on one foot. Anne Boleyn could outbid this with an extra finger on her left hand and three breasts. (The supernumerary nipple has also been described more modestly as a cyst on her neck.) Mickey Mouse has only four fingers on each hand.

□ See also: *accidents, Andorra, Buckingham Palace, Catherine de Medici, circumnavigation, elegance, hair, homosexuality, idiocy, leeches, Nobel, pyjamas, robbery, Zoroaster.*

FRANCE, Anatole (1844–1924)

Pen-name of French author and satirist Jacques Anatole Thibault.

□ See **BOOKS.**

FRANKENSTEIN

Horror story creation by Mary Wollstonecraft Shelley (1797–1851), wife of Percy Bysshe Shelley.

□ See **CHEMISTRY.**

FRANKFURT

German city on the River Main. Four men reading constantly for eighteen hours a day would take a lifetime to work through everything on offer at the 1983 Frankfurt book fair. But if they did take on the task it would at least give them a ready excuse never to have to go to another Frankfurt book fair.

□ See also: *Frederick William I, sausage.*

FRANKLIN, Benjamin (1706–90)

American statesman, scientist and son of an English tallow chandler. Quite apart from inventing the rocking chair and **BIFO-CALS**, Benjamin Franklin was responsible for the discovery of the Gulf Stream. He was the youngest son of a youngest son of a youngest son of a youngest son.

An old American Indian cure for jaundice was to administer powdered lice, or to have boiled worms administered by a seventh son. Perhaps, if no seventh son was immediately available, Ben Franklin might have been persuaded to step in as a substitute.

☐ See also: *Churchill, W., Louis XVI.*

FRAUD

The correct collective noun for lapwings is a deceit of lapwings.

☐ See **PTOLEMY.**

FRECKLES

Spots of yellow or brownish pigment in the deeper layers of the epidermis. The Pennsylvania Germans had two remedies for removing freckles: either wash your face with water gathered from tombstones, then come away without looking back; or, if you do not fancy tombstones, you can smear the freckles with frog spawn.

Figures for frogs are not immediately available, but the mother codfish lays between 4 and 6 million eggs at a single spawning.

FREDERICK, Prince of Wales (1707–51)

Son of George II and father of George III, banished from court in 1737 because he kept arguing with his father.

☐ See **CHARLES VIII** of France.

FREDERICK THE GREAT (1712–86)

Frederick II of Prussia, also known as Frederick the Great, used to ride into battle with a doctor alongside. He liked to have his veins opened from time to time in order to calm his nerves. Sometimes at less

stressful moments, he would calm himsel with a cup of coffee, which he liked to have made with champagne. The pressure in a bottle of decent champagne is the same as that in the tyres of a London bus.

Frederick the Great and Ian Fleming both died on 12 August, the opening day o the English grouse shooting season.

☐ See also: *Frederick William I.*

FREDERICK WILLIAM I, King of Prussia (1688–1740)

Father of Frederick the Great, Frederic William I did not give his offspring a happ childhood. His mealtime habits included spitting into the dish to prevent his childre from eating properly, and he tried to strangle his famous son for refusing to renounce his rights to the succession.

Frankfurt was one of the major cities o Prussia but now has the most expensiv taxis on earth.

☐ See also: *breeding, repartee.*

RENCH

The French for a French letter is *une capote anglaise*. The cor anglais is not the French for a French horn. The German for a black eye is a blue eye (*blaues Auge*). The Czech for a beautiful life sounds exactly the same as the Russian for a red stomach.

REUD, Sigmund (1856–1939)

Sigmund Freud, father of **PSYCHO-ANALYSIS**, was breast-fed.

RIEDMAN, Milton (*b.* 1912)

Milton Keynes is not what you get if you cross a Keynesian with a monetarist.

☐ See **ECONOMICS.**

RIGHT

(From the Old English: *fyrhto*, fear, fright.) An important discovery concerning how to frighten a Jersey cow was announced at the 134th meeting of the American Association for the Advancement of Science: if you burst a paper bag next to the ear of a Jersey cow, its milk flow will be interrupted for thirty minutes.

FRISBEE

A popular and healthy modern pastime.

☐ See **SEX.**

FROG

Smooth-skinned member of the order Ecaudata (without tail) of the class Batrachia. In 1972 soldiers of the Cambodian army opened fire at the sky in order to prevent an eclipse of the moon. They were shooting at a mythical monster frog named Reahou which they believed was trying to eat the moon. In the resulting chaos, two people were killed and fifty injured, but the moon was saved.

☐ See also: *carpentry, chameleon, earthquake, eye, freckles, potato.*

FROZEN FOOD

☐ See **DEATH, SHOPLIFTING.**

A typical problem for the Cambodian army

FRUITFLY

An insect of the genus *Drosophila*. Research has proven that sex shortens the life of the male fruitfly. A celibate fruitfly can expect to have, if not actually enjoy, a life of sixty-five days, but experimental fruitflies, tempted with one luscious virgin female fruitfly each day, only survived an average of fifty-six days. The lucky sample who were offered, and accepted, eight virgin females daily found their life expectancies cut to forty days.

FUNERAL

Funeral is an anagram of 'real fun'.

☐ See **REINCARNATION.**

FUSSINESS

The giant dung beetle will neither feed on nor lay its eggs in, anything less tha elephant droppings.

G

GABON

Libreville, the capital of Gabon, was originally formed in 1849 as a place of refuge for escaped slaves. In Gabon a woman's life expectancy is 45 years, whereas a man can only expect to reach the age of 25. If you want to live a long life, your best bet is to arrange to be born in Sweden (72 for men, 77 for women). Guinea is a good place to avoid (26 for men, 27 for women).

In general, larger mammals have longer lives than smaller ones, though man, the longest lived of all mammals, is an exception to this rule. Among dogs, the smaller breeds live longer.

☐ See also: *pygmy, viper.*

GALILEO GALILEI (1564–1642)

Italian astronomer who, in his spare time, composed music for the lute. Music has three patron saints: St Gregory the Great, St Cecilia and St Dunstan, though the last of these also moonlighted as patron saint of blacksmiths and metalworkers.

GALL-BLADDER

Receptacle on the under surface of the liver where bile is stored. A good place to look for gall-stones.

☐ See CAMEL.

GALL-STONES

(*Biliary calculi*)

☐ See APOPLEXY.

GALSWORTHY, John (1867–1933)

British novelist and dramatist who in 1918 declined the offer of a knighthood.

☐ See HARDY.

GALTIERI, General Leopoldo Fortunato (*b.* 1926)

Leader of the opposition to the British Government in 1983.

☐ See KINNOCK.

GALTON, Sir Francis (1822–1911)

British anthropologist and meteorologist, founder of 'Eugenics' which later provided important ideas in the fields of genetics and Nazism.

☐ See DARWIN.

GAMBLING

☐ See COFFEE, MONACO, QUIZ.

GAMESMANSHIP

Term coined by Stephen Potter for the art of winning games by employing means not directly covered by the rules of the game in question, calculated to distract or disturb the opponent. Before a fight, two hippopotamuses defecate profusely. The one who produces more excrement is usually the eventual winner of the fight, boosted to victory by the smell of his own dung. If that fails, they are wont to confound the enemy with foul-smelling belches. And if it finally comes to making a bolt for it, the hippopotamus can run faster than a man.

GANNET

The gannet or Solan Goose (*Sula bassana*) enjoys eating so much that after a good meal it may find itself too heavy to fly. According to a law passed in the reign of Edward III, it was illegal to eat more than two meals a day. The law did not apply to gannets.

☐ See also: *newt.*

GARBAGE

If all the household garbage produced in Tokyo in a single day was piled into a square column with a base one foot wide, it would be over 100 times as high as Mount Everest. And it would make an awful mess when it fell over. The fastidious English produce an average of only one-third of a ton of rubbish per person per annum.

GARBAGE DISPOSAL

In the Middle Ages an edict banned pigs from town streets in France, after one such animal had caused a death in the royal family by tripping the regal horse. The effect of the ban was a massive increase in the amount of garbage rotting in the street with no pigs around to eat it any more.

GARDENING

In early Babylonia, one feature of New Year's Day celebrations was the election of a commoner to be king for the day. Come midnight, he would be sacrificed. This dubious honour fell one year on Enlil-Bani, gardener to King Erra-Imitti. On New Year's Day, however, Erra-Imitti died. The ex-gardener remained on the throne until his own death twenty-four years later.

GARFIELD, James Abram (1831–81)

American statesman, elected president in 1880. When he was shot in 1881, a metal detector was specially designed by Alexander Graham Bell to search for the assassin's bullet. But for interference from the spring in the mattress upon which he lay, President Garfield might have been saved by the Bell.

☐ See also: *United States of America.*

ARIBALDI, Giuseppe (1807–82)

Italian patriot and son of a fisherman.

☐ See **URUGUAY.**

GARLIC

Pungent bulb of the onion family, genus *Allium.*

☐ See **NUT, RHEUMATISM.**

ARROTTING

(From the Spanish: *garrote*, a cudgel.)

☐ See **KNACKERS.**

ASTRONOMY

The science or art of good food.

☐ See **LION, REINDEER.**

AUGUIN, Paul (1848–1903)

Self-taught French painter who spent his last years in Tahiti.

☐ See **PANAMA.**

ELLER, Uri (*b.* 1946)

Israeli psycho-kineticist specialising in spoons.

☐ See **COMPENSATION.**

GENEROSITY

(From the Latin: *generosus*, of noble birth.) Mrs Mary Kuhery of New Jersey left two dollars to her husband in her will, on the sole condition that he spent half of it on a rope to hang himself.

GENESIS

The first book of the Old Testament.

☐ See **CHLOROFORM, CREATION.**

GENETICS

The best way for a young man to discover whether he will go bald, is to look at his maternal grandfather. Baldness is hereditary, but the gene responsible is on the sex-linked chromosome and skips a generation. An average non-bald human scalp has about 100,000 hairs, but redheads have fewer than blondes or brunettes. Research shows that marriages to brunettes tend to last longer than those to blondes.

☐ See also: *colour-blindness.*

GENGHIS KHAN (1162–1227)

(Alias Jenghiz Khan, etc.) The first great Mongol emperor, also a sporting type who liked to play polo using the skulls of enemy generals for the ball.

☐ See also: *massacre.*

GENIUS

(From the Latin: *genere*, to produce.) The remarkable advances in modern civilisation are owed mainly to the genius of those men and women whose imaginations have enabled them to transcend the commonplace and produce ideas of genuine inspiration to make life easier and more pleasurable for the rest of us. Here, in chronological order, are some of the patented inventions of the past three centuries.

In 1718 a patent was granted by George I to James Puckle for the manufacture of a machine gun which could be adjusted to fire square bullets at Turks and round bullets at Christians.

The year 1860 was a vintage one for useful creativity. It saw a piano with a curved keyboard, to help pianists with short arms to reach all the notes. Also boots with pockets were introduced to come to the aid of nudists.

In 1884 in Germany, finally came what the world had been longing for: the musical cigar. Who could then have blamed the Director of the US Patent Office when, in 1899, he urged President McKinley to abolish his job and the whole organisation on the grounds that: 'everything that can be invented has been invented'.

Four years later, in 1903, he was proved wrong, by Mayer's Improved Toilet Paper. At last a bog roll which enabled advertising matter to be printed on the sheets without any prejudice to the demands of hygiene. The adverts could appear either on detachable sheets or 'in such places as not to come into use for toilet purposes'. Indeed 1903 was a great year for improvements. Pardo's Improved Umbrella, of that date, could be hung from a tree allowing its mosquito net curtain to hang down to the ground providing simultaneous protection from rain and insects.

But we still had to worry about rats. That is, until Joseph Barad's 1908 invention, designed to frighten away the rats from any infested building. It consisted of a chain with bells attached. This would be dropped upon, and cling to the fur of, the first bold rat which ventured out of its hole. This rat would then surely rush back to the nest where the accompanying noise of the bells ringing would frighten away all the other rats in the colony. We had to wait until 1943 for the handbag with the translucent bottom. It is hard to believe, in these present enlightened times, that until that date one had to tip out the contents of a bag to see what was inside it. The ultimate labour-saving device, however, came in 1952 – the revolving spaghetti fork, to eliminate all that tiresome twiddling.

But above all the 'fifties were the decade for infants' improvements. The musical potty (1957) would play a tune only when it was peed into. The following year the babies fought back. A lady in Pennsylvania patented nappies with pistol holsters. Perhaps she was hoping that some sweet child might shoot the man who gave us the musical potty.

And so we come to the man who seems to be the greatest genius of the modern era, William C. Loughran who, in 1960, patented the champagne bottle for launching ships. After seeing film of numerous embarrassing ceremonies at which the bottle had refused to shatter against the side of a ship, he designed a specially tapering bottle, with the glass becoming thinner towards the neck to ensure its successful breakage. Furthermore (showing that Mr Loughran has taste as well as genius) it is filled with a fizzy imitation thereby saving the waste of good champagne. These bottles are now in widespread use at launching ceremonies. As a sideline Mr Loughran also makes 'millionaire's confetti', consisting of shredded banknotes.

?EOGRAPHY

There is a town called Å in Sweden, not to be confused with the villages of the same name in Denmark and Norway. The village of Y is in France and the town of O is in Japan. This latter should on no account be mistaken for the yellow-thighed Oo bird, which lives on Kuan Island, Hawaii. The Hawaiian alphabet has only twelve letters.

☐ See also: ***Bohemia, Kipling.***

?EOLOGY

The science concerning the history and development of the earth's crust. Geologists aspire to the state of geognosy, knowledge of the general structure of the earth.

☐ See **BUCKLAND.**

?EORGE I, King of Great Britain and ?eland (1660–1727)

King George I died on a Saturday. He was succeeded by George II.

☐ See also: ***English, marital stress.***

GEORGE II, King of Great Britain and Ireland (1683–1760)

King George II was the last British king to fight in a battle – at Dettingen in 1743. His death occurred on a Saturday. He was succeeded by George III.

GEORGE III, King of Great Britain and Ireland (1738–1820)

King George III was the grandson of George II. He was terribly short-sighted and died on a Saturday. He was succeeded by George IV.

☐ See also: ***diarist, George III of Saxony, statue, trees.***

GEORGE III OF SAXONY

So pleased was George III of Saxony at the marriage of Princess Sophia of Dresden to the Margrave of Brandenburg in 1662, that he organised a fancy dress hunt to celebrate the event. He went dressed as the goddess Diana. His namesake, George III of England, had more legitimate children than any other British monarch.

George III was too short-sighted to appreciate the plainness of his daughters

GEORGE IV, King of Great Britain and Ireland (1762–1830)

The official cause of death of King George IV was: rupture of blood vessels in his stomach, alcoholic cirrhosis, gout, nephritis and dropsy. With all those afflictions he was evidently lucky to last until the weekend. He died on a Saturday.

☐ See also: *Caroline, James I, shoes.*

GEORGE V, King and Emperor (1865–1936)

King George the Fifth's constant companion was a parrot called Charlotte.

☐ See also: *last words.*

George V in his young days

GERBIL

(From the French: *gerbille*, a gerbil.) The Canadians have a squad of gerbils train to sniff out drugs in their jails. There see to be no collective noun for gerbils, but right expression for ferrets is a 'business ferrets'. The effect of drugs on prison may take various forms, but amphetamir are known to improve the ability of m keys to read facial expressions.

GERMANY

When Charles the Bald was King Germany, Wilfred the Hairy ruled Ca lonia. The two men did not get on well a fought a brief war in AD 878.

☐ See also: *asthma, bat, beer, defection, ukelele.*

GERM WARFARE

Possibly the first use of germ warfare v recorded in the fourteenth century wh the Tartar armies were besieging the wall town of Caffa in the Crimea. Geno merchants in the town had to contend w the threat of infection from bodies of Tar soldiers who had died from bubonic plag catapulted over the town walls. Eau Cologne was originally developed to act a protection against the plague.

GERTRUDE, St (*d.* 659)

Daughter of Pepin the Short and half-sis to Charlemagne.

☐ See **RATTLESNAKE.**

GESTATION

Birth statistics in the United Kingd reveal that the sixth month after marriag the most likely month for a first child to produced.

☐ See also: *vole.*

GHANA

(Formerly the Gold Coast.) Eating is ov ten times more expensive in Ghana than the United Kingdom. Anyone looking a cheaper gastronomic holiday might advised to consider going to jail in Mo omery, Indiana. In 1982, charges were initiated for short-term residents of around 9 a day for the room plus 60p for each meal.

HOST

An apparition.

☐ See **KEVIN, PORCUPINE.**

BBON

Not only birds sing a dawn chorus, the gibbon (*Hylobates*) does so too. The song of the gibbon has been reported as starting in the key of E but sharpening quickly to reach an octave higher after half an hour. Then a gradual flattening in pitch brings it slowly back to its starting point. The latter half of this procedure might be referred to by naturalists as Gibbon's decline and fall.

When Nero was singing in the theatre, none of the audience was allowed to leave the building. Women were said to have given birth as he sang, but some of the more daring or desperate of the listeners feigned death in order to have their bodies removed from the scene.

The collective noun for apes is a shrewdness of apes.

BRALTAR

☐ See **POTATO.**

LBERT, Sir William Schwenk 836–1911)

Arthur Sullivan had a light bulb fitted onto the end of his baton by Thomas Edison so that he could conduct in the dark. His collaborator, W. S. Gilbert, was kidnapped at the age of two when he was in Naples, and was ransomed for £25. He was called to the bar in 1863. Gilbert was by no means the youngest ever kidnap victim. That dubious honour is held by Miss Carolyn Wharton, born at 12.46 pm on 19 March 1955 in Texas and abducted by a woman dressed as a nurse twenty-nine minutes later. In the USA ransom money paid to kidnappers is tax deductible.

GIRAFFE

(From the Arab: *zaraf.*) An even-toed ungulate with long legs and **NECK.** Giraffe's milk is seven times richer in protein than cow's milk. Its heart weighs about 25 lb and its blood pressure is two or three times that of man, quite necessary considering how high the blood must be pumped. There is a special valve in a giraffe's neck to stop the blood rushing to its head when it stoops.

☐ See also: ***boredom, colour-blindness, lemur, maternity, musical composition, telephone.***

GIRL

The word 'girl' (origin obscure) occurs only once in the Bible, but there are eighteen dogs, no cats, and 46,227 uses of the word 'and'.

GLADIATOR

(From the Latin: *gladius*, a sword.) Gladiatorial combat was introduced into Rome in 264 BC.

☐ See **JULIUS CAESAR.**

GLADIOLUS

Any plant of the genus *Gladiolus* of the natural order Iridaceae. From the same linguistic root as 'Gladiator', owing to its sword-like appearance. The plural is gladioli.

☐ See **MALTA.**

GLADSTONE, William Ewart (1809–98)

Prime Minister William Gladstone was born at 62 Rodney Street, Liverpool. He liked to chew each mouthful of food thirty-two times. 'Man has 32 teeth, therefore he should chew each mouthful 32 times.' This profound thought inspired a health cult in America led by Horace Fletcher. 'Nature will castigate those who don't masticate,' pronounced Fletcher, who lost five stones in weight through taking so long to eat. He died in 1919 and the cult faded away.

GLASGOW
□ See **PORNOGRAPHY.**

GLAUCOMA
(From the Greek: *glaukos*, bluish-green.) Disease of the eye marked by increased tension within the eyeball.

□ See **MARKSMANSHIP.**

GLOUCESTER
(Pronounced: Gloster.) At the time of Edward the Confessor there was a bye-law of Gloucester 'to protect Gloucestershire women from marauding Welshmen'. The tallest recorded Welshman was William Evans (1599–1634) of Monmouthshire, standing 7 ft 6 in. high. He was a porter to King James I.

James I considered bear-baiting, mimes, short plays and bowling to be unsuitable activities for a Sunday. His views of marauding forays into Gloucestershire are not known.

GLOVES
There is an old belief that it will bring ba luck to say 'thank you' when someon returns a lost glove. In 1941, 26,000 pairs gloves were lost on London Transport, b there were over 30,000 lost handbags a purses, which carry no similar curse on th return.

□ See also: *etiquette.*

GLOW-WORM
The beetle, *Lampyris noctiluca*, of whi the larvae and wingless female are lum nous. Quite apart from the inconvenien and indignity of not having wings, t female works harder by pulsing every 2 seconds, while the male only pulses eve 5.8 seconds.

GLUE
Impure gelatin obtained by boiling anim refuse. Properly manufactured, fish glue said to be as good as hide glue.

□ See **ALBATROSS.**

GLUTTONY
Honoré de Balzac (1799–1850) at o sitting once consumed 110 oysters, 2 p tridges, 1 duck, 12 cutlets, 12 pears an selection of desserts. In a controlled expe ment, one dragonfly ate forty houseflies two hours. This feat may be compared w the world record set at the 1981 Wo Fly-swatting Championships in Eaglehaw Australia. On a system which awarded o point for a housefly, ten for a blowfly a twenty for a greenfly, 'Blowfly' Mick By scored 148 points, almost doubling previous record. His technique includ the adornment of his person with pieces rotting meat and fruit, a glass of beer, an ferret, all of which helped to attract flies his trusty swatter.

□ See also: *Arpocras, Edward VII, platypus, shrew.*

GOAT
The domestic goat (*capra hircus*) has

highest blood temperature of any mammal. Like the pig, it has around 15,000 taste buds; pretty impressive compared with the 9,000 of humans and hares, but comparatively tasteless beside the rabbit's 17,000. Rooks have only 60 taste buds. A trip of goats is the correct collective expression for these beasts.

☐ See also: *cat, dancing, ordeal by goat, yak.*

The South American Goat-sucker

GOD

The supreme deity.

☐ See **ARABIC**

GOERING, Hermann (1893–1946)

German politician and war criminal. Hermann Goering was perhaps the only man in history to have a prosthetic umbilicus. The poison with which he took his own life just before he was to be hanged, was later found to have been concealed beneath a false naval.

GOETHE, Johann Wolfgang von (1749–1832)

German poet and author of Faust.

☐ See **NEWTON.**

GOLDFISH

Small fish of the carp family native to China and Japan. A goldfish will turn white if left long enough in a darkened room. It can survive being frozen to 310° below zero. Neither a goldfish nor any other fish can survive in the Vinegar River of Colombia, which is too acid for any such creatures to live there. Rather odd when you realise how well fish and vinegar usually go together.

☐ See also: *drowning, fishing, hearing, knowledge, lost property, pets, Pompadour.*

GOLF

(Pronounced *golf*, sometimes *gof*, or in Scotland *gowf*.)

☐ See **KIPLING.**

GONORRHOEA

(From a Greek misunderstanding concerning the nature of the disease: *gonos*, seed; *rheein*, to flow.)

☐ See **MEASLES.**

GOOSE

Name applied to various genera of the order Anseres. The correct collective term for geese is a gaggle, but only if they are on the ground. As soon as they take off they become a skein of geese.

☐ See also: *fidelity, flea.*

GORILLA

Largest of the anthropoid apes, the gorilla sleeps for fourteen hours a day, is a vegetarian, has no hair on its chest and the erect penis of the male measures only two inches. The flatworm's penis comes out of its mouth and is accorded with spikes and poison glands. The penis of the spider, on the other hand, is at the end of one of its legs.

☐ See also: *brain, snoring, swimming.*

GORMLESSNESS

During rainstorms, turkeys have the habit of looking upwards, with their mouths open. Many have been known to drown by doing so. This all-American bird was originally marketed in Europe by Turkish merchants, hence the misnomer.

GOUT

Constitutional disorder obtainable in three sizes: acute, chronic and irregular.

☐ See also: *footwear, George IV, Pitt.*

GRABLE, Betty (Elizabeth Grasle, 1916–73)
☐ See **HARRIS, Frank.**

GRAFFITI

Plural of graffito (from the Greek: *graphein*, to write). A mural scribbling or drawing.

☐ See **MORALITY.**

GRAMOPHONE

Of all his inventions, Thomas Edison took greatest pride in the phonograph. What he did not think of, however, was the chocolate gramophone record. Patented in 1903, this was a chocolate disc, wrapped in tinfoil upon which grooves had been cut to make it playable on a gramophone. After the overture the chocolate could be eaten as a main course. This groovy chocolate bar was evidently too far ahead of its time to be a commercial success.

☐ See also: *Bhutan.*

GRANT, Sir Robert (1779–1838)

British governor of Bombay.
☐ See **METEMPSYCHOSIS.**

GRANT, Ulysses Simpson (1822–85)

American soldier and President of the USA for two terms. Ulysses S. Grant's wife was cross-eyed. He liked her that way and would not allow her to undergo the minor surgery needed to correct the squint.

GRASSHOPPER

Saltatorial orthopterous insects of the Locustidiae and Acridiidae families.

☐ See **BLOOD, SAUSAGE.**

GRAVEYARD

The sort of place one would not mind being seen dead in.

☐ See **SOMALIA.**

GRAVY

Juices from meat while cooking, often found in gravy-boat.

☐ See **FOOD.**

GREECE

Formerly part of the East Roman Empire. Constantine V reigned over the area including Greece from AD 741–75. The Greeks gave him the name Copronymus because he is said to have defecated in the font at his baptism. *Copros* is the Greek for dung. Compared with Constantine the Incontinent, Ethelred the Unready was a minor offender; his baptism was marked by urination in the font.

The Greek national anthem has 158 verses.

☐ See also: *death, marital customs.*

GREEK SCHOLARSHIP

A branch of classical learning.
☐ See **POGO STICK.**

GREENE, Graham (*b.* 1904)
☐ See **WRITING.**

GREENLAND

If a child dies in some parts of Greenland, a

live dog is buried with it to guide it to the next world. Greenland is the world's largest producer of icebergs. The Jakobshavn Glacier alone sends a new iceberg into the sea every five minutes.

☐ See also: *confidence tricksters.*

GRENADA

When the United States marines launched their 1983 invasion of the Caribbean Island of Grenada, the Soviet television news condemnation of the act lost some of its conviction through the newscaster's error in pointing vigorously at Granada in Spain throughout his commentary. Such an error would hardly have been noticed in Libya, where there is only one television set for every 2,000 people.

GREYHOUND

Of all dogs, greyhounds have the best eyesight. But their sense of smell is poor and they are much noisier than the Basenji, which do not bark. The greyhound is also untidier than the poodle, which does not moult.

The first time artificial insemination was performed on a dog was in 1885. The experiment was conducted by the priest Lazzaro Spallanzi who, six years earlier, had been the first to establish the necessity of sperm for fertilisation.

GROPIUS, Walter (1883–1969)

☐ See **GROUPIES.**

GROUPIES

Marie Budberg (1892–1974) was a Russian aristocrat who lived most of her life in London. Maxim Gorky and H. G. Wells were among those with whom she had amorous liaisons, but the all-time greatest cultural groupie must have been Alma Maria Schindler. Her first husband was composer Gustav Mahler. She was widowed, then married painter Oskar Kokoschka. Moving on after a divorce to architect Walter Gropius, she ended up with playwright (and Oscar winner) Franz Werfel. All her husbands had good claims to be the leading exponents in their fields at that time.

GUATEMALA

Republic of Central America of which the capital is called (with stunning lack of originality) Guatemala City.

☐ See **QUETZAL.**

GUILLOTINE

The first execution by guillotine in France was performed in 1792. It was such a success that they immediately made eighty more guillotines and trained 160 men to operate them. The last public guillotining in France was of the murderer Eugen Weidmann on 17 June 1939. This was just short of fifty years after the first use of judicial electrocution in the United States, which took place in 1890. That had not been an unmitigated success; the victim, William Kemmer, took eight minutes to die.

☐ See also: *heredity, poetic justice.*

GUINEA

There is a not particularly friendly tribe in Guinea, West Africa, called the Kissi. The unit of currency is more aptly named: the syli.

Tongues of Guinea fowl were considered to be an aphrodisiac in Georgian England. Or you could try an extract from the sinews of octopus tentacles. Should that sound a trifle syli, it might be borne in mind that Equatorial Guinea (a different country just below the bump on the left of Africa) had three kings named Bonkero.

☐ See also: *Gabon.*

GUINEA PIG

Small domesticated rodent having no connections with Guinea, but possibly some with Guyana. Penicillin is fatal to guinea pigs.

GUSTAVUS III, King of Sweden (1746–92)

King Gustav III of Sweden imposed one of the most benign death sentences on record when he ordered a convicted murderer to drink himself to death on coffee. The good king thought coffee to be poisonous. The murderer proved that it was not.

In the sixteenth and seventeenth centuries, drinking coffee was itself a crime in Turkey, carrying a death penalty with more conventionally prompt action.

H

HAAKON HAAKONARSON, King of Norway (1204–63)

Friendly Norwegian King who liked to send his friends polar bears. Also known as King Haakon IV, or King Haakon the Old.

☐ See **HENRY III.**

HAAKON VII, King of Norway (1872–1957)

Born Prince Charles, second son of Frederick VIII of Denmark, he took the name Haakon when elected king on Norway's separation from Sweden in 1905. He married Maud, youngest daughter of Edward VII.

☐ See **DEATH, TRANSVESTISM.**

HAEMOPHILIA

(From the Greek: *haima*, blood; *philia*, friendship, tendency to.) Congenital tendency towards bleeding.

☐ See **MUSSOLINI.**

HAGGIS

Ancient Scottish dish made from the insides of a sheep. The largest haggis ever made weighed a quarter of a ton and took twelve hours to cook.

HAIR

King Francis I of France introduced the death penalty for anyone wearing a beard or moustache. The more liberal regime of Peter the Great of Russia merely imposed a beard tax in 1698, though it was later decreed that offenders would be shaved with a blunt razor or plucked clean, one hair at a time, with pincers. It is not known whether these laws were inspired by a fear of beards, if so, pogonophobia would be the right word to describe the condition.

Francis I was the first owner of the 'Mona

Lisa', which he kept in his bathroom. True to the hairless fashion of the time, the 'Mona Lisa' has no eyebrows. The model's enigmatic smile conceals dentures, fashioned for her by Leonardo da Vinci from a copper frame and three teeth purloined from corpses. She lost her own teeth between sittings.

☐ See also: ***Baudelaire, Germany, polar bear, Scotland, Shakespeare.***

HAIRCUT

The wartime record for giving a US Marine a haircut was six seconds. For alacrity, this may be compared with the speed of Mrs James E. Duck of Memphis, Tennessee, who gave birth to triplets in 1977 within the space of two minutes. This was the fastest ever recorded natural birth of triplets.

Barbers in the Yemen also perform circumcisions. Speed records are not kept.

☐ See also: ***Disraeli.***

Typical erection of a haircut in the Yemeni style. The model is from Natal

HAITI

One of the worst jobs in history was tha of the royal guards to Henri Christoph (1767–1820), King of Haiti. He demande a high standard of loyalty in his guards an was known to order them to march over 200-foot cliff as a test. Those who obeye plunged to their deaths on the rocks below the disobedient fared less well, bein mutilated before their execution.

☐ See also: ***dolphin.***

HALIFAX

'From Hell, Hull and Halifax, Good Lorc deliver us.' This old beggars' and vag bonds' prayer (of the sixteenth or earl seventeenth century) named Hull, too we governed for beggars to make a dece living, and Halifax, because of the summar executions for theft on the Halifax gibbe Under the Gibbet Law, the gaol and the ax were kept by the Bailiff of the Lord of th

THE HALIFAX GIBBET-LAW.

Manor. Execution was the punishment for crimes involving theft of goods to the value of 13½ pence or more. A jury of sixteen men valued the goods and established the guilt of the accused. The gibbet was a type of guillotine with an iron axe hauled up by cord and pulley. Execution was immediate if it was a market day, otherwise saved for the next day when a crowd would be assured. A nice further point of procedure was that if an ox, sheep, horse or other animal had been stolen, that beast was attached to the rope holding the axe and by being freed would cause it to fall.

HALITOSIS

(From the Latin: *halitus*, a vapour.)

□ See **ALLIGATOR.**

HALLEY, Edmund (1656–1742)

English astronomer who saw a comet in 1682, identified it as the same one which had appeared in 1607 and 1531, and predicted its return in 1757. He died fifteen years too soon to enjoy it.

□ See **ENTREPRENEURS.**

HAMBURG

McDonalds have sold more than 25 billion hamburgers since the company began.

□ See also: *politeness.*

HAMLET

Shakespearean tragedy first performed in 1602.

□ See **BEQUESTS, PORCUPINE, THESPIANS.**

HAM SANDWICH

□ See **OHIO.**

HAMSTER

A rodent (*Cricetus*). Every golden hamster is a direct descendant of one of three members of a family of thirteen hamsters dug up in a Syrian desert in 1930. They are all totally colour-blind.

HAND

Prehensile extremity of the arm.

□ See **ARTIFICIAL LIMB, AUSTRIA, BONE.**

HANDCUFFS

□ See **DARWIN, MISOGYNY.**

HANDEL, George Frederic (1685–1759)

Musical son of a barber-surgeon, born at Halle in Saxony. In 1923, the American publishers of Handel's *Messiah* sued the writers of the popular song 'Yes, we have no bananas' claiming that the melodic line had been pinched from the Allelujah chorus. The court found in favour of Mr Handel.

HANDKERCHIEF

In 1785 Louis XVI of France decreed that all handkerchiefs must be square. Whatever shape of handkerchief you have, it is impossible to sneeze with your eyes open.

□ See also: *Richard II, waxworks.*

HANG-GLIDING

□ See **SWITZERLAND.**

HANGING

Judicial execution by constriction or dislocation of the neck. The oldest person to be hanged for murder in the United Kingdom was Charles Frembd, aged 71, who did away with his wife and paid the penalty at Chelmsford in 1914. One of the luckiest men to be hanged was John Smith, convicted of robbery and strung up in 1705. After fifteen minutes his body was cut down and found to be still alive. He recovered and was reprieved.

During the reign of Edward VI, **TYBURN** came out as the top spot for hangings, averaging about 560 a year.

□ See also: *adolescence, excursions, incompetence.*

HANGMEN

Arthur Ellis was dismissed from his post as official hangman in 1935 after bungling the execution of a woman. The 18-foot drop was far too much and resulted in her decapitation. This one error followed 500 successful hangings. How the accident happened is difficult to understand, since any good hangman knows the right length of drop for a given weight: 10 feet for 8 stone, 8 feet for 12 stone and so on.

After his dismissal, Arthur Ellis left England for Canada. Three years later he died in a Montreal hospital after being found in a starving condition on a city street.

☐ See also: *Tyburn.*

HARDY, Thomas (1840–1928)

At birth, Thomas Hardy had been aban-

doned as stillborn until a nurse saw hi suddenly move. Victor Hugo, on the othe hand, was born prematurely. He was als responsible for what must surely be th briefest exchange of telegrams ever. Inqui ing about the sales of *Les Miserables*, Hug cabled his publishers with the single symb '?'. Their enthusiastic reply came equall succinctly: '!'. Thomas Hardy left £91,00 £3,000 more than John Galsworthy.

HARE

Beneficial properties of the hare, if old fol remedies are to be believed, include th power of its ankle bone to ward off cram and its brains taken in wine to cu oversleeping. But the hare is not without i dangers to humans. In 1948, a motorist Johannesburg, South Africa, shot a ha and threw it onto his back seat. The ha was only stunned by the bullet, regaine consciousness shortly after and leapt out the car window. As it bounded out, touched the trigger of the gun and wounde the motorist in the neck. The top speed of hare is 45 mph.

☐ See also: *goat, rabbit.*

HARLOW, Jean (1911–37)

Film Star.

☐ See **ACTING.**

HAROLD II, King of the English (c. 1026–66)

Brother-in-law of Edward the Confesso no relation of Harold I, known as Harol the Harefoot (*d.* 1040).

☐ See **MAORI, PLATO.**

HARRIS, Frank (1854–1931)

Frank Harris, the literary lecher, had a car index of his 2,000 claimed conquests, whic he insured with Lloyd's of London fe $150,000. None of the ladies could hav meant very much to him when this sum compared with the $500,000 for whic Betty Grable insured her legs in 1942.

HAT

An item of **HEADGEAR**. The invention of the silk hat in the USA at the time of Lincoln had the curious geographical side-effect of creating many small lakes and bogs. The reduced demand for beaver fur hats caused by the new silk fashion, led to an increase in the beaver population and consequently a boom in the dam-building industry.

It is not generally realised that a beaver 68 feet long with a 51-foot tail could have built the Kariba dam.

□ See also: *common cold, taboo.*

materialised. Instead he locked them in and set fire to the barn. His reasoning was that the famine ought to end sooner if the poor were sent more quickly to receive their heavenly reward. 'They are like mice, only good to devour the corn,' he said. Later, however, a plague of mice pursued Archbishop Hatto and devoured him in his last stronghold, a tower on the Rhine.

Among others said to have been devoured by mice are Bishop Adolf of Cologne in 1112 and Widerolf, Bishop of Strasburg, in 997.

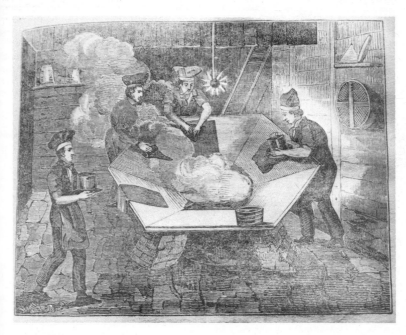

HATTO II (*d. 970*)

During the great famine of AD 970 Archbishop Hatto II of Mainz lured a vast number of poor and oppressed people into a barn at Caub with the promise of food. But this Mad Hatto's Tea Party never

HAWAII

An owl's eye occupies one-sixth of the total volume of its head. Curiously, this is exactly the same ratio as exists between the number of letters in the Hawaiian alphabet and the number of letters in the Cambodian alphabet (cf. **CAMBODIA, GEOGRA-PHY**).

HAYDN, Franz Josef (1732–1809)

☐ See **ALEXANDER THE GREAT, FINGERPRINTS.**

HAZLITT, William (1778–1830)

British essayist, critic and uncomplaining sort of character. Hazlitt's first ambition was to be a portrait painter, but he failed in that endeavour. He proposed to Miss Railton and later to Dorothy Wordsworth. Both rejected him. Finally marrying Sarah Stoddart, he had to travel to Scotland to obtain a divorce. He was separated from his second wife. After being declared bankrupt, he drank too much tea, which ruined his health and digestion. His last words were: 'Well, I have had a happy life.'

HEAD

Part of the body, usually found on the end of the neck, containing the brains and organs of sense. The kings of ancient Scythia divided the spoils of war victories among their troops in proportion to the number of enemy heads each soldier could bring in for counting. If you want to get ahead, get a head.

☐ See also: *Charles I, Cromwell, flamingo, Shelley.*

HEADACHE

It was an old English belief that the noose which was used to hang a criminal would bring relief to the sufferer of a headache. A more recent, and perhaps less unpleasant, American belief was that Coca-Cola was a good tonic for headache or hangover. When the drink was first brewed by John Pemberton in 1886, his intentions were purely medicinal.

☐ See also: *fox.*

HEADGEAR

Though an excellent way of preserving warmth (since up to 80 per cent of the body's heat may escape through the head) the **HAT** seems destined to be a constant source of misunderstanding. John **HETHERINGTON**, inventor of the top hat, was arrested and fined £50 for causing a breach of the peace the first time he wore it in public. Other hats guilty of misrepresentation are the Panama hat, which comes from Ecuador, and the ten-gallon hat which holds only about six pints.

HEALING

Until the mid-fifteenth century, English physicians were not allowed to marry owing to the prevalent belief that bachelors were better healers than married men. In modern times, the shortage of married Catholic priests seems to account for Vatican City having the lowest birth rate in the world.

HEARING

Goldfish have an exceptionally keen sense of hearing; they can distinguish between sound signals one 150-millionth of a second apart. This is considerably better than King John IV of Portugal, who had to have a special throne designed in 1819 as a hearing aid. It had hollow arms which served to carry conversation to his ears.

☐ See also: *Canada.*

HEATHROW AIRPORT

☐ See **AIRCRAFT, LONDON.**

HEDGEHOG

Common British mammal (*Erinaceus europaeus*). There are no hedgehogs in the Americas, no snakes in Ireland, no Income Tax in Kuwait and no soda in soda water.

☐ See also: *flea, homosexuality, lion.*

HEINE, Heinrich (1797–1856)

German Jewish poet converted to Christianity in 1825 and to Parisian life in 1831.

☐ See **BEQUESTS.**

HELL

Hell is mentioned twenty-one times in the Authorised Version of the New Testament. In eight instances this translates the Greek *hades* (a place of rest and gloom for departed spirits), in twelve cases the word was *Gehenna* (much worse than *hades* – a place of eternal torment) and once only the word was *Tartarus* (a sort of classicist's *hades*).

Actually, Hell is a town in Norway. You can take a train there from Trondheim. Norway was the first country to give the vote to women.

HEMINGWAY, Ernest (1899–1961)

American writer who thrived on rye crisps, peanut butter sandwiches, and raw green vegetables.

☐ See **BEETHOVEN.**

HENRY I, King of England (1068–1135)

Third surviving son of William the Conqueror and the only one to have been born in England. Had Henry I been a dwarf, the yard would be much shorter than it is today. For he it was who decreed that a yard would be the length of his own arm, from finger to nose.

☐ See also: ***death.***

HENRY II, King of England (1133–89)

Son of Geoffrey of Anjou, who was the second husband of the Empress Matilda (or Maud), daughter of Henry I of England. In 1176 Henry II ordained the amputation of the right hand and right foot of anyone convicted of robbery, murder, arson or false coining. A bit of a let-off for the left-handed criminal.

In 1984 in Karachi a man was sentenced to have a hand and foot amputated because he had robbed a taxi.

HENRY III, King of England (1207–72)

King Henry III of England had a pet polar bear which he kept in the Tower of London and let out for swims in the Thames on the end of a rope. The king issued a writ 'directing the sheriffs of London to furnish six pence a day to support our White Bear in our Tower of London; and to provide a muzzle and iron chain to hold him when out of the water; and a long strong rope to hold him when he was fishing in the Thames'. It is thought likely that the bear was a present from King Haakon IV of Norway. Haakon often sent Henry gifts and had given him six gyrfalcons and a few goshawks in 1223–4. He also gave polar bears to Emperor Frederick II and to the Emperor of Germany.

In later years the Norwegians stopped giving people polar bears and started to give Christmas trees to the English. Probably a wise decision; a polar bear would look silly and feel undignified standing in Trafalgar Square draped in fairy lights.

One of the sad facts of nature is that no polar bear has ever met a penguin in the wild, owing to their dwelling at opposite poles.

HENRY IV, King of England (1367–1413)

Earl of Hereford, Earl of Derby, Duke of Lancaster, eponymous star of Henry IV Part One, and its sequel Henry IV Part Two.

☐ See **STARLING, TURKEY.**

HENRY V, King of England (1387–1422)

Known as Henry of Monmouth or 'Madcap Hal'.

☐ See **DIFFERENTIALS,
    NECROPHILIA.**

HENRY VI, King of England (1421–71)

☐ See **APOLLONIA.**

HENRY VII, King of England (1457–1509)

Henry Tudor, Earl of Richmond, was recognised as the legitimate king after he slew Richard III at the battle of Bosworth in 1485. The position was secured by his marriage to Elizabeth of York. Elizabeth was later to be the model for the Queen in packs of playing cards. Half the English words indicating trickery or deceit are taken from the vocabulary of card games.

☐ See also: ***Henry VIII, Plato.***

HENRY VIII, King of England (1491–1547)

Henry VIII, second son of Henry VII, was a noted hammer-thrower in his youth. Later he settled down to a more courtly pace and decreed that anyone striking a blow in his palace or court would be punishable by loss of his right hand.

☐ See also: ***aural sex, Boleyn, Buckingham Palace, coronation, Edward VI, paternity, Plato.***

HENRY FREDERICK, Prince of Wales (1594–1612)

Henry Frederick, eldest son of James I, brother of Charles I, was the first known person to die of typhoid. According to a Mexican remedy, two freshly killed pigeons can be used to treat typhoid. They should be rubbed with vinegar and cut in half, then one pigeon tied to the stomach and one to the back of the patient. This pigeon poultice should be applied daily as long as the fever lasts. For those too poor to buy pigeons, newborn puppies were recommended as an alternative.

HERACLITUS (540–475 BC)

Misanthropic Greek philosopher who maintained that fire was the origin of all things; nothing is born, nothing dies; birth and death are but rearrangements. He improvised an early form of underfloor heating by building his house on a dungheap. Despite this healthy state of affairs he could not avoid being rearranged in his sixty-fifth year.

☐ See **CREATION.**

HEREDITY

When his father died in 1726, Charles Jean-Baptiste Sansom inherited the office of Chief Executioner of Paris. Since Charles was only 7 years old at the time, h had to employ an assistant to perform hi duties until he was able to do them himsel: At the age of 35, years of hard executing le him too ill to carry on. He was succeeded b his son, Charles Henri Sansom, aged 15 who continued to serve for fifty years, eve adapting to the modern technology of th guillotine.

HEROISM

Never underestimate a shrew. The Centra African hero shrew (*Scutisorex*) has oddl shaped nodules on its spine which enable to withstand the weight of a 12-stone ma standing on its back. The salivary glands o the short-tailed shrew contain enoug poison to kill 200 mice.

HERRING

Fish (*Clupea harengus*) belonging to th same genus as the sprat or pilchard Nowadays the medicinal properties of th herring tend to be underestimated. An Iris folk remedy for sore throat advocates th application of salt herring to the feet. I Russia, the following prescription wa recommended for cases of malaria: Tak two salted herrings, remove their heads wash, dry and fillet them. Bandage on herring to each foot against the bare sole with the head end towards the balls of th foot. Leave overnight. In the morning was the feet in warm water and dry thoroughly A baby herring is called a fry.

HETHERINGTON, John

For appearing in London streets with a to hat on his head (see **HEADGEAR**) Joh Hetherington was hauled before the Lor Mayor on 5 January 1797. He was charge with having 'appeared on a public highwa wearing upon his head a tall structur having a shining lustre and calculated frighten timid people'. He was bound ove to keep the peace in consideration of a sun of £50.

In 1418 the castle at Vincennes in Franc had its doorway raised by order of th queen, in order to accommodate the fashion for tall ladies' hats without the ladies having to stoop or duck in an undignified manner.

The royal doorway tester at Vincennes

INTING

When a painted owl was shown to prisoners in ancient Ethiopia, they were expected to take the hint and kill themselves.

IPPOCRATES (c. 460–377 BC)

Greek physician and one of the very first scientific medical men. Hippocrates disapproved of abortions but suggested that jumping up and down seven times might be the way to induce one.

☐ See **BEANS, CHILDREN.**

IPPOPOTAMUS

(From the Greek: *hippos*, a horse; *potamos*, a river.) Large African artiodactyl ungulate. The adjectives meaning hippopotamus-like are hippopotamian or hippo-

potamic. Hippocrepian means horse-shoe shaped.

☐ See **COCONUT, GAMESMANSHIP, REPRODUCTION, SNAKEBITE, SWIMMING, TEARS.**

HIROHITO, Emperor of Japan (*b.* 1901)

☐ See **CORMORANT.**

HITLER, Adolf (1889–1945)

Unity Mitford, one of the Fuhrer's greatest admirers, had a pet snake called Enid.

☐ See also: ***Brighton, Chaplin, horse.***

HOATZIN

The crested Hoatzin, Hoactzin or Hoazin (*opisthocomus cristatus*) emerges from its egg with four legs. Soon after birth, however, its foreclaws drop off and the stumps develop into wings. Its name comes from the Nahuatl, *uatsin*. It is also known as the stink-bird and is found in South America.

HOBBIES

When not writing books, Sir Arthur Conan Doyle was an ophthalmologist. When not being Prime Minister (in fact before he turned to politics at all) Disraeli was quite a successful novelist. Sir Christopher Wren devised a language for the deaf and dumb.

HO CHI MINH (1890–1969)

Born Nguyen That Thanh.

☐ See **RITZ.**

HOG

A castrated boar; swine generally. (From the Old English: *hogg*.)

☐ See **LONGEVITY.**

HOLLAND

Country of Europe, nucleus of the Kingdom of the Netherlands. The village of Staphorst in Holland is one of the last strongholds of the Reformed Association Church. On Sundays cocks and hens are kept apart and no one is permitted to have sex. Neither may any girl be married until she is pregnant.

☐ See also: *tulip.*

HOLLY, Buddy (1936–58)

American songwriter and vocalist, real name Charles Hardin.

☐ See **LONGEVITY.**

HOLMES, Sherlock

The mystery, my dear Watson, lies in the precise location of your old war wound. For in Conan Doyle's 'A Study in Scarlet' it is in the good doctor's shoulder, but when writing 'The Sign of Four' the author moved it to his leg. Irritating stuff this movable shrapnel.

HOMING INSTINCT

☐ See **MONGOLIA.**

HOMOSEXUALITY

Leonardo da Vinci and Michelangelo are both reputed to have been homosexuals,

though Michelangelo might not have bee very fussy. Homosexuality has been legal i France since 1810, but is still punishable b imprisonment in Spain. A higher perce tage of homosexuals than heterosexua become alcoholics. Two out of every thre hedgehogs are male. They have nine spines per square inch and were popul pets in ancient Rome. Homosexuals we also not unpopular in ancient Rome.

HONDURAS

Honduras is to be found somewhere i Central America. Its capital is Tegucigalp its currency is the lempira and it is th leading grower of bananas in the region.

HONEY

(From the Old English: *hunig*; Old Norse *hunang*.) As a method of execution, hone is no longer in great demand, though suficed well enough in the first century fo Marcus, Bishop of Arethusa. He was hun in a basket, smeared all over with hone and stung to death by wasps. A **BEE** incidentally, would be able to cruis 4 million miles on a gallon of nectar.

HONG KONG

British Crown colony in the South Chin Sea.

☐ See **CYPRUS, SURGERY.**

HOOVER, J. Edgar (1895–1972)

Beats as he sweeps as he cleans.

☐ See **COMMUNISM.**

HOPS

The hop (*Humulus lupulus*) is a perennia twining plant of the natural order Urti caceae.

☐ See **CAPITAL PUNISHMENT.**

HORMONES

☐ See **SHELLFISH.**

ORROR

Horror-film actors Christopher Lee and Vincent Price were both born on 27 May. Peter Cushing misses sharing the same birthday, but not by much; he was born on 26 May. Perhaps by getting there one day earlier he assured himself of all the good-guy parts.

Lon Chaney's parents were both deaf mutes.

ORSE

Family of the odd-toed group of the Ungulata. The horse is immune to tear-gas, has no collar bone, and can fall asleep standing up. When Hitler was in power, German farmers and policemen were forbidden to name their horses Adolf.

◻ See also: *artificial limbs, brain, Curie, hospital, indecency, knackers, manure, perfume, speed, statue, yak.*

OSPITAL

The 2nd Earl of Montague built a hospital in the early eighteenth century for old horses and cows. There is a present day hospital in Israel for camels, where the Bedouins can take their beasts for blood tests and X-rays. If any Bedouin has a sick owl, however, he would do better to take it to Ontario, Canada, where there is an owl hospital.

◻ See also: *Finland.*

OUNSLOW CENTRAL

Station on the Piccadilly Line of the **LONDON** Underground Railway, situated to the east of Hounslow West, and to the west of Hounslow East.

OUNSLOW WEST

◻ See **HOUNSLOW CENTRAL, LONDON.**

OUNSLOW EAST

◻ See **HOUNSLOW CENTRAL, LONDON.**

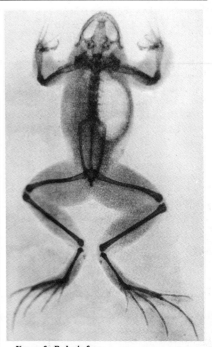

X-ray of a Bedouin frog

HOUSE OF COMMONS

The lower house of the British Parliament.

◻ See **OBSCENITY, POGO STICK, SQUINTING.**

HOUSE OF LORDS

The upper house of the British Parliament.

◻ See **DWARF.**

HUGHES, Howard Robard (1905–76)

American millionaire recluse.

◻ See **BREASTS.**

HUGO, Victor-Marie (1802–85)

Prolific French writer, who died of pneumonia and by his own direction was carried to his grave in a pauper's hearse. The effect was spoiled a little by the decision to locate the grave in the Pantheon and to have a mighty procession accompanying the funeral.

☐ See **HARDY.**

HUMMING-BIRD

Large family of small birds, Trochilidae. The feet of the humming-bird are of no use for walking, but serve only as a perch. It is the only bird which can fly backwards. The ruby-throated humming-bird migrates 2,000 miles from eastern USA to South America beating its wings fifty times a second. Among faster flappers are wasps (100 wing beats per sec), houseflies (190), mosquitoes (500) and midges with an amazing 1,000 wing beats every second.

HUMOUR

The funniest joke in the world appears to have been discovered by the Greek comedy writer, Philemon, who laughed himself to death around 263 BC apparently at one of his own jokes. Fortunately, perhaps, the joke itself has not been passed down to posterity, but it may have something to do with a donkey and a fig. Chrysippus, Greek philosopher and contemporary of Philemon, died of laughter brought on by the sight of a donkey eating figs.

HUNCHBACK

Deformity caused by a curvature of the spine. The most famous hunchback in history was probably not a hunchback at all. There is no evidence during the lifetime of Richard III to suggest that he had any such deformity. The hump seems to have been a malicious invention of his detractors grafted onto his reputation after his death.

When a hunchback shot at Queen Victoria in an assassination attempt in 1842, so efficient were London's police that by nightfall sixty hunchbacks were behind bars.

UNGARY

Magyar homeland, formerly part of the Austro-Hungarian Empire, a kingdom from 1001 until 1918.

☐ See **MARX, SNAKEBITE.**

UNTING

Seal-hunting: see **SOUP;** snail-hunting: see **DISCIPLINE;** camel-hunting: see **CAMEL.**

YENA

(Also Hyaena.) Family of carnivorous mammals (Hyaenidae), striped, spotted or brown. Among carnivores and primates, the hyena is the only beast apart from man not to have a penis bone. Perhaps through a sense of empathy at this shared deficiency, the ancient Egyptians were rather fond of hyenas, which they bred in captivity and ate. According to Pliny the Elder, the consumption of hyena's eye, mixed with liquorice root and anise, is a cure for sterility in a woman. It is so powerful that it will ensure she conceives within three days.

☐ See also: *flea.*

HYGIENE

Raccoons often wash their food before eating it. The hygienic benefit of this habit is considerably reduced by their habit of using water dirtier than the food they are washing.

I

ICE

Eighty per cent of all the ice in the world is in Antarctica. If all the ice in the world melted, the sea-level would increase to such an extent that the Empire State Building would be submerged up to the twentieth floor. People visiting floors above the twentieth would probably also complain that the refrigerators were malfunctioning.

ICEBERG

(From Scandinavian or Dutch: *berg*, a hill or mountain.)

□ See **BELGIUM, GREENLAND.**

ICE CREAM

In Lexington, Kentucky, it is illegal to carry an ice cream cornet in your pocket. Anywhere else on earth, it is inadvisable to carry an ice cream cornet in your pocket.

□ See also: *calendar.*

ICELAND

Telephone directories in Iceland are arranged in alphabetical order of first names. Icelanders have no family surnames, only their given first name plus a patronymic formed by adding the suffix *-son* (in the case of a male) or *-dottir* (in the case of a female) to the first name of the father. Dogs are illegal in Reykjavik, the capital city of Iceland.

Pronunciation of Icelandic can be confusing, but follows certain clear rules. For example, the letter *f* may be pronounced five different ways:

(i) at the beginning of a word, or when followed by *k* or *s*, it is pronounced as *f*;

(ii) if it occurs between two vowels, it is voiced as *v*;

(iii) occurring in the combinations *-lft* or *-lfs*, the *f* is silent;

(iv) when followed by the letters *l* or *n*, the *f* is pronounced as *b*;

(v) when followed by *-nd* or *-nt*, the *f* sounds like *m*.

It is a difficult language to learn, but it helps if you already speak Anglo-Saxon or Old Norse.

□ See also: *Denmark, literacy, newt.*

ICOSAGRAM

(From the Greek: *eikosi*, twenty; *gramma*, a letter.) A word having twenty letters. The most commonly used English icosagram is 'uncharacteristically'. (If that information is found useful it might restore the disproportionateness of the other inconsequentialities in this book, pseudoscientifically speaking.)

IDIOCY

St Mathurin is the French patron saint of idiots and fools. He was a priest in the third century and is said to have been highly popular in the Middle Ages, when there were presumably a large number of fools around. St Agnes is the patron saint of young virgins. She was martyred about AD 303 at the age of 13. St Agnes' Day is 21 January, so St Agnes' Eve, of which Keats wrote (Young virgins might have visions of delight) is presumably 20 January.

GLOO

(Eskimo word.)

☐ See **ESKIMO.**

LLITERACY

Illiteracy was an occupational qualification for the job of janitor at Alamagordo, New Mexico, during the Second World War. The atomic bomb was being developed there and they did not want to employ anyone who might be able to read something carelessly thrown into a waste bin.

Had the Emperor Charlemagne lived in New Mexico at the time, he might have had the chance of a part-time job there. He could read, but not write, though he had tried to learn.

☐ See also: **Newton.**

MMORALITY

☐ See **RASPUTIN.**

MPALA

The South African antelope (*Aepyceros melampus*).

☐ See **MATING.**

MPOTENCE

(From the Latin: *impotentia*, incapacity.) When the mummified penis of Napoleon Bonaparte was offered at auction at Christies of London in 1972, it failed to reach the reserve price. Napoleon, incidentally, had a morbid fear of cats. The correct term for a fear of cats is 'ailurophobia' (alternatively ailourophobia). There seems to be no single English word for a mummified penis,

but 'coprolite' is fossilised faeces, especially those of fish.

☐ See also: **Roosevelt, F. D.**

INCEST

(From the Latin: *in*, not; *castus*, chaste.) Pyemotis mites are born in a state of full sexual maturity. A newly born girl mite is likely to be pounced on immediately by one of her brothers.

INCOMPETENCE

No Persian carpet made by Moslems is free from mistakes, since only Allah may make things perfectly. British hangmen do not have an impeccable record of excellence either: in 1728 Margaret Dickson, hanged for infanticide at Edinburgh, sat up and got out of her coffin when the hearse driver stopped for refreshment. (Her innocence was later established, so all was for the good in the end.) In 1740, William Duell was hanged for murder at Tyburn. He came to life again when the knife was applied in the dissecting room. Rather than give the hangman a second chance, the sentence was reduced to one of transportation. In 1650, the Oxford University anatomy department must have been disappointed when the body of Anne Green, hanged for murder, came to life and prevented their further investigations. Anne Green made a complete recovery.

INDECENCY

The Society for Indecency to Naked Animals was probably originally founded for a joke, but many of its members took the activities seriously. In 1963 they picketed the White House in an attempt to persuade Mrs Kennedy to put clothes on her naked horse. A spokesman asserted that by 1969 it would be quite normal to see a dog wearing boxer shorts, or a horse trotting down the street in Bermudas.

A naked horse is capable of shocking us by displaying eighteen pairs of ribs compared with the human's twelve. There are

75 million horses on earth, almost all of which run around in the nude.

Somewhere is Australia, however, there may still be a very old kangaroo bounding about clad in a waistcoat. In 1945, William Thompson, a Sydney farmer, found a kangaroo trapped in his wire fence. 'Acting on impulse' (his own description) he put his waistcoat on the marsupial before freeing it. Only as it bounced away did Mr Thompson remember that he had left £5 in the pocket of the kangaroo's waistcoat. He never saw the money, kangaroo or waistcoat again.

☐ See also: *decency.*

INDEPENDENCE

United States Independence Day has been a popular choice of date for presidents of that country to die. Thomas Jefferson, John Adams and James Monroe all died on 4 July. It was also the birthday of Calvin Coolidge.

INDIA

In India you can hear about a thousand different languages spoken (estimate range from 845 to over 1,200). You can also meet a quarter of the world's cattle encounter more than 20 per cent of the world's 6 million eunuchs, and enjoy the company of 40 per cent of the world' illiterates. Nevertheless, Indian ink come from China.

☐ See also: *adultery, Ceylon, debt, demography, fashion, fertiliser, marital customs, murder, party spirit, weather, wind.*

INDIVIDUALITY

Venus is the only planet in the solar system which appears to rotate clockwise when viewed from the earth. But Pluto is the coldest (at around −220°C). In France Walt Disney's cartoon dog Pluto is called 'Dingo', but that nomenclature does not extend beyond the earth's atmosphere. The dingo also has strong claims to individuality, being Australia's only indigenous carnivore.

KIRALFY BROS. GRAND PRODUCTION

BLACK VENUS.

INDONESIA

The last time anybody bothered to count, Indonesia comprised 13,667 islands of which 12,675 are uninhabited and 7,600 have not even been named. Seventy-seven of the 167 volcanoes in Indonesia are kown to have erupted at some time in history.

INDUSTRIAL ACCIDENT

A rat-catcher employed by the council of Daventry in Northamptonshire was paid £7.45 compensation for a pair of spectacles which he lost down a rat-hole. Norwegian rat-catchers may have even more rat-holes to peer down than exist in Daventry. Each litter of the Norway rat has ten young, and this fecund little rodent is capable of producing ten litters a year.

INDUSTRIAL DISPUTE

The earliest strike on record occurred in 1160 BC when the workers on the tomb of Rameses III went on strike for higher wages.

INFANTICIDE

(From the Latin: *infans*, infant; *caedere*, to kill.)

☐ See **INCOMPETENCE, MURDER.**

INFERIORITY

☐ See **PYGMY.**

INFIDELITY

(From the Latin: *infidelis*, faithless.)

☐ See **TUVALU.**

INFLUENZA

A highly infectious epidemic disease. The longest case of suspected influenza ended in 1978, according to a report by geriatrician Dr Peter Rowe in the British Medical Journal. An unnamed lady had been ordered to bed with the 'flu by her doctor in 1935. He told her to 'stay in bed until I return'. He forgot to return. She stayed in bed. Forty years later another doctor called and took seven months of patient coaxing to get her up again. She lived for another three comparatively active years.

☐ See also: *Ecuador, mortality.*

INLAND REVENUE

An organisation for collecting money.

☐ See **CHARITY.**

INSANITY

A mental derangement due to a diseased brain.

☐ See **MARRIAGE, SEX, ROOSEVELT, F. D.**

INSECT

The largest class of the arthropoda. There are a million billion (10^{15}) ants on earth. Only the females work. Well, with that many of them why should the men bother? Despite the fact that there are half a million billion girl ants toiling away, none of them produces a food eaten by man (or woman). Of all insects, only the bee performs this useful service.

☐ See also: *discovery.*

One of the insect's natural enemies

INSOMNIA

(From the Latin: *insomnis*, sleepless.)
Alexandre Dumas (fils) was advised to eat
an apple each morning at 7 o'clock beneath
the Arc de Triomphe as a cure for his
insomnia. Winston Churchill, Napoleon
Bonaparte and Catherine the Great were
all sufferers from this condition. The latter
advocated sex six times a day as a cure.
Historical precedent indicates that this is
indeed the ideal frequency, since Queen
Joanna II of Naples decreed that a man may
not force his wife to have sex more than six
times a day.

No comparative study has ever been
performed to determine the relative effi-
cacies of Dumas's cure and Catherine's,
but if it must be done beneath the Arc de
Triomphe, eating an apple is less likely to
frighten the horses.

☐ See also: *lettuce.*

INSPIRATION

(From the Latin: *in-*, in or into; *spirare*, t
breathe.) That which breathes into th
mind an uplifting influence.

☐ See **SAUSAGE.**

INSURANCE

Before the battle of the Little Big Horn
General Custer took out $5,000 insuranc
on his life. Other items insured for greate
sums include: Jimmy (schnozzle) Durante'
nose for £70,000; Ben Turpin's squint fo
$500,000; Fred Astaire's legs for $650,000

The value of the 'Mona Lisa' wa
assessed for insurance purposes at 10
million dollars. There is a South America
millipede with 784 legs. If Fred Astaire ha
had that number of legs and insured then
pro rata, he would stand to gain enough t

buy three 'Mona Lisas' on the proceeds of a particularly nasty accident.

☐ See also: *Harris.*

NTELLIGENCE

From the time of Aristotle until the Middle Ages, the seat of human intelligence was believed to reside in the heart. For sheer braininess, it is hard to beat the silkworm moth. It has eleven brains. But the male emperor moth is even more remarkable in its accomplishments; it can smell a virgin female up to seven miles away upwind.

NTERCOURSE

☐ See AUCTION, CAMPANOLOGY.

NTERMENT

(From the Latin: *in*, in; *terra*, the earth. cf. BURIAL.) In 1970, a Belgrade electrician, Milutin Velkjovic, broke the world record for interment by spending 463 days buried underground. Purist grave-dwellers may contest this achievement, since he was accompanied by two Canadian ducks. During the period of his subterranean sojourn, Mr Velkjovic was divorced by his wife for 'unreasonable behaviour'. The ducks were not cited as co-respondents.

This experience contrasts with that of William White of Fort Worth, Texas, who chose to be buried alive with a telephone in his coffin. As a result of publicity on an English radio programme, he emerged from the grave engaged to Miss Beryl Wilson, a barmaid from Leeds.

NTESTINE

Part of the alimentary canal divided into the small intestine (duodenum, jejunum and ileum) and large intestine (caecum, colon and rectum).

☐ See CRIME, JAPAN, PYTHON.

RAN

(Formerly Persia.) If you want to get married in Iran, do not forget to bring along some proof of your virginity.

☐ See also: *puberty.*

IRAQ

(Formerly Mesopotamia.) More than 80 per cent of the world's dates are grown in Iraq (about half a million tons of dates each year). The only date until the twenty-fourth century which requires as many as thirteen Roman numerals is 1888. (MDCCCLXXXVIII if you prefer.) In old Iraq, surgeons who lost the lives of a gentleman patient paid for their ineptitude with the loss of a hand.

☐ See also: *bee.*

IRELAND

An Irishman convicted at St Albans Crown Court in 1981 on a charge of stealing microwave ovens, was given a suspended sentence and discharged. It came out in the trial that he had thought he was taking television sets; the judge considered it unfair that anyone so stupid should go to prison.

St Patrick, patron saint of Ireland, was not Irish. Authorities differ as to his origins, but Welsh, English or French seem most likely.

☐ See also: *hedgehog, newt, peanut, rabies, whooping cough.*

ISRAEL

Israel boasts more university professors per head of population than any other country. The Israelis also eat more eggs than any other nation. The Japanese, however, eat the most fish. Per capita, they consume each day 90 g of fish and 60 g of meat; the Americans eat only 20 g of fish each. Every day, however, 1,250 Americans are injured by falling off bicycles. Another 7,000 or so are hurt in other ways while indulging in sport or recreation.

☐ See also: *road safety.*

ITALY

The Italians drink more wine per head than the Austrians drink beer. Any sense of pride the Italians may have in this achievement is undoubtedly diminished by the knowledge that their flag was designed by a well-known Frenchman, Napoleon Bonaparte. Further indignity is suffered by those Italians who realise that there are 22 miles more of canals in Birmingham than there are in Venice.

☐ See also: *business, prostitution, San Marino, vocational guidance.*

IVAN THE TERRIBLE (1530–84)

Ivan IV, Czar of Russia, known as Iva Grozny (the Terrible), was the first Russia ruler to agree a treaty with England. S great was the pride of Ivan the Terrible a the magnificence of St Basil's Cathedral i Moscow, which he had had built, that h had the architect's eyes put out to preven him from building a similar church else where. Ivan's death is said to have bee hastened by his remorse for killing his so in a fit of temper in 1580.

☐ See also: *Mahomet.*

J

JACK THE RIPPER

Murderer of at least six and probably eight women in London's East End between 1887 and 1889, never captured by the police.

☐ See **SYRIA.**

JACOBITES

Supporters of James II and his descendants. *Jacobus* is the Latin for James.

☐ See **BARRISTERS, SCROFULA.**

JAGUAR

(*Felis onca*) Large American spotted cat. March 1987 could be the start of a good year for jaguars according to Aztec beliefs. The Aztecs who lived near Mexico City in the twelfth century had two calendars: one of 365 days for agricultural purposes, another of 260 days for religious calculations. Every fifty-two years these calendars would coincide, when strange and terrible things were predicted. In particular, one should be warned at such times to beware of flood, wind, fire, earthquake, and being eaten by jaguars. The next such coincidence will occur in March 1987.

JAMAICA

(From the Indian: *Xaymaca*, Land of springs.) Some oysters live in trees in Jamaica, but even the average non-Jamaican oyster can survive for up to four months out of water. A healthy human adult, on the other hand, can survive for eight weeks on water alone. It is not known for how long a human can survive on oysters alone (but see **CASANOVA).**

JAMES I, King of Great Britain (1566–1625)

King of Scotland from the age of 1, he was the sixth James to rule that country and became the first of England on the death of Queen Elizabeth in 1603. King James I was more active in the publishing world than many of our monarchs. In 1599 he wrote an influential treatise on witchcraft called 'Daemonology'. This was followed in 1604 by his 'Counterblaste to Tobacco', as vehement against cigarettes as he had been against witches. James I was left-handed, as were also King George IV and Queen Victoria, but no other British monarchs.

☐ See also: *consolation, Gloucester, thespians.*

JAMES II, King of Great Britain and Ireland (1633–1701)

Younger son of Charles I and brother of Charles II, the greatest achievement of James II was to father two English queens, Mary and Anne.

☐ See **CORONATION, PRAGMATISM.**

JAMES IV, King of Scotland (1473–1513)

A popular, if somewhat licentious king,

who was, at any rate, more successful than his court alchemist, a man named John Damian. One day, Damian took off from the battlements of Stirling Castle attached to a pair of feathered wings, announcing that he was attempting to fly to Paris. He dropped like a stone and broke a leg. In retrospect he decided that it had been a mistake to include feathers of barndoor fowl, little accustomed to flight.

James IV enjoyed playing dice and cards with his alchemist, and was not above doing his own scientific investigations. He performed one historic experiment by sending two newly born babies to live with a dumb woman on Inchkeith Island in the Firth of Forth, in order to discover what language they would grow up speaking. It was reported that the children spoke good Hebrew, but there is no first-hand corroboration of this fact.

☐ See also: *Siamese twins.*

JANUARY SALES

In fourteenth- and fifteenth-century Eng land there was a great shortage of pir which resulted in a parliamentary decre that they might only be sold on 1 and 2 c January each year. Women would there fore save 'pin money' for the January sales

JAPAN

The name of Japan is derived from tw Chinese ideographs meaning 'the Origin c the Sun'. Dr Tadao Yagi of Japan is one c the pioneers of cosmetic intestinal surgery He claims that the Japanese have a bigge large intestine than Westerners and tha this is in part responsible for their pig mentation. By removing up to four feet c intestine, he can improve a patient's con plexion.

Conventional ideas of beauty have changed since the Middle Ages when Japanese woman would paint her teet

Alchemists at the Scottish Court

black to look more beautiful. Without wishing any disrespect to Dr Yagi, one might suggest that the old recipe is less trouble than having your intestines hacked about. The Japanese, incidentally, are so polite that the men bow to each other 2,000 times a day in normal conversation.

☐ See also: *Cameroon, Carter, communism, cormorant, etiquette, garbage, geography, Israel, kamikaze, lost property, photograph, politeness, umbrella.*

AUNDICE

(From the French: *jaunisse*, yellowness.) One old cure for jaundice recommended taking the head of a mad dog, pounded and mingled with wine. What wine one should take with mad dog is unspecified; perhaps something from the Alsace region would be appropriate.

In 1981 in Paris the former director of a French eye bank was charged with manslaughter following the death of a corneal transplant patient. The donor had been a rabies victim. The bank was later closed.

☐ See also: *Franklin.*

AVA

Island of the Malay archipelago. One of the best hotels in Java has a room with bath permanently reserved in the name of Njai Loro Kidul, the goddess of the South Sea.

AZZ

Musical form introduced into Britain in 1918, of which syncopation and improvisation form important parts. Perhaps the most sincere critic of jazz was Mr Nicola Coviello, professor of a music school in Balham, South London. At the age of 79, on a trip to Coney Island, USA, he was taken to hear a jazz band. Saying, 'That isn't music; stop it!' he swayed, fell, and dropped dead.

JEFFERSON, Thomas (1743–1826)

Barrister and (from 1801–9) President of the United States; he purchased Louisiana from the French for £3 million.

☐ See **INDEPENDENCE.**

JEFFERSON AS FIGHTING BOB

JEFFREYS, George (1648–89)

Best known as Judge Jeffreys (the hanging judge), he was a leading prosecutor who became Chief Justice in 1683 and was created a baron in 1685. Arrested in 1688 as a supporter of James II he died a prisoner in the Tower.

☐ See **MONMOUTH.**

JEROME, Jeanette (Jennie) (1850–1921)

Daughter of Leonard Jerome of New York, wife of Lord Randolph Churchill, mother of Winston Churchill, great-granddaughter of the 7th Duke of Marlborough. No relation at all to Jerome K. Jerome, whose middle initial stood for 'Klapka'.

☐ See **MANHATTAN.**

JESUS CHRIST (c. 4 BC–AD 32)

Ernest Digweed died in 1977 leaving £30,000 in his will to the Son of God, so that He would have some ready cash on His second coming. There have been more than twenty claimants, but none has yet given sufficient proof of identity to satisfy the Public Trustee Office in London.

☐ See also: *films.*

JET-LAG

The oyster appears to suffer from something very similar to jet-lag in humans. After a change of domicile, transplanted oysters have been observed opening their shells at the time of high tide in their original homes. It takes about two weeks for them to acclimatise and begin opening up at high tide of the new environment.

JOGGING

☐ See **DISEASE.**

JOHN, King of England (1167–1216)

A quarrelsome king (he reigned 1199–1216) who picked fights with his barons, the Pope, and France. He died of a surfeit of peaches and too much of a new type of beer. King John was buried in Worcester Cathedral, clad in monk's habit in the hope of fooling the recording angel on the day of judgement. An old trick, but it might just work. The only angels mentioned by name in the Bible are Michael and Gabriel. (Apparently one has to be an archangel to have one's name remembered.) The Koran lists another two archangels: Azrael (the angel of death) and Israfel (trumpeter of the resurrection).

JOHN III, King of Poland (1624–96)

Known as John Sobieski, he succeede Michael Wisniowiecki as King of Poland i 1674. After a brilliant military caree specialising in the annihilation of Turkis armies, he died of apoplexy.

☐ See **BIRTHDAY.**

JOHN IV, King of Portugal (1604–56)

Known as 'The Fortunate'.

☐ See **HEARING.**

JOHNSON, Samuel (1709–84)

Dr Johnson, lexicographer and schola never trod on the cracks between pavin stones, and always touched each woode post he walked past.

☐ See also: *apoplexy, electricity, scrofula, Voltaire.*

JOHNSTON, Sir Harry Hamilton (1858–1927)

British explorer, writer and diplomat.

☐ See **LLAMA.**

JONSON, Ben (c. 1573–1637)

English poet and dramatist, tutor to the so of Sir Walter Raleigh, the first Englis playwright to publish his works. The he bone of Ben Jonson, which had been stole from his grave by William **BUCKLAN** when the plot was disturbed in 1849, late turned up in a furniture shop in 1938. Be Jonson's father died before Ben was born

☐ See also: *burial, right of clergy.*

JUGGERNAUT

(From the Sanskrit: *Jagannatha,* Lord (the World.) A Hindu idol kept in a temp at Puri in India. On important festivals th figure is dragged through the streets on huge car some 50 feet high. The name cam to be used erroneously for any huge mobi structure which threatened the lives (those in its path.

☐ See also: *snakebite.*

ULIUS CAESAR (102–44 BC)

Gaius Julius Caesar was proclaimed Dictator of Rome in 48 BC. Successful military commander, with an elegant literary style, he was also an epileptic and has been accused of seducing one of the vestal virgins. The best treatment for epilepsy, according to normally reliable Roman sources, was to drink the fresh blood of a gladiator, preferably just before he expires. Paracelsus had a more scientific treatment, placing the negative pole of a magnet on the head and the positive pole of another magnet on the stomach. The flow of magnetic energy through the body would arrest the flow of nervous fluid to the brain.

☐ See also: *clock, road safety, uniqueness.*

JUSTICE

In Selvio in northern Italy in 1519, the local fieldmice were convicted of having caused damage to food crops. The penalty was banishment, but in order to ensure that justice was done, they were given safe conduct into exile with an escorted trip out of town and all cats kept locked away. By special order, older mice and nursing mothers were allowed fourteen extra days in which to make their preparations for the journey.

JUSTINIAN II (669–711)

East Roman Emperor 685–695 and 705–711. Justinian II celebrated the beginning of his second reign with a great massacre.

☐ See **CONSTANTINOPLE.**

K

KAMIKAZE

In 1281, the Mongol army of Kublai Khan launched an invasion of Japan. Its fleet was wrecked by a hurricane, and the troops which did manage to land were easily dealt with by the Japanese. The Japanese named the hurricane 'kamikaze', a divine wind, and the term was borrowed by later kamikaze pilots.

☐ See also: *bat.*

KANGAROO

Genus of marsupials found only in Australia and New Guinea. The kangaroo (*Macropus*) cannot jump from a position with its tail off the ground. Its meat is totally free of cholesterol.

☐ See also: *entrepreneurs, indecency, lost property, misunderstanding, potoroo.*

KARIBA DAM

Dam at Kariba in Zimbabwe/Zambia.

☐ See **HAT.**

KEATS, John (1795–1821)

Medical student who turned to poetry.

☐ See **SCHOENBERG, SOPHOCLES.**

KENNEDY, John Fitzgerald (1917–63)

President of the United States from 1960 until his assassination in 1963. President Kennedy holds the record for the fastest ever rate of delivery of a public speech, set when he was timed at 327 words a minute in 1961.

Since 1840, every American president elected in a year ending in zero, has died in office. At the time of writing we are still waiting to see if President Reagan (elected 1980) insists on following this pattern.

The favourite food of the late President Kennedy was fish chowder, of which he once ate twelve bowls at a sitting.

☐ See also: *indecency.*

KENT

English county in the south-east, formerly the name of a kingdom of which Ethelbert was King.

☐ See **OHIO, PRAGMATISM.**

KENTUCKY

East central state of the USA best known for fried chicken.

☐ See **ICE CREAM.**

KENYA

Some strange ideas of beauty come from Kenya. Quite apart from the fetching toothlessness of the Luo tribe (see **EXTRACTION**), the Masai tribeswomen though hanging on to their teeth, shave their heads. Bald is beautiful. Kenya has the highest birth rate in the world, so there must be something in it.

☐ See also: *spitting.*

KETCHUP

(From a Malay word: *kechap*.) A sauce of tomatoes.

□ See **MONET.**

KEVIN, St (*d.* 618, feast day 3 June)

St Kevin was a sixth-century Irishman who sought solitude on a remote island upon which he vowed no woman would ever land. A lady called Kathleen succeeded in tracking him down, so he hurled her to her death from a rock. Her ghost was said never to have left the place where she was killed. For suffering this ordeal and having to put up with the unwanted ghost, Kevin was canonised.

KIDNAP

Illegal abduction of a human, often for ransom.

□ See **GILBERT, ZAIRE.**

KIDNEY

Organ weighing about 4½ oz in the male, a little less in the female. The two kidneys cleanse about 1,750 litres of blood a day, during which time about a kilogram of salt will have passed through them too. The blue whale has approximately 2,000 gallons of blood.

KINNOCK, Neil Gordon (*b.* 1942)

Neil Kinnock was elected leader of the British Labour Party in 1983. His name is an anagram of 'I knock Lenin'. Ken Livingstone (leader of the Greater London Council's ruling Labour group) is an anagram of 'Votes Lenin king'. Konstantin Chernenko makes 'Another Ten N. Kinnocks'.

General Galtieri (former Argentine president) is an anagram of 'El large Argie nit'.

□ See also: *bellows.*

KIPLING, Joseph Rudyard (1865–1936)

Bombay-born British poet and author, winner of the Nobel prize for literature in 1907. Had there been a Nobel prize for geography, Kipling's poem 'Mandalay' would have been a non-starter. In it, he wrote the memorable lines: 'An' the dawn comes up like thunder outer China 'crost the Bay.' But Mandalay, in the west of Burma, is across the bay from India, not China. Of course, 'outer China 'crost the mainland' would neither have scanned nor had the poetic force of the original.

Geography apart, Kipling should be remembered for his invention of snow golf, played with red balls. He left £155,000, but before he died he had given away his manuscript of *The Jungle Book* to the nurse who looked after his first child. Kipling advised her: 'If you are in need of money you may be able to sell it at a handsome price.' She was, she did, and later lived in comfort on the proceeds.

KISSING

A 24-year-old man was convicted of assault in Oklahoma in 1976 and fined $200 for

kissing the elbow of a parking warden while she was giving him a ticket. The punishment seems very fair compared with the early nineteenth-century penalty of two hours in the stocks for any man seen kissing his wife in public on a Sunday in England.

The world kissing record was broken by two young Americans called Paul and Sadie in 1975, who managed 20,009 kisses in two hours.

KITE

Airborne appliance or bird of prey (*Milvus ictinus* is the common kite).

☐ See **BANGKOK.**

KITSCH

(From the German.) Work of art that is inferior or in bad taste (see illustration).

KITTEN

A young cat.

☐ See **EISENHOWER.**

KIWI

Flightless bird of **NEW ZEALAND** also known as apteryx (of the class Apterygota).

KNACKERS

Until the 1930s men could be whipped in England under five separate statutes:
  (i) slaughtering horses without a licence (under the Knackers Act of 1786);
 (ii) being an incorrigible rogue (Vagrancy Act of 1824);
(iii) treason (Treason Act of 1824);
 (iv) aggravated robbery with violence, and garrotting (Larceny Acts of 1861 and 1916, Garrotters Act of 1863);
  (v) procuration and living on earnings of prostitutes (Criminal Law amendment Act of 1912).

KNEE

Hinged joint at head of femur, tibia and patella.

☐ See **BEAVER, DICKENS, ELEPHAN MOLEOSOPHY.**

KNICKERS

Abbreviated form of knickerbocker dating back to a Cruikshank illustratic of a Dutchman named Knickerbocker Washington Irving's humorous *History New York.*

☐ See **BEQUESTS.**

KNOWLEDGE

Throughout history, human achievement and knowledge have only progressed thanks to the diligent efforts of dedicated researchers. Here are some of the important additions to the data bank of wisdom:

Poultry: In the chicken world, hens are better peckers than cocks; the female has first strike accuracy between 48 per cent and 82 per cent under laboratory (or indeed farmyard) conditions, while the male manages only 14–52 per cent of grains picked at first peck. If you want your turkeys to eat more, however, it helps to have them fitted with rose-tinted contact lenses. The turkey which looks at the world through rose-coloured glasses has been shown to become less aggressive and spend more time eating.

Aquatic creatures: Artificial waves made in a goldfish bowl during a scientific study have been shown to cause seasickness in the occupants. And if your problem is not a seasick goldfish but a randy salamander, you might do well to cut off its tail. According to experiments by Dr Virginia Maiorana of the University of California, salamanders with their tails cut off are less likely to breed. The most significant research, however, has been that carried out on the spiny lobster (*palinurus argus*). These creatures migrate by walking along the seabed in an orderly tail-to-antenna queue. Research has demonstrated convincingly that such a lobster queue serves to reduce drag and hence enable the creatures to travel more quickly. Experiments have been carried out towing lobsters along the bottom of a tank, with the use of capstan, pulley and weighted pendulum, which confirmed that such lobster queues can travel at 35cm per second, compared with a lone lobster's top speed of 28cm per second.

Asparagus: In 1981, in an epoch-making controlled experiment on urine-sniffing, the old asparagus theory was finally debunked by researchers in Jerusalem. For many years, the production of odd-smelling urine after the consumption of asparagus had been thought to be a genetically transmitted trait, but the 1981 result proved that the ability to produce the relevant smell is universal; it is the ability to detect the smell which some of us have and others do not. This was discovered by a series of trials in which people sniffed their own urine and that of others, all of whom had been asparagus-fed. It is not yet known whether the asparagus sniffing ability has a genetic component.

The human world: research at the Ear, Nose and Throat Department of St Mary's Hosptial in London showed that a really rasping snore can register 69 decibels. (A pneumatic drill manages between 70 and 90 decibels.) Decency is no doubt observed among the snorers of St Mary's, but in the privacy of their own homes, according to research by nightwear manufacturers, one in five people sleep nude.

And finally, do remember, in case you are slightly inebriated while absorbing this information, that according to an experiment in 1969, knowledge acquired while drunk may vanish again when you are sober. But fear not! For it will have a good chance of returning when you get drunk again. On the whole that sounds a more enjoyable experiment in which to have participated than the urine-smelling one.

KOALA

(*Phascolarctus cinereus*) Marsupial mammal known as the Australian native bear, though not numbering any bears among its relatives. The Koala is only 2ft 6 in. long, but its appendix may measure 8 feet. The name 'koala' derives from an Aborigine word meaning 'to drink'. The French drink 140 bottles of wine per person each year.

☐ See also: *eucalyptus.*

KÖCHEL, Ludwig Ritter von (1800–77)

(Usually known as K.)

☐ See **PROCRASTINATION.**

KOKOSCHKA, Oskar (1886–1980)

☐ See **GROUPIES.**

KORAN

(From the Arabic: *Qur'an*: that which should be read.) Holy book of the Moslems, revealed to Mahomet during the last twenty-three years of his life.

☐ See **JOHN.**

KOREA

When South Korea launched a national campaign against Decadent Trends, one of the immediate results was 50,000 long-haired youths being given compulsory haircuts. The Emperor Nero, though never in Korea in his youth, must have had no difficulty obtaining haircuts. He was brought up by a barber and a male ballet dancer. His father had died and his mother was exiled when he was very young.

☐ See also: *Cameroon, etiquette, tennis.*

KUBLAI KHAN (1216–94)

First Mongol Emperor of China (also known as Kubla Khan), grandson Genghis Khan.

☐ See **KAMIKAZE.**

KUNG FU

Oriental philosophy and means of se defence. The expression Kung Fu is in fac translation of the words 'leisure time'. karate blow to the knee is shown in t illustration.

KURU

Kuru is a really exclusive disease, claime to be the rarest in the world. It is confined a cannibal tribe in New Guinea. One theo claims that kuru is spread only by the ha of eating human brains, but you may st have to wait forty years after the meal f the first symptoms to appear. One of t symptoms of kuru is hysterical laughter.

KUWAIT

☐ See **HEDGEHOG.**

L

(From the Latin: *lac*, *lactis*, milk.) According to Pliny the Elder, mother's milk has many uses in medicine, but if the baby is a girl then the value of the milk is limited to treatment of diseases of the face. It is compulsory in England to wash a cow's teats before milking if the milk is to be sold to the public. An experienced milker can wash a set of four teats in 30 seconds.

LAST WORDS

Several techniques may be recommended to anyone who wishes his last words to be recorded for posterity. One tried and tested procedure is the short and apt farewell. For example: 'Goodnight' (Byron), or 'If this is dying, then I don't think much of it' (Lytton Strachey), or 'Ah, my God, I am dead' (Catherine de Medici) or 'Oh, I am so bored with it all' (Winston Churchill) or 'Get my swan costume ready' (Anna Pavlova). To take things to a ridiculously logical extreme it would be hard to better 'Decay is inherent in all component things' (Buddha) but one cannot help having the feeling that this may have lost something in the translation.

On the other hand, peculiarly inappropriate sentiments tend to be recorded too: 'Go away, I'm all right' (H. G. Wells), or 'Die, my dear doctor? That's the last thing I shall do' (Viscount Palmerston, who was proved absolutely correct somewhat sooner than he expected), but the most incorrect of all was General Sedgewick, killed at the battle of Spotsylvania in the American Civil War, after uttering these last memorable seven-and-a-half words: 'They couldn't hit an elephant at this dist . . .'

Though not his last words, W. C. Fields's chosen epitaph, 'On the whole, I'd rather be in Pennsylvania', expressed more succinctly the sentiments of the final statement of Somerset Maugham: 'Dying is a very dull, dreary affair, and my advice to you is to have nothing whatever to do with it.' But neither of these has the pedantic finality of grammarian Dominique Bouhours, who exited on the line: 'I am about to, or, I am going to die. Either expression is used.'

Another trick to be recommended is to record two alternative sets of last words, to leave future anthologisers and historians arguing about which was really the tailpiece. Oscar Wilde, as might have been expected, left his fans with the choice of two witticisms: 'I am dying as I have lived – beyond my means' or 'Either this wallpaper goes or I do.' George V of England may have asked 'How is the Empire', but more probably, replying to a comment that he would soon be well enough to convalesce at Bognor Regis, snapped 'Bugger Bognor'. William Pitt the Younger, having presumably uttered the well-rehearsed 'My, country, oh my country' woke up again and said 'I think I could eat one of Bellamy's meat pies.' (There is even considerable dispute about this version, and whether he ordered 'meat', 'pork' or 'veal' pie.)

A proper sense of occasion is all too lacking in many of these above last words. That accusation cannot be made of the following: 'Carry my bones before you on your march. For the rebels will not be able to endure the sight of me, alive or dead' (King Edward I). Or the exit of Marie Antoinette, on tripping over the foot of the executioner at the guillotine: 'Monsieur, I beg your pardon. I did not do it on purpose.' Equally dignified at the guillotine was Henri Desire Landru (1869–1922), murderer of a dozen or so women: 'I want to wash my feet.' But neither of these, proud though they were, could quite match the presence and dignity of the Duc de Lanzon de Biron, guillotined in 1793: 'I beg a thousand pardons, my friend, but permit me to finish this last dozen of oysters.'

LAUNDRY

□ See **SOCKS**.

LAWRENCE, David Herbert (1885–1930)

In his spare time, British poet and novelist D. H. Lawrence liked to take off his clothes and climb mulberry trees. He left only £2,500.

LAWRENCE, St

St Lawrence is the patron saint of curriers. He was martyred by being broiled alive on a grid iron in AD 258. His last words are reported to have been: 'This side enough is toasted, so turn me, tyrant, eat and see whether raw or roasted I make the better meat.'

Though it might well be considered entirely appropriate for him to be the patron saint of makers of hot food, the curriers whom he patronises are those w[.] dress leather.

LEECH

An order (Hirudinea) of annelid worm[.] When gorging itself on blood the leech c[.] expand in size from 2 to 12 centimetr[.] One good meal can satisfy it for up [.] twelve months. The use of leeches [.] medicine has recently been revived as [.] means of removing traces of blood [.] delicate grafting operations. But the pr[.] tice is still far short of the level reached [.] the Parisian heyday of leeching arou[.] 1930, when France was importing leeches[.] a rate of 40 million a year.

LEFT-HANDEDNESS

According to a 1981 study at Manches[.] University, the chances of having a le[.]

handed child increases as the mother gets older. For first-time mothers aged 39 or over, the chance of giving birth to a sinistromanual child is 43 per cent.

A nineteenth-century piece of medical advice in Mexico was to take medicine with your right hand for complaints of the liver, but with your left hand for kidney ailments.

☐ See also: ***James I, polar bear, Syria.***

EG

Hind limb useful for walking.

☐ See **ARTIFICIAL LIMBS, BARBERS, HARRIS, F., SPIDER.**

EGLESSNESS

The state or condition of having insufficient of the preceding.

☐ See **AMPUTEES, BERNHARDT, S., DANCING, EMERGENCY, MISSIONARY.**

LEGISLATION

A multiplicity of laws is a sign of bad government (Aristotle). The Americans get an average of 150,000 new laws every year.

LEMMING

Genus of small rodents including the European lemming (*Myodes lemmus*). They have an odd habit of migrating occasionally for no clear reason.

☐ See **HAITI.**

LEMUR

The lemur was given its name by Carl Linnaeus (1707–78) who likened their nocturnal habits to those of ghosts; *lemures* is the Latin for ghosts. The ring-tailed lemur miaows like a cat. If you prefer a quiet pet, try a giraffe. It is the only

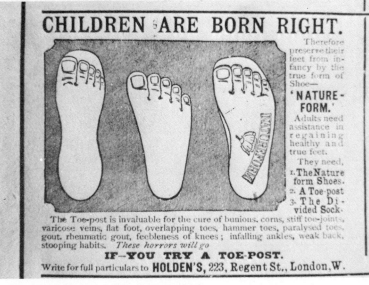

The wrong way to make love with a one-legged partner

naturally silent quadruped. Giraffes show affection by pressing their necks together.

☐ See also: *birth.*

LENIN (1870–1924)

Vladimir Ilyich Ulyanov travelled under many pseudonyms, of which Lenin became the best known. With these identity problems, it is hardly surprising that he did not learn to walk until he was 3 years old. Stalin spent five years studying for the priesthood. He was a model student but was expelled from the seminary for becoming a member of the Social Democratic Party and a Marxist.

When Lenin died, his brain was removed and cut into 20,000 pieces so that it could be studied by the Soviet Brain Institute.

LEO VIII, Pope (*d.* 965)

☐ See **DEATH.**

LEO X, Pope (1475–1521)

Second son of Lorenzo the Magnificent, a cardinal at the age of 13.

☐ See **MEDICI.**

LEONARDO DA VINCI (1452–1519)

Leonardo da Vinci was born in the village of Vinci, the illegitimate son of a lawyer and a peasant woman named Caterina. Apart from inventing breech-loading guns and scissors, he designed the first model of a helicopter. And for an encore he could break a horseshoe in half with his bare hands. His artistic fecundity might in part be explained by his ability to write with one hand while drawing with the other. Though, of course, he was unable to do either while breaking horseshoes.

☐ See also: *dog show, hair, homosexuality.*

LEOPOLD I, King of Belgium (1790–1865)

Son-in-law of George IV (after his marriage to Princess Charlotte), uncle of Queen Victoria. In 1831, Leopold became the first king of the Belgians.

☐ See **NAPOLEON III.**

LEPROSY

(From the Greek: *lepros*, scabby.) Infec tious disease caused by the *bacillus leprae* By an edict of Edward III in 1375, porters a the gates to the City of London had to tak an oath to prevent lepers entering, on pai of the pillory. There were no porters at th gates of Burgundy to prevent the passage c lepers in 1610, but that year saw a ba imposed on potatoes in the town since thes vegetables were suspected of being a caus of leprosy.

The pillory was abolished in England i 1816 (when there was already considerabl less leprosy in the City), except as a penalt for perjury, which it still functioned to dete until 1837.

☐ See also: *beauty, Benin, birth,*
   Buckingham Palace.

LERMONTOV, Mikhail Yurievich (1814–41)

Russian poet born to a noble family c Scottish descent (from George Learmonth who had settled in Russia in the seven teenth century).

☐ See **PEANUT.**

LESBIANISM

Whiptail lizards have been observed in dulging in overtly lesbian love-makin activity. They have little choice actually since they are all female and reproduce b parthenogenesis.

☐ See also: *ordeal by goat.*

LESOTHO

When the prime minister of Lesotho, Chie Jonathan, found himself losing the electio of 1970, he suspended the constitution, an arrested his opponents and the King Moshoeshoe II. A low trick, perhaps, bu do not forget that the lowest point c Lesotho is higher above sea level than th lowest point of any other country.

☐ See also: *Mexico.*

Emulating the whiptail lizard

LETHARGY
☐ See **APOPLEXY.**

LETTUCE

Hardy annual vegetable of the natural order Compositae and genus *Lactuca*, the lettuce is the most widely eaten green vegetable in the world. The Americans eat more than anyone else, munching their way through $700 million worth of lettuce a year. In Mexico it is believed that a baby may be cured of insomnia by bathing in lettuce water.

Another supposed cure for insomnia is to go to bed with a wolf's head under your pillow. No empirical evidence is available but there are some grounds for believing that this last remedy might also run the risk of causing insomnia in someone who was not already a sufferer.

LIBERAL PARTY
☐ See **OBSCENITY.**

LIBYA

In 1974 a dog was put on trial in Libya on the charge of biting a human. On conviction, it was sentenced to a month in jail on bread and water. The sentence seems fair when you consider that until 1819 you could be hanged in Britain for impersonating a Chelsea pensioner or damaging Westminster Bridge.

☐ See also: *Grenada.*

LIECHTENSTEIN

The principality of Liechtenstein covers an area of 61 square miles. It has had no army since 1868 but is one of the world's leading exporters of dentures.

LIFE EXPECTANCY

Life expectancy of the Greeks and Romans was 36 years, exactly the number for which Byron managed to survive. But Burns, Van Gogh and Raphael all managed to reach 37 before dying. Between 1900 and 1974, life expectancy in the United States rose from 47.3 to 71.9 years. In fifth-century England it was only 30 years.

☐ See also: *Gabon.*

LIFE-STYLE
☐ See **BLOOD.**

LIGHTNING

Two men were hanged in the South African village of Mogoboya in 1984, for allegedly causing a woman to be struck dead by a lightning bolt. The hanging was ordered by a witch doctor. Police arrested eight.

☐ See also: *traffic.*

LILY

Genus of bulbous herbs of the order Liliaceae.

☐ See **NUT.**

LINCOLN, Abraham (1809–65)

Throughout his life, Abraham Lincoln was convinced, wrongly, that he was illegitimate. He was shot in 1865 by John Wilkes Booth. The illustration is neither of President Lincoln nor of his assassin but portrays Charles Wyndham, an English actor whose first appearance on stage was at Washington, where he played Osric to the Hamlet of John Wilkes Booth. He was sacked by the latter for incompetence, but later gained the reputation of a fine light comedian.

☐ See also: *hat.*

LINCOLN, City of

The county town of Lincolnshire, England.

☐ See **PYRAMID.**

LION

(*Felis leo*) The largest member of the cat genus, one lion weighs as much as 10,000

mice, 250 hedgehogs or 1¼ giraffes. According to reliable gastronomic sources, pig-muzzled hedgehogs taste better than the dog-muzzled variety. Whale meat is very rich in vitamin C, but you need 480 lions to equal the weight of a blue whale.

☐ See also: *premarital sex.*

IP

Muscular organ bounding the mouth. A man in Australia was awarded $142,000 damages after a car crash had left him with numb lips and unable to enjoy the delights of kissing. Medically, a kiss has been defined as: 'The anatomical juxtaposition of two orbicularis oris muscles in a state of contraction.' The longest such juxtaposition on screen was the three-minute plus smackeroo shared between Regis Toomey and Jane Wyman in 1914 in the film 'You're in the Army Now'.

IP-READING

Deaf viewers have complained to the BBC television authorities about the bad language of footballers on 'Match of the Day'.

ISZT, Franz (1811–86)

Hungarian pianist and composer.

☐ See **MONTEZ.**

ITERACY

The Icelanders read more books per capita than any other nation on earth. Their literacy rate is 100 per cent. Algerian women are not far behind on 80 per cent literacy, but they are badly let down by their menfolk, only half of whom can read.

The average temperature in Reykjavik is higher than in New York. It is much hotter in Algeria, of course, where even all the rivers have dried up.

☐ See also: *India.*

ITERARY CRITICISM

The French literary critic Charles-Augustin Sainte-Beuve (1804–69) was once chal-

lenged to a duel by an irate journalist who considered himself insulted by the critic's writings. Seizing the opportunity afforded to him by choice of weapons, Sainte-Beuve replied: 'I choose spelling – you're dead.'

LITERATURE

Ernest Vincent Wright in 1939 published a 58,000 word novel *Gadsby*, which contained no letter 'e'. This feat more than redressed the balance which had been upset in 1824 by the publication of Lord Holland's short story *Eve's legend*, which contained no vowel other than 'e'. Tryphiodorus, a sixth-century Greek poet of Egypt, wrote an epic poem in twenty-four books on the destruction of Troy. Each book avoided using a different letter of the Greek alphabet, starting with alpha in Book 1, through to omega in Book 24.

☐ See also: *anti-social behaviour, Frankfurt, Peter the Great.*

LIVER

The largest glandular organ in the human body, weighing an average of 3 lb.

☐ See **LEFT-HANDEDNESS, SHARK, TERRAPIN, VITAMINS.**

LIVERPOOL

English city on the Mersey estuary.

☐ See **AUCTION.**

LIZARD

(From the Latin: *lacerta*.) A four-legged scaly creature with movable eyelids, member of the order Lacertilia. Some types of lizard keep cool in the sun by urinating over themselves. Urine used to be used as a detergent in ancient Rome. It was collected in 'public lavatories' (wash-places, from the Latin: *lavare*, to wash) and saved for the bleaching properties of its ammonia content.

☐ See also: *lesbianism, toe.*

LLAMA

The llama (from the Spanish: *llama*, a llama) has bad breath, but it can wiggle its ears independently. The okapi (discovered in 1901 by Sir Harry Johnston while looking for a unicorn) can wash its own ears with its 14-inch tongue. Dogs have seventeen different muscles controlling their ears, humans have only nine. Female humans in the US Army, according to an edict of 1983, may wear ear-rings, but they must be spherical, made of gold, silver or pearl, fit snugly against the ear, and be not more than ¼-inch in diameter.

☐ See also: *earthquake, Peru.*

LLEWELYN AP GRUFFYDD, Prince of Wales (*d.* 1282)

Grandson of Llewelyn the Great. Llewelyn is old Welsh for lion-like.

☐ See **SAHARA.**

LOBSTER

(Corruption of the Latin: *locusta*, spiny lobster.) A ten-footed crustacean. The most effective bait for catching a lobster is a brick soaked in paraffin. It is not known whether this was used by French dramatis Gerard de Nerval, but he was frequentl seen taking his pet lobster for walks on th end of a blue ribbon in Paris. When aske why, he replied: 'Because it does not bark and it knows the secrets of the sea.' H hanged himself in 1855 from a lamp-pos by an apron string which he maintained wa the garter of the Queen of Sheba.

☐ See also: *flamingo, knowledge.*

LOCUST

The desert locust (*schistocera gregaria*) often too cold to fly first thing in th morning. The common commuter (*hom Londoniensis*) knows just how he feels.

☐ See also: *aural sex.*

LONDON

Capital city of England, situated on th River Thames (pronounced *Temz*). Unt the Piccadilly line extension was opened i 1977, Chorleywood, Chalfont & Latime. and Chesham, on the Metropolitan line was the longest sequence of consecutiv London underground stations all beginnin

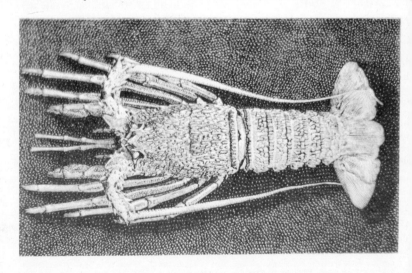

with the same letter (though necessitating a change at Chalfont for the Chesham line). Thanks to huge capital investment, the commuter can now enjoy an unbroken alliterative sequence from Hounslow East, via Hounslow West, Hounslow Central and Hatton Cross, to Heathrow Central.

ONGEVITY

Jane Lewson died in London in 1816 aged 116 years. She never washed the inside of her windows and never took a bath. Her daily cleansing ritual was to smear her face with hog's lard. Whether this performance contributed to her survival is a matter for conjecture, but it should be noted that the average clam can live for 100 years.

The world's oldest living organism is, however, believed to be a creosote bush living in the Mojave desert in California. Its age has been estimated as 11,700 years. Buddy Holly died when he was 22.

☐ See also: *Parsee.*

ONG JUMP
☐ See **MELON.**

OS ANGELES
(From the Spanish: *los angeles*, the angels.) City of California, USA.

☐ See **POPULATION, THEFT.**

OST PROPERTY

In 1979 on public transport in Tokyo, quite apart from the almost predictable quarter of a million **UMBRELLAS** left by passengers, also mislaid were seventeen goldfish bowls, complete with goldfish, two rhinoceros horns, a stuffed kangaroo, and eight crematorial urns with ashes inside.

☐ See also: *barrel-organ, gloves, milk powder, Wellington.*

OUIS I, King of Bavaria (1786–1868)

King Louis I of Bavaria was the father of Otto, King of Greece.

☐ See **MONTEZ.**

LOUIS XI, King of France (1423–83)
☐ See **SOOTHSAYING.**

LOUIS XIII, King of France (1601–43)

Son of Henry IV and Marie de Medici, manipulated by Richelieu, father of Louis XIV.

☐ See **AGE OF CONSENT.**

LOUIS XIV, King of France (1638–1715)

Louis XIV reigned for 72 years and was the first person to wear high-heeled shoes. He only took three baths in his life, but changed his linen three times each day. His wife, Spanish princess Maria Theresa, had a 13-inch waist. He and she were the only ones at the French court permitted to sit in chairs with arms. When Maria Theresa died, Louis did the decent thing and married his mistress, Madame de Maintenon. His son and grandson both died before him, so he was succeeded by his great-grandson Louis XV.

☐ See also: *accidents, Buckland, Richard III, Versailles.*

LOUIS XVI, King of France (1754–93)

Though generally lacking in insight, judgement or knowledge, Louis XVI had a good line in insults. Annoyed to hear the Duchesse de Polignac praising Benjamin Franklin, when the latter was American emissary in Paris, the King arranged for the Duchess to be presented with a chamber pot displaying Franklin's face on its bowl.

☐ See also: *accidents, diarists, handkerchief.*

LOUSE

Name given to a small group of parasitic wingless insects. The louse used to determine mayors of the Swedish town of Hurdenburg. Eligible candidates would place the points of their beards on a table top. A louse was then dropped in the centre of the table. Whichever beard it chose determined the mayor for the next year.

Since lice have the habit of fleeing from a feverish body, the possession of these creatures used to be considered a sign of good health.

LOVE

What is this thing called love? According to the first International Conference on Love and Attraction, it may be defined as: 'The cognitive–affective state characterised by intrusive and obsessive fantasising concerning reciprocity of amorant feeling by the object of the amorance.'

This definition appears to preclude any objective acceptance of a state of unrequited amorance.

LOVE-SICKNESS

An old Egyptian cure for love-sickness is t drink beer out of an old shoe. The beer ma be purchased, for example, in a bee parlour of Saskatchewan, but on suc premises it is illegal to drink water.

LUCK

☐ See **GARDENING.**

LUFTWAFFE

(From the German: *Luftwaffe*, air force.)
☐ See **BRIGHTON.**

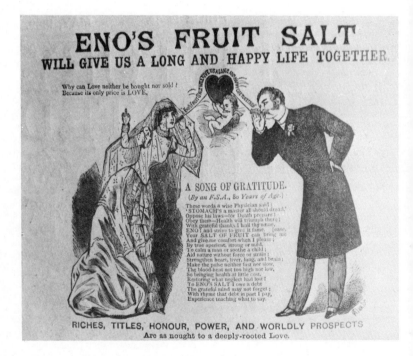

ENO'S FRUIT SALT

WILL GIVE US A LONG AND HAPPY LIFE TOGETHER.

RICHES, TITLES, HONOUR, POWER, AND WORLDLY PROSPECTS
Are as nought to a deeply-rooted Love.

ULLY, Jean-Baptiste (1633–87)
French composer, born in Italy.
☐ See **DEATH.**

UST
The male Australian marsupial mole, *Antichinus stuarti*, is doomed to die of lust. This little digger has only a four-day mating season, after which all the males then die from excessive hormone levels caused by copulation.
☐ See also: *chocolate.*

LUTHER, Martin (1483–1546)
German reformer.
☐ See **PITT.**

M

MACARONI

According to the regulations of the American Public Health Service of Food and Drug Administration, macaroni may be sold to the public provided a tested sample does not exceed a defect level of twenty-five insect fragments in 225 grams. This seems rather harsh compared with the allowed levels of up to 2,500 aphids per 100 g of hops, and strawberries which are permissible with a mould count of 55 per cent.

MACDONALD, James Ramsay (1866–1937)

British Prime Minister.

☐ See **BACHELOR.**

MACEDONIA

A part of Yugoslavia; also a mixture of fruit (or more rarely vegetables) embedded in jelly.

☐ See **SOAP.**

MACINTOSH, Charles (1766–1843)

British chemist, elected Fellow of the Royal Society in 1823. Performed important research into the manufacture of steel.

☐ See **RAINCOAT.**

MADAGASCAR

Island in the Indian Ocean off the east coast of Africa. The Madagascans are an extraordinarily superstitious people who believe that the number eight is unlucky and that Friday is red. The capital is Antananarivo and there are no poisonous snakes in Madagascar.

☐ See also: *birth, dream, etiquette, taboo.*

MAGELLAN, Ferdinand (c. 1480–1521)

Portuguese navigator whose real name was Fernao de Magalhaes. He made all his important voyages of discovery after being lamed in a Moroccan campaign in 1512. Had the weather not been so good when he became the first European to enter the Pacific, he would probably have given that ocean a totally different name.

☐ See also: *Antigua.*

MAGNETISM

☐ See **DICKENS, JULIUS CAESAR.**

MAHLER, Gustav (1860–1911)

Austrian composer.

☐ See **SATIE.**

MAHOMET (570–632)

The founder of Islam, his original name was Halabi. Or it may have been Kotham. And he is sometimes known under the alias Mohammed (or various alternative spellings all of which mean 'the praised one'). Anyway, his father, Abdallah, was said to have been so beautiful that two hundred

Madagascans preparing the vegetables

virgins died of broken hearts when he married Amina.

Ivan the Terrible, who was crowned Czar at the age of 16, had a thousand virgins assembled so that he could choose a suitable bride. The 999 unsuccessful applicants were probably more relieved than heartbroken. Ivan was the sort of man who would kill an elephant if it did not bow down before him. Indeed he did have put to death the only elephant known to have offended him in this manner.

MALARIA

(From the Italian: *mala aria*, bad air.) Disease once thought to be caused by the bad air from swamp marches.

□ See **HERRING.**

MALAYSIA

Enough rubber is produced each year in Malaysia to produce tyres for more than 55 million cars. In Bermuda, this information became a matter of concern only in 1946, before which year cars were not legal. There are no mammals or reptiles native to Bermuda.

□ See also: *premarital sex.*

MALI

(Formerly French Sudan.) The natives of Mali have the highest fertility rate in the world. The Dogon tribe have one of the most perplexing religions too, worshipping Sirius B, one of the moons of the Dogstar, Sirius. They have been doing this since centuries before Sirius B was discovered by astronomers. Its period of revolution about Sirius is also accurately known to the Dogons and forms part of the religious ritual, though the details seem calculable only by modern methods.

□ See also: *Niger.*

MALORY, Sir Thomas (fl.1469)

English writer of romance.

□ See **SPELLING.**

MALTA

Many churches in Malta have two clocks, one showing the correct time, the other deliberately wrong, in order to confuse the devil about the times of church services.

It is forbidden to import Maltese gladioli into the United States. Early in 1958, *Life* magazine published a nine-page interview with the devil. Perhaps significantly neither Maltese clocks nor gladioli featured as a topic in the discussion.

☐ See also: *Arabic.*

MANCHESTER

City and seaport on the River Irwell in England.

☐ See **RECYCLING.**

MANDARIN

☐ See **CHINA, CIVIL SERVICE.**

MANHATTAN

Island at the mouth of the Hudson River, USA. The Manhattan cocktail was invented by Jennie Jerome, mother of Winston Churchill.

MANSFIELD, Jayne (1932–67)

American actress born Jayne Palmer.

☐ See **BREASTS.**

MANSION HOUSE

The official residence of the Lord Mayor of London, who may live there free, on condition that he does his own repairs and cleans his own windows. This condition may have been waived in the case of Brook Watson, Lord Mayor in 1796, whose ability to perform menial tasks was impaired by his losing a foot to a shark in Havana harbour.

MANSLAUGHTER

The unlawful slaying of another person without malice aforethought. In Aborigine tribes the punishment for manslaughter is to be stabbed in the thigh by a tribal elder.

Brook Watson's accident

MANURE

The British horse population peaked i 1902 at 3½ million. At that time thes animals were estimated to be leaving 1 million tons of manure in the streets eac year.

Between 1850 and 1880 the single mos common cause of death among America cowboys was to be dragged by their hors while caught in the stirrups.

☐ See also: *fertiliser.*

MAORI

The Maoris of New Zealand regard tattooed chin as a sign of rank. After th battle of Hastings in 1066, no tattooe Maoris were found, but King Harold's bod was identified by a tattoo over his heart. read: Edith and England.

MARBLE ARCH

London monument, modelled by Joh Nash. Originally intended as an entranc to Buckingham Palace, Marble Arch wa

A Maori of extremely high rank

iscovered to be too small to admit the state oach, so was moved to its present location t the top of Park Lane, on the central line.

ARIE ANTOINETTE (1755–93)

Queen of France.

❒ See **ACCIDENTS, BREASTS, CROCKERY, LAST WORDS.**

ARIGOLD

(*Calendula officinalis*) Annual herb of the natural order Compositae.

❒ See **CONJUNCTION.**

ARITAL CUSTOMS

Male Spartans unmarried by the age of 30 lost the right to vote and to attend orgies. In India nine out of ten girls are married by the time they are 20. In ancient Greece, however, a woman's age was only counted from the day of her marriage.

❒ See also: *Babylonia.*

MARITAL STRESS

When George I came over to take the throne of England in 1714, he left his wife behind. She did not become queen because she had committed adultery. In fact the two of them did not seem to get on well at all and she was kept under house arrest for thirty-two years in Ahlden castle. Even the existence of the 'Prisoner of Ahlden' was kept a secret.

MARKSMANSHIP

The worst case of marksmanship on record seems to be that of a duel which took place in an apartment house hallway in Cleveland, Ohio, in 1981. The combatants, aged 77 and 76 years respectively, finally decided to settle an old grudge with antique pistols. They stood five feet apart and emptied the barrels at each other, but all twelve bullets missed. Their aim may have been affected by the fact that one suffered from glaucoma, while the other needed a stick to prop himself up. Police called to the scene decided to take possession of the pistols for safe-keeping.

MARRIAGE

Recent research indicates that marriage can be good for you. Statistics show that bachelors are three times more likely than married men to go mad; they are also more liable to commit suicide and suffer from accidents or disease. (Alternatively, one might deduce that women are more likely to prefer sane, non-suicidal, healthy partners.)

Husbands were not permitted to beat their wives after 10 pm in sixteenth-century Britain. The illustration shows a suitable stance for wife-beating.

☐ See also: *genetics, healing.*

MARS

Planet of eccentric orbit, average distanc 141,384,000 miles from the sun.

☐ See **APHRODISIAC, RATS.**

MARX, Heinrich Karl (1818–83)

Founder of international revolutiona socialism. Two of Karl Marx's daughte committed suicide, as indeed did Stalin wife and one of Trotsky's daughters.

Sweden has the world's highest suicid rate, but the Hungarians are putting in strong challenge for leadership in th demanding field. Stalin's son did not con mit suicide, but died in a German prisc camp in the Second World War after Stali had declined an offer to exchange him for German prisoner.

MARY, Queen of Scots (1542–87)

Daughter of James V of Scotland, who die when she was five days old, leaving he Queen.

☐ See **EXECUTION, FINGERPRINTS, REMARRIAGE.**

MASSACRE

If reports of the carnage are accurate, th greatest massacre in history was at Nish. pur in north-east Iran in 1221 when, in th space of one hour, Genghis Khan's troo slaughtered 1¾ million people. Continuin at that rate, they could have disposed of th whole of the present world population i fourteen weeks.

For a massacre where the instrument c destruction was non-human, we need on go back to near the end of the Secon World War and the fierce battles o Ramree Island, off the coast of Burma, i February 1945. One thousand retreatin Japanese soldiers waded waist deep i swamp waters in order to escape the British pursuers. The British troops did n get them; the crocodiles did. Only twen survived.

ATA HARI (1876–1917)

The real name of exotic dancer and spy, Mata Hari, was Gertrude Zelle. She showed a possibly unique sense of occasion and elegance in ordering a specially tailored suit and new gloves to be worn for her execution by firing squad.

☐ See also: *Rasputin.*

ATCHSTICKS

According to Lawrence Shaw, a miner from Stoke-on-Trent, it takes 156,000 matchsticks to build a 7-foot tall grandfather clock. Mr Shaw knows, because he did it while unemployed in 1982.

ATERNITY

The giraffe gives birth standing up, which means that the first experience of each baby giraffe is a fall to earth from a height of about 6 feet. The African elephant has no such traumatic beginning to its life, but it does sleep in a standing position.

ATING

Probably from the Middle Low German, *nate,* or earlier Dutch, *maet.*) The snail only makes love once in its life, but the act can last for up to twelve hours. The fastest love-making is probably that of the impala, seen copulating on the gallop at speeds of 30 mph.

☐ See also: *auction, bedbug, cricket, eyelid, porcupine, Raleigh.*

ATISSE, Henri Emile Benoît (1869–1954)

Matisse's father did not like his son's paintings and cut off his allowance; for a time his career had to be supported by his wife's millinery shop in Paris.

☐ See **ARTISTIC APPRECIATION.**

ATTERHORN

Alpine peak of 14,800 ft between Italy and Switzerland.

☐ See **MOUNTAINEERING.**

MATTHIAS CORVINUS, King of Hungary (1443–90)

Hungarian king and founder of Budapest University.

☐ See **UGLINESS.**

MAUGHAM, William Somerset (1874–1965)

English novelist who thought *Moby Dick* to be the tenth greatest novel of all time.

☐ See **LAST WORDS, STAMMERING.**

MAURITANIA

There are less than four people per square mile in the north-west African republic of Mauritania. In England, however, there are approximately 2 million spiders in every acre of field land. The capital of Mauritania is Nouakchott.

☐ See also: *motorcycling.*

MAXIMILIAN I, Emperor of Austria (1459–1519)

Son of the Hapsburg emperor Frederick III, he married Mary, daughter of Charles the Bold, Duke of Burgundy.

☐ See **AUSTRIA.**

MAYFLY

A plectopterous insect (Ephemera) which lives only a day or so as an adult. During that period it moults twice, mates and lays its eggs in water. Even if it had time to eat, it could not do so, since it has no mouth or stomach. The only appropriate way to greet a mayfly is with the words: 'Have a good day.'

McCARTHY, Charlie

☐ See **OVERQUALIFICATION.**

McKINLEY, William (1843–1901)

American president, shot by a Polish-American anarchist named Czolgosz.

☐ See **GENIUS.**

MEASLES

(Perhaps connected with Old High German: *masala*, a blister.) Also known as Rubeola. According to an old German remedy, children suffering from measles should be washed in water in which peas have been boiled.

After measles, the world's second most infectious disease is gonorrhoea.

MEDIA

The influence of the media may be overestimated; 70 per cent of the world's population have no newspapers, radio, telephone or television. Between the ages of 5 and 14 the average American child will have seen 13,000 deaths on television. In an average week's viewing he will see crimes committed for which convictions of those responsible would merit 6,000 years imprisonment.

MEDICI

Ruling family of Florence, flourishing between the thirteenth and eighteen centuries. Quite apart from producir **CATHERINE DE MEDICI**, the Medi clan gave the world two popes (Leo X ar the illegitimate Clement VII), and Lorenz the Magnificent. But their most lastir claim to fame ought to rest with Ferdinar II, Grand Duke of Tuscany, who in 165 invented the first sealed bulb thermomete

A normal adult gives off the san amount of heat as a 120-watt bulb. Th daily output would be enough to boil litres of ice-cold water.

MEDICINE

Research on different coloured pills havir the same chemical composition shows th yellow pills work better than other colou as tranquillisers on depressed patients. you are out of yellow ones, the next best a red or green pills, followed by blue ar brown. Worst of all are black pills.

It is not known whether this result st holds true for depressives in Czech slovakia, where the highest known rate red–green colour-blindness is found.

MELBOURNE

Capital of the state of Victoria, Australia, usually pronounced *Mel'bn*. In 1975, Melbourne became the world's first city to use chickens to control the traffic in a park.

MELON

(*Cucumis melo*) Plant of the natural order Cucurbitaceae. The annual melon pip spitting contest in France in 1983 was won by a lorry driver from Agen. He spat his pip 24 ft 6 in. to outdistance the other forty-eight contestants. This winning distance is longer than the world record for the women's long jump.

MENELIK II, Emperor of Abyssinia 1844–1913)

With little evidence, Menelik II claimed direct descent from Solomon and the Queen of Sheba. But he did abolish slavery in Abyssinia.

☐ See **ELECTRIC CHAIR.**

MENSTRUATION

(From the Latin: *menstruus*, monthly.) According to old superstitions, a menstrual woman can, by her mere presence, blunt steel, take the polish off ivory, corrode brass, rust iron, and cause the fruit to fall from trees. But her touch can bring help to those suffering from mumps, swellings, boils, or scrofulous tumours.

MERMAID

According to Athanasius Kircher, a mid seventeenth-century microscopist, plague was caused by the rotting bodies of dead mermaids. But it was also believed at about the same time that eating cucumbers caused cholera, so it might not have been the mermaids' fault after all.

METEMPSYCHOSIS

The transmigration of souls. On the evening of the death of Sir Robert Grant, Governor of Bombay, in 1838, a cat was seen leaving Government House and walking Sir Robert's usual route. For the next twenty-five years, any cat passing through the front door of Government House was saluted and addressed as His Excellency.

MEXICO

Every day, seventy-five murders are committed in Mexico, one of the highest rates in the world but still way behind the leaders, Lesotho. Mexico can, however, claim two world records (one shared). The border between the United States and Mexico is crossed by more people each year (about 120 million) than any other frontier. Also Mexico has more mules than anywhere else; its 12 million mules account for 28 per cent of the world's total. Vietnam, however, has 27 per cent of the world's ducks.

☐ See also: *scorpion, worm.*

MICHELANGELO (1475–1564)

Despite being sent off to school in Florence to rid him of his vulgar artistic proclivities, Michelangelo survived beatings from father and teachers to indulge his passion for art and for Luigia de Medici at the court of Lorenzo the Magnificent, where his nose was broken by a fellow student. Later he sculpted a huge monument to Pope Julius II, which was too big to put in St Peter's church, so the Pope had the church rebuilt to accommodate it. A bit slow as an interior decorator, Michelangelo could take four years to paint a ceiling.

☐ See also: *homosexuality, Pitt, technology.*

MICROWAVE OVEN

☐ See **IRELAND.**

MIDWIFERY

(From the Old English, *mid*, with; *wif*, woman.)

☐ See **BRIDGET, TOAD.**

MIGRAINE

(From 14th to 18th century, *Megrim*.)

☐ See **APOPLEXY.**

MILAN

City of Italy called Milano by the Italians.

☐ See **PROCRASTINATION, VERDI.**

MILDEW

Fungal disease of plants.

☐ See **THEOLOGY.**

MILK

Liquid secreted in the udder of a female animal.

☐ See **DENTISTRY, GIRAFFE, LACTATION, PLATYPUS, PRODUCTIVITY, RABIES, TANZANIA.**

MILK POWDER

Skimmed milk solids, vegetable fats, dried glucose syrup, emulsifier E471, anti-caking agent silica, lecithin, Vitamin A and Vitamin D are what may be found in a packet of milk powder; though the milk solids may be optional and substituted by flavourings and colours E102 and E110. Another thing once found in a packet of milk powder in Peru was a bunch of keys which a New Zealander had lost in Hamilton two years before.

MILLIPEDE

Order of arthropods forming, with the **CENTIPEDE**, the zoological class Myriapoda.

☐ See **INSURANCE.**

MILTON, John (1608–74)

Richard Porson (1750–1808), reputedly England's greatest classical scholar of the time, could recite the whole of Milton's 'Paradise Lost' backwards.

MISOGYNY

The hatred of women. (From the Greek: *miseein*, to hate; *gyne*, a young woman.) In Spanish the word *esposa* means both 'wife' and 'handcuff'. In Chinese, the ideograph showing two women under one roof means 'trouble'.

MISPRINT

The most potentially lethal misprint must have been that of the Warrenton Fauquier Democrat newspaper of Virginia, USA. The correction read as follows:

'Important: in our Easy Sky Diving book, please make the following correction: On page 8, line 7, the words "State zip code" should have read "Pull rip cord".'

☐ See also: *physics.*

MISSIONARY

The Reverend Elisha Fawcett of Manchester taught the natives of the Admiralty Islands in the South Pacific the Commandments of God and the Laws of Cricket. When he died around 1817, his parishioners could not afford to have a proper monument erected on his grave, so they adorned it with his wooden leg as a headstone. And the leg did take root and flower. Taken as a sign by the natives, the resulting tree was used to provide wood for cricket bats for generations thereafter.

MISUNDERSTANDING

When Captain Cook saw an odd creature bounding past in Australia, he asked a native what was the name of the animal. The Aborigine replied 'Kangaroo'. Only some years later, after the name had stuck, did the good captain learn that 'kangaroo' in the local dialect meant, 'I don't understand what you are saying.'

☐ See also: *Yucatan, Zaire.*

MODESTY

Paul Cézanne trained his parrot to say 'Cézanne is a genius.'

MOLE

Family of insectivorous mammals (*Talpidae*). A mole can shift 10 lb of soil in twenty minutes, dig a 100-yard tunnel in a single night, and bury itself in five seconds flat. The collective noun is a labour of moles.

☐ See also: *barrister, cramp, lust,*

survival, swimming, William III of England.

Modesty

MOLEOSOPHY

Fortune-telling by the position of moles on the body. A mole on the right side of the forehead is predictive of talent and success; on the left it is indicative of a stubborn and extravagant personality. A happy marriage is foretold if you have a mole on the right knee, but on the other knee it is said to indicate only a bad temper.

MONACO

Principality of southern Europe, bounded to the north by France. The 3,500 native Monegasques are heavily outnumbered by the 25,000 foreign residents of Monaco and the million or so visitors to the principality each year. Of all these, only the Monegasques are prohibited from gambling.

John B. Kelly, father of Princess Grace of Monaco, won two Olympic gold medals for rowing in 1920, retaining the gold for the double sculls in 1924. He may have looked a bit like the man in the illustration.

☐ See also: ***civilisation.***

MONA LISA

Name given to a painting by Leonardo da Vinci of Lisa di Anton Maria di Noldo Gherardini, who married Francesco di Bartolommeo del Giocondo in 1495. Leonardo himself claimed the portrait to be unfinished, but there have been few complaints.

☐ See **ARTISTIC APPRECIATION, HAIR, INSURANCE.**

MONDALE, Walter (*b.* 1928)

☐ See **TAYLOR, Elizabeth.**

MONET, Claude Oscar (1840–1926)

In 1883, Monet began to paint a particularly splendid oak tree during the winter months. His work was interrupted by a period of particularly bad weather, which obscured his view of the tree. When work resumed, the previously bare tree had grown buds and leaves. At Monet's request, the mayor of the village organised teams to remove all the leaves from the tree to enable the painting to be completed. Monet makes the leaves go aground.

Another case where art and nature came into conflict was Carl André's exhibition in 1973. The display lasted only one day (1 January to be precise) because of the smell. The exhibit 'American Decay' consisted of 500 lb of cottage cheese, 10 inches deep on a piece of tar paper 18 ft × 12 ft; the cheese was covered with 10 gallons of ketchup.

MONEY

(From the Latin: *moneta*, money, a mint. *Moneta* was a surname of Juno, in whose temple at Rome money was minted.) Cree Indians used pipes as their sole form of currency. In nineteenth-century China, however, bamboo was used for money. The Bank of England is evidently rather frugal in its use of resources. Used banknotes, a

One ſhilling & ſix pence Lawful Money. NEW-LONDON: Printed by Timothy Green, 1ſ6. 7 7 6. 1ſ6.

the end of their lives, are burned, thereby producing enough warmth to heat the factory which produces new notes. In early US trading, the buckskin was a common form of currency; hence the word 'buck' coming to mean a dollar.

MONGOLIA

With only three people per square mile, Mongolia is the most sparsely populated country on earth. It can therefore be very difficult, if you get lost in Mongolia, to find anyone from whom to obtain directions. Mongol horsemen had a bright way round this problem when they used to go on raiding expeditions into Siberia. They would ride on mares, leaving the foals at home. When they wanted to return, they simply slackened the reins, and let the mares find their own way back to their families.

Penguins have a similarly uncanny knack of knowing which iceflow will take them home, but the Mongolians have so far failed to utilise this ability.

☐ See also: *coffin.*

MONKEY

Any mammal of the Primates, except man

and (usually) the anthropoid apes. A useful rule of thumb (or rump) to determine the place of origin of a monkey is to see whether it can hang from its tail. In general, monkeys from Central and South America have prehensile tails, those from Africa and Asia do not. South African monkeys do, however, seem to have other talents. Pretoria art school examiners once gave a pass mark to a chimpanzee's scrawlings which had been submitted as a joke by a student. Actually the chimpanzee is an anthropoid ape, so not really a monkey at all.

☐ See also: *art, musical appreciation, pregnancy.*

MONMOUTH, James Scott, Duke of (1649–85)

English prince, born in Rotterdam. The official portrait of the Duke of Monmouth was painted after his decapitation in 1685. The severed head was stitched back onto the torso, the body dressed, and the corpse posed for sittings with the artist.

After the Duke of Monmouth's unsuccessful rebellion against King James II, Judge Jeffreys sentenced 350 to hang and 841 to be transported for periods of ten years or more.

MONOPOLY

(From the Greek: *monos*, alone; *polein*, to sell.) The street names on the American version of the game of 'Monopoly' are taken from Atlantic City. The 'Monopoly' lobby once successfully restrained the city council from changing the name of a street which was represented on the 'Monopoly' board.

To go from the Atlantic to the Pacific, take the Panama Canal, the only canal in the world linking two oceans. The area of the Pacific Ocean is larger than the combined area of all land on earth.

MONOSODIUM GLUTAMATE

A white crystalline salt which stimulates the

taste buds; MSG to its friends and enemies.

☐ See **DISEASE**.

MONROE, James (1758–1831)

American president for two terms beginning in 1816.

☐ See **INDEPENDENCE**.

MONTEZ, Lola (1818–61)

Stage name of the Irish dancer Marie Dolores Eliza Rosanna Gilbert. It is one of the great tragedies of history that Lola Montez did not live at the same time as Isaac Newton. Had she but done so, he might not have died a virgin. For Miss Montez liked men with teeth. Before becoming mistress of Ludwig I of Bavaria, her lovers included Alexandre Dumas, père, and Franz Liszt. And she refused to sleep with the Viceroy of Poland because he had false teeth. At the age of 80 not only did Newton have all but one of his own teeth, but he didn't need glasses for reading.

MONTREAL

The largest city of Canada.

☐ See **ANTARCTICA**.

MOON

Natural satellite of the earth, revolving in 27.32 days at an average distance of 238,800 miles.

☐ See **FROG**.

MORALITY

Alexander Cruden compiled his 'Concordance to the Bible' (a sort of Biblical index) in 1737. He was then appointed corrector to the press which published it. Taking his duties perhaps too seriously, he appointed himself Corrector to the Morals of the Nation in 1755. On several occasions he was confined to asylums, but during his spells of freedom he was wont to wander round the streets with a sponge, ready to erase any chalk scribblings which he considered licentious, coarse or profane. A worthy opponent for eighteenth-century graffitists, but perhaps in some small way responsible for the paucity of graffiti collections among our early literature.

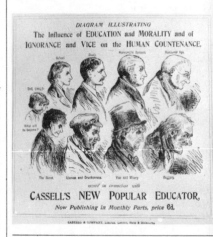

DIAGRAM ILLUSTRATING
The Influence of EDUCATION and MORALITY and of IGNORANCE and VICE on the HUMAN COUNTENANCE,

issued in connection with

CASSELL'S NEW POPULAR EDUCATOR,
Now Publishing in Monthly Parts, price 6d.

MORNING SICKNESS

☐ See **LOCUST**.

MOROCCO

The last Sharifian Emperor of Morocco was Moulay Ismail (1672–1727), known as The Bloodthirsty. Evidently blood alone was not enough to slake his voracious appetites. He reputedly fathered 548 sons and 340 daughters. This is comparative celibacy compared with the 80,000 fathered in one year by Grove Speculator, an 11-year-old Friesian bull in 1983. He is England's most prolific bull, so virile that he attends the artificial insemination clinic three times a week, once more than most bulls. It is believed that Moulay Ismail gave a personal service, preferring not to trust to artificial insemination methods. A female mosquito can produce 150 million offspring in a year.

☐ See also: *divorce, Niger.*

MORSE, Samuel Finley Breese (1791–1872)

Originally a portrait painter (he exhibited

at the Royal Academy) Samuel Morse turned later to science, but had almost a decade of struggle in convincing European or American governments that there might be some use in a telegraph service.

☐ See **BELL.**

MORTALITY

More people were killed in Europe by the influenza epidemic of 1918–19 than had been slain during the preceding World War. More Roman infantry were killed at the battle of Cannae in 216 BC than the total number lost by the Royal Air Force in both World Wars put together.

Nobody is believed to have been killed during the 110 years of hostilities between Berwick-upon-Tweed and Russia between 1856 and 1966. Since Berwick had changed hands so frequently between England and Scotland, the town was usually mentioned explicitly in declarations of war, and was particularly so mentioned at the outbreak of the Crimean War. When the treaty was signed at the end of that war, however, Berwick was omitted from mention, with the result that the war officially raged on until a Soviet delegation arrived in Berwick in 1966 to shake hands and call it all off.

MOSCOW

The city of Moscow, capital of the Soviet Union, was built in 1147 by Prince Yuri Dolguruki, whose mother was an English-woman. In Russian 'Dolguruki' means 'long-armed'. In English, dolichocercic means having long forearms, while dolicho-podous is long-footed (cf. **BERTHA**).

☐ See also: *Ohio.*

MOSES

Hebrew lawgiver.

☐ See **TINTORETTO.**

MOSQUITO

(From the Spanish, a little fly.) A fly of the family Culicidae found in warm and hot climes. Only the female mosquito bites. It

has forty-seven teeth and prefers blondes.

☐ See also: *humming-bird, Morocco.*

MOTH

A lepidopterous insect which does not eat clothes. It is the moth larva which does the damage. Having no mouth or stomach, the moth cannot eat at all.

☐ See **EDWARD VII, INTELLIGENCE, NAPOLEON I.**

MOTHER-IN-LAW

☐ See **FERRET.**

MOTORCYCLING

Bermuda has more motorcycles per capita than any other country, Mauritania has the least. If all the bees in the United States were divided equally among the population of that country, there would be enough for everyone to have half a million.

MOTORING

In 1864 the speed limit in England for steam-driven cars was 2 mph. In 1888 the Sultan of Turkey became the first member of any royal family to drive a car. It is considered unlucky in Turkey to step on a piece of bread. Perhaps the Sultan motored about to avoid this possibility of misfortune.

MOULTING

☐ See **GREYHOUND, MAYFLY.**

MOUNTAINEERING

The greatest ever feat of mountaineering was that of the 4-month-old kitten which climbed to the top of the Matterhorn. The greatest ever error by mountaineers (happily not fatal) was that perpetrated in 1974 by the West German expedition which set out to climb Annapurna 4, but reached the summit of Annapurna 2 by mistake. Probably the signposts are not all they might be in that part of the world, but the Nepalese authorities accepted no responsibility and

refused permission for the climbers to have another go.

☐ See also: ***Albert I, Everest.***

MOUSE

A small rodent (*Mus*) of which the most common in Great Britain is the house mouse (*Mus musculus*). Experiments have shown that a female mouse which preserves her virginity has a longer life expectancy than either a spayed female or a sexually active one. The sexually active ones live shortest of all. Neutered tom cats live on average two years longer than those which have not felt the vet's scalpel. But spaying does not appear to affect the lifespan of the female cat. Only the quality of her life is altered. Research has also shown that mice prefer women to men.

MOUSE, Mickey (*b.* 1927)

☐ See **FRANCE.**

MOZART, Wolfgang Amadeus Chrysostom (1756–91)

Researchers at University College, Cardiff in 1970 announced an important discovery concerning the formation of musical taste in rats. A group of experimental rats were played Mozart all day long during their infancy. They heard *The Magic Flute*, the Fifth Violin Concerto K.219, and two symphonies (unspecified), each four times a day. In later life these rats grew up preferring Mozart to Schoenberg, given the choice. Sceptics might claim that any rat with taste would do so anyway.

☐ See also: ***billiards, da Ponte, fingerprints, musical composition, procrastination, Satie, whipping.***

MULBERRY TREE

Tree of the genus *Morus*, family Moraceae.

☐ See **LAWRENCE, D. H.**

MULE

A hybrid between a male ass and a mare.

☐ See **MEXICO, PROCREATION.**

MUMMY

(From the Arabic and Persian: *mumiya*, bitumen.) From the twelfth to the seventeenth centuries, mummies were in great demand for their supposed medicinal properties. This was based largely on an enormous misconception. The supposed value of the mummy was that of natural bitumen, produced from the Dead Sea and thought to be used in the ancient Egyptian mummification process. In fact the embalming agent used was resin, but mummies were originally powdered for their non-existent bitumen content. Later even this connection was lost and the mummified flesh itself was credited with medicinal properties.

On a 1685 list for London Apothecaries and Druggists, mummy was priced at 5s 4d a pound. Boars' teeth were also good value at one shilling each.

☐ See also: ***amusement, artists, auction.***

MUMPS

An acute infectious disease also known as epidemic parotitis. To effect a cure for mumps, all you need to do, if old folk remedies are to be believed, is to lead the patient by an ass-halter three times round a pigsty. But do be careful what you do with the pig. In May 1982 in the town of Baracaldo in Spain, a riot appears to have been caused by Señor Ferdi Garcia who entered a local bank and tried to pay off a hire-purchase debt with a pig.

☐ See also: ***menstruation.***

MURDER

(From the Old English: *morth*, death.) The unlawful killing of any human being who is in being and under the King's (Queen's) Peace, with malice aforethought, either express or implied. Only the mother of a child can commit infanticide. The father can commit insecticide if he wishes, but it isn't the same thing at all. Over half the murders in the United States are committed by a friend or relative of the victim.

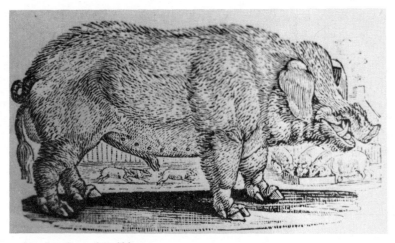

A boar's tooth, complete with boar

Comparable figures are not available for India, but they may have been distorted by Buhram, a member of the Thuggee sect who strangled over 900 people in the space of five years; few of his victims could honestly have described him as a friend. He was the sort of man who gave thugs a bad name.

MUSCLES

☐ See **CATERPILLAR, ELEPHANT.**

MUSHROOM

Fungus (*Psalliota campestris*) of the order Agaricineae.

☐ See **CHEMISTRY, TAIWAN.**

MUSICAL APPRECIATION

In an experiment at London Zoo, a recital of music by a string and wind ensemble showed that alligators and crocodiles are most appreciative of a slow and mournful air, but exactly the same music only irritated the rhino. The cheetah was bored, but seemed to enjoy jazz.

This improved on the results of Tommy Dorsey and his band, who left the monkeys totally unimpressed in Philadelphia in 1940. Playing Beatles songs underwater, however, is reported to be an effective way to frighten sharks.

☐ See also: *Mozart.*

MUSICAL COMPOSITION

The principal theme of the last movement of Mozart's Piano Concerto K.453 was suggested to the composer by a tune whistled by his pet starling. Two other composers have written pieces supposedly suggested by a cat running across a piano keyboard. Chopin's Waltz No. 3 in F is known as the Cat's Waltz, while Domenic Scarlatti's cat was more contrapuntal an gave him a Cat Fugue in D Minor.

Whereas most quadrupeds walk advancing a front leg, followed by a re leg on the opposite side of the body, cat camels and giraffes follow the front advan with the rear leg on the same side. Or might therefore speculate that Chopin an Scarlatti would have produced similar con positions had a camel or giraffe walked ov the keys.

☐ See also: *Satie, silence, vexations.*

MUSSOLINI, Benito (1883–1945)

Ian Fleming, creator of James Bond, w once the owner of Mussolini's passport. O Fleming's death, the passport was au tioned in 1972 and fetched £1,200. Th price compares highly favourably with th £110 for which two pairs of Queen Vi toria's silk stockings were knocked down Bonham's in 1978. Perhaps their value w reduced in the light of the fact that Quee Victoria was a carrier of classic haemophilia.

MYTHOLOGY

(From the Greek: *mythos*, talk, story myth.)

☐ See **EARTHQUAKE.**

MYXOMATOSIS

One hundred million rabbits were elimin ated in Britain when myxomatosis w introduced to reduce their population. Th indiscriminate slaughter also brought abo the deaths of 7 billion innocent bystander the rabbit fleas which were deprived of the homes and essential living·environmen Copulation between fleas lasts betwee three and nine hours.

N

Three recent legal decisions in the United States have been of great importance in establishing what is and is not a suitable name for a human being. In 1977 the New York Supreme Court, after three years' litigation, finally allowed Ellen Cooperman to change her name to 'Cooperperson'. This overturned the decision of a lower court which had described her wish as 'inane and nonsensical'.

In 1978, however, the council of Woonsocket, Rhode Island, dropped its plans to refer to manholes as 'personholes'. In Minneapolis the same year, Mr Michael Herbert Dengler applied to change his name to '1069'. This was not allowed, since a number was deemed to be 'totalitarian and an offence to human dignity'. Mr Dengler said that his desired name 'symbolised his interrelationship with society and reflected his personal and philosophical identity'.

The successful coup in Burma in 1962 was led by a general named U Win.

☐ See also: **Christening.**

NAPKIN

Everything you need to know about napkins can be found in a book published in 1682. Entitled *The Perfect School of Instructions for Offices of the Mouth* and written by Giles Rose, chef to Charles II, it contains instructions for folding table napkins into twenty-six different shapes.

NAPOLEON I, Emperor of the French (1769–1821)

In his spare time, Napoleon Bonaparte liked to shoot the swans on Josephine's

ornamental lake. One of his letters to her, announcing his imminent return from a campaign, contained the amorous instruction: 'Home in three days. Don't wash.'

A male silkworm moth can smell a female 7 miles away.

☐ See also: *Alexander the Great, barbers, Caroline, food preservation, impotence, insomnia, Italy, Richard III, shaving.*

NAPOLEON III (1803–73)

Nephew of Napoleon Bonaparte, Emperor of the French. Charles Louis Napoleon Bonaparte became head of the Bonapartes on the death of the Duke of Reichstadt, Napoleon II. The Emperor Napoleon III suffered from bladder stones. So, curiously enough, did King Leopold I of Belgium. In 1877, just four years after the death of Napoleon III, a society was founded in Belgium to improve the morals and mental faculties of the domestic cat.

NASAL SEX

It is an essential feature of the mating ritual

of otters, for the male to nip the nose of t female with his teeth. The precise functic of this behaviour is not properly unde stood, but one theory is that it helps induce ovulation in the female. The Ca fornian sea otter eats floating on its bac using its chest as a table. Its flippers are th free to use rocks to break open shellfish.

The average length of the nose of United States air hostess is 2.6 inches.

NAVEL

(From the Old English: *nafu*, the nave central part of a wheel. *Nafela* was t diminutive form of *nafu*.)

☐ See **CRIME, GOERING.**

NAVIGATION

☐ See **PREGNANCY.**

NAVY

The major responsibility for the successf build-up of British naval power in t nineteenth century has been attributed the absence of termites on Britannia

shores. Other termite-ridden nations found it impossible to build and store wooden boats without their falling victim to these voracious beasts.

Fried termites have 560 calories per 100 g. Their contents include 46 per cent protein and 44 per cent fat (compared, for example, with the 23 per cent protein and 32 per cent fat of sirloin steak).

☐ See also: *coconut, sex change, whipping.*

NEANDERTHAL MAN

Elvis Presley died at the age of 42, which is thirteen years longer than the average Neanderthal man could expect to survive. After his first concert, Elvis Presley was advised to pursue a serious career as a lorry driver.

NECK

(From the Old English: *hnecca*.) The neck

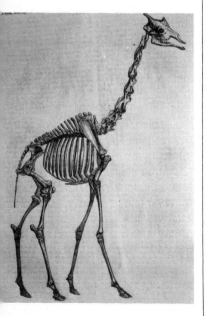

of the giraffe has seven vertebrae, the same number as in the human neck.

☐ See also: *carpentry.*

NECROPHILIA

(From the Greek: *nekros*, dead body; *phileein*, to love.) Samuel Pepys chose an odd way to celebrate his thirty-sixth birthday. He went to Westminster Abbey and kissed the embalmed body of Catherine de Valois, late wife of Henry V. The object of his affection had been dead for more than 200 years.

NEGLIGENCE

☐ See **BASINGSTOKE.**

NELSON, Horatio, Viscount Nelson (1758–1805)

Admiral Lord Nelson was only 5 ft 2 in. tall and suffered from seasickness. When he was killed at the battle of Trafalgar, his body was shipped back to England, preserved in a cask of rum. He is buried in what amounts to a second-hand coffin, being a black marble sarcophagus originally provided by Cardinal Wolsey and intended for his own use.

☐ See also: *confidence tricksters.*

NEPAL

Nobody wants an ex-goddess in Nepal. The Kumari Deva is a pre-pubescent girl chosen as a goddess to live in a temple in Kathmandu. She leaves her quarters only once a year for a religious ceremony. When she reaches puberty, she is handsomely pensioned off and retired, and another young girl chosen to take her place. But no one will marry her because ex-goddesses are bad luck.

☐ See also: *mountaineering, tiger.*

NEPHRITIS

Inflammation of the kidney.

☐ See **GEORGE IV.**

NEPOTISM

(From the Latin: *nepos*, a grandson.)

☐ See **HEREDITY, NICARAGUA.**

NERO, Emperor of Rome (AD 37–68)

Nero Claudius Domitius Caesar, son of Gaius Domitius Ahenobarbus, did not fiddle while Rome burned since the violin was not to be invented for several centuries. He may have played the lyre.

One violinist who never achieved the international acclaim he undoubtedly deserved was Otto E. Funk who, in 1929, walked the 4,165 miles from New York to San Francisco, playing the violin every step of the way.

☐ See also: *cosmetics, gibbon, Korea, racehorse, royalty, Wales.*

NERVAL, Gerard de (1808–55)

Adopted name of French writer Gerard Labrunie.

☐ See **LOBSTER.**

NETHERLANDS

In 1568 the entire population of the Netherlands was condemned to death by the Spanish Inquisition. The British use twice as much soap as the Dutch, but that is hardly enough reason to wipe out a whole nation. Four billion pounds weight of soap are produced annually in Great Britain.

☐ See also: *fertiliser, Holland.*

NEWFOUNDLAND

Former dominion of the British Empire.

☐ See **SOUP.**

NEW GUINEA

Island of the East Indian Archipelago.

☐ See **KURU, POSSUM, SEXUALITY.**

NEWT

The newt, or eft (*Molge*) is the only reptile indigenous to Ireland. That country does, however, have more hospital beds per capita than any other nation except Finland. But for the world's biggest gannet colony, you have to go to Iceland.

NEWTON, Sir Isaac (1642–1727)

Isaac Newton was born on Christmas Day but never knew his father, who was illiterate and had died two months previously. Newton never knew (in the Biblical sense) any women either, and died an 85-year-old virgin. His only recorded speech in his period as a Member of Parliament was a request for a window to be opened. The last words of Johann Wolfgang von Goethe are reported to have been 'Mehr Licht!' (more light), indicating that he too desired a window to be opened. But some think that what he actually said was 'Mehr nicht', meaning 'That's all, folks'.

☐ See also: *Montez.*

NEW YORK

Commercial metropolis of the USA. In the city of New York, there live more Italians than in Rome, more Jews than in Tel Aviv and more Irish than in Dublin. It is against the law in New York to leave a naked dummy in a shop window.

☐ See also: *artistic appreciation, literacy, Nero, politeness, shock, starling, transvestism.*

NEW ZEALAND

New Zealand has twenty times as many sheep as people, its only native mammals are bats, and the importation of birds' nests (even as bird's nest soup) is prohibited. The kiwi is the only bird with a sense of smell. This may be connected with the fact that it is the only bird with nostrils at the tip of its beak. The kiwi's egg can weigh as much as a quarter of the weight of its body.

☐ See also: *Maori, milk powder.*

NGULTRUM

☐ See **APOPLEXY.**

*The one on the left is the kiwi; his friend is an
extinct ancestor*

NIAGARA FALLS

Thanks to steady erosion, the Niagara Falls are now 10 miles further upstream than their position 10,000 years ago. Despite this constant exercise, they froze solid in the winter of 1925.

Charles Dickens converted a waterfall into a shower bath at his house on the Isle of Wight. He left £93,000.

NICARAGUA

Central American republic, filling in the space between Honduras and Costa Rica. The Nicaraguan army holds the record for the youngest soldier to attain the rank of colonel. President Somoza's grandson was appointed a colonel on full pay on the day of his birth.

NICHOLAS I, Czar of Russia (1796–1855)

☐ See **PARANOIA.**

NIGER

Central African republic in which one of the languages spoken is called Beri-beri. Between 1970 and 1975 Niger had the highest birth rate of any country on earth. But Mali claims the highest fertility rate, and Morocco has the largest sardine fishery.

NIGERIA

☐ See **COCONUT, ETIQUETTE, SUGAR.**

NIGHTINGALE, Florence (1820–1910)

(From the Anglo-Saxon: *nihtegale*, singer of the night.) Miss Nightingale had a pet owl which she carried everywhere with her. Only the cock nightingale can sing. Hen canaries can sing, but only if they are sterile.

☐ See also: *Scarborough.*

NILE

African river.

☐ See **BUTTERFLY.**

NIPPLE

(A diminutive of neb or nib, something small and pointed. From the Old English: *nebb*, beak or face.)

☐ See **BABOON, FRANCE, PLATYPUS, SEX-CHANGE, YAK.**

NIXON, Richard Milhous (*b.* 1913)

President of the United States.

☐ See **UNIQUENESS.**

NOBEL, Alfred Bernhard (1833–96)

The founder of the Nobel prizes was the son of Immanuel Nobel, inventor of plywood. Although Alfred Nobel had no wife, he was an advocate of euthanasia and invented dynamite.

Trinity College, Cambridge, has produced more Nobel prizewinners than the whole of France.

☐ See also: *Curie.*

NOISE

A sound of any kind, particularly un-musical.

☐ See **AVALANCHE, BEE, CAMPANOLOGY.**

NORWAY

Country of northern Europe wherein may be found the most northerly brewery, pub and university in the world.

☐ See **DEATH, GEOGRAPHY, HELL, HENRY III, SEA.**

NORWICH

Cathedral city of Norfolk, England, packed with churches.

☐ See **ARTIFICIAL LIMBS, NUTRITION.**

NOSE

Ants have five noses.

☐ See also: *adultery, Charlemagne, Constantinople, insurance, potoroo, Richard II, road safety.*

NOSE-IMPROVERS

Professor Lees Ray, of Wavertree near Liverpool, invented the Nose Improver in the 1890s. A compact device of brass and screws, it was designed to press an un-beautiful nose into the desired shape, 'from nez retrousse to the nose Hebraic'. He did a good trade, selling 600 nose machines a year, and treating an additional 2,500 persons 'cursed with red or fiery noses'. Prices ranged from 9s 6d to 2½ guineas. He even had one request from a middle-aged man who wanted his nose put awry, so as to induce the girl to whom he was engaged to give him up. (He had gone away on prolonged business and got engaged to another girl.) He trusted the machine to be able to restore the nasal *status quo ante*, after it had accomplished its dastardly mission.

NOSTRIL

(From the Old English: *nosu*, nose; *thyrel*, opening.)

☐ See **AARDVARK, NEW ZEALAND.**

NUDITY

A court in Tel Aviv in September 198… ordered a 16-year-old girl to stop walking around her house naked. Her 80-year-old stepfather claimed that she was trying to induce him to suffer a heart attack in order that she might more quickly inherit his fortune. Her actions would have been more justified if there had been bulls in the house. The bull is known to be more likely to attack clothed people than nudists.

☐ See also: *eating, genius, indecency, knowledge, Lawrence, D. H., New York*

NUMERACY

You can spell all the numbers from one to ninety-nine without using the letter A.

☐ See also: *Waterloo.*

URSING

One in five of the policemen in Birmingham marries a nurse. This phenomenon is believed to be connected with policemen's balls. Nurses get free tickets. But the long arm of the law in Birmingham reaches beyond the nurses' hostels; after 8 am in Birmingham, it is forbidden to beat your doormat against a wall.

UT

The ancient Egyptians believed the universe to be the body of a goddess named Nut. The cashew nut is a member of the poison ivy family. Garlic belongs to the lily family. These days it is simply not enough to come from a good family.

☐ See also: ***dormouse.***

NUTRITION

In 1632 the weekly ration per child in Norwich children's hospital included 2 gallons of beer.

☐ See also: ***navy.***

O

OAK

Large genus (*Quercus*) of trees of the order Amentaceae.

□ See **PERSPIRATION**.

OBESITY

(From the Latin: *ob-*, completely; *edere*, *esum*, to eat.) It has been estimated that the population of North America is collectively about 100,000 tons overweight.

OBSCENITY

In 1886 Liberal Member of Parliament Robert Graham was suspended from the House of Commons for using the word 'damn' in a speech. The Queen is forbidden to enter the House of Commons. And a good thing too if that is the sort of foul language she might otherwise be forced to encounter.

OBSTETRICS

(From the Latin: *obstetrix*, a midwife.) The potential hazards of obstetrics can rarely have been better illustrated than by the scientist who was bitten by a sand tiger

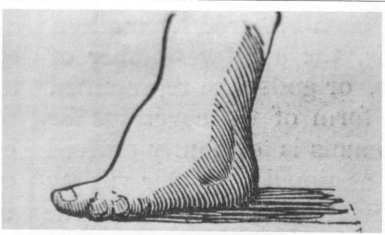

There is no obscenity greater than that of a Chinese lady's foot (cf. Prudery)

shark embryo while he was examining its pregnant mother. Sharks give birth to live young rather than laying eggs, but unlike mammals the newborn have no placenta. An animal which gives birth to live young is termed 'viviparous', unless the young has hatched from an egg within the parent's body, in which case the correct term is 'ovoviviparous'.

OCEAN

Enough water evaporates from the earth's oceans each day to fill 5 million Olympic size swimming pools.

☐ See also: ***Bolivia, monopoly, pianoforte, secrets.***

OCTOPUS

A genus (*Octopus*) of eight-armed cephalopods. The most common and vulgar octopus is the common octopus, *octopus vulgaris*.

☐ See **BEER, GUINEA.**

OHIO

North central state of the USA. Amsterdam, Berlin, Dublin, Moscow, Rome, Toronto, Venice, Vienna and Warsaw are all towns in Ohio. Altogether there are eight towns called Rome in the United States. More significantly, Ham and Sandwich are both places in Kent. The standard sandwich for attempts on sandwich-eating records measures 6 in. × 3¾ in. × ½ in.

OIL

The first oil slick in history was in 1889 in the English Channel, when the sailing ship *Vandania*, full of oil from Canada, collided with the ss Duke of Buccleugh. The only fatality resulting from the accident was a ship's dog.

OKAPI

(*Ocapia johnstoni*) Ruminant mammal related to the giraffe, with yellow legs striped with black.

☐ See **LLAMA.**

OKLAHOMA

State of the USA turned into a musical.

☐ See **ANGLING, ELITISM.**

OLIVE

Small evergreen tree (*Olea europea*) of the Oleaceae order.

☐ See **BUSINESS.**

OLYMPIC GAMES

An international athletic festival, often incorrectly termed Olympiad, which strictly means the period of four years between each celebration of the Olympic Games.

☐ See **MONACO, ROYALTY.**

OMAN

The only national holiday in Oman is 18 December, the Sultan's birthday. Until 1970, it was illegal to play the drums in Oman.

OMAR KHAYYAM (c. 1071–1123)

Persian poet, astronomer, mathematician, author of a treatise on algebra, founder of the secret Assassins sect, nowadays remembered almost solely for his *Rubaiyat*. Rubaiyat is the plural in Persian of the word Rubai, meaning a quatrain (a four-line verse).

☐ See **BROWNING**.

OMNIBUS

The introduction of the omnibus (from the Latin: *omnibus*, for all) into London on 4 July 1829 led to considerable reforms of both language and law. The word 'bus-stop' was first recorded in 1930, but we had to wait until 1945 for a 'bus-shelter'. And the 'bus-conductress' dates back linguistically only to 1952.

The law permits us to stand and wait for a bus, but only in the proper place. In general a footpath is for free passage, not for standing around. In 1959 a man was fined £3 for standing still outside his own house and refusing to move on when requested to do so by a policeman.

ONAN

☐ See Genesis, 38, verse 9, or **PARKER**, Dorothy.

ONION

(*Allium*) Hardy bulbous plant of the natural order Liliaceae. Often eaten, the onion may instead be used for cromniomancy – divination by onions. To make a forecast from a number of different possibilities, plant one onion for each of the runners, each identified with the name or description of whatever it represents. The first onion to sprout will give the prediction. If you can't be bothered waiting for onions to come up, a more limited technique which might be employed is scarpomancy – character reading from old shoes.

☐ See also: ***antisocial behaviour, Edison, flea, footwear.***

OPHTHALMOLOGY

(From the Greek: *ophthalmos*, an eye.)

☐ See **HOBBIES**.

ORANGE

(From the Arabic: *naranj*.) Despite man works of art providing contrary indications there were no oranges eaten at the La Supper. They were introduced to th Mediterranean area from China at a late date. There is record of a tree in Forfarshir which grew apples in 1902 and pears i 1903.

☐ See also: ***artists, contraception.***

ORCHID

The orchid gets its name from the Gree word *orkhis*, meaning testicle. It is said tha some types of orchid do bear a resemblanc to justify the name. Another word with similar derivation is 'testimony' from th Latin *testis*. The meaning stems from th practice in Roman courts of a male witnes placing his hand over his reproductiv organs when taking an oath. Linguistically it is interesting to note how terms for th reproductive organs have changed fro having connotations of trust to a mor derogatory usage.

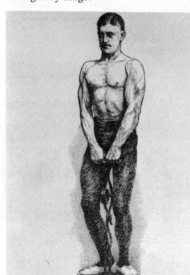

Man training to take oath in Roman court

ORDEAL BY GOAT

Now no longer part of the legal system, Ordeal by Goat was an ancient Egyptian method of determining the innocence or guilt of a young girl accused of lesbianism. The accused would be presented to the goat and the reaction of the animal would decide matters. If he appeared to fancy her, she was innocent, but the goat's disdain was interpreted as a guilty verdict.

ORGY

☐ See **MARITAL CUSTOMS.**

ORIENT EXPRESS

☐ See **PYJAMAS.**

ORTHOPAEDICS

(From the Greek: *orthos*, straight; *pais*, child.) Strictly, the art of curing diseases and deformities of children's bones.

☐ See **ABORIGINE.**

OSIRIS

Egyptian deity, brother and husband of Isis. His brother Set, god of darkness, threw him into a coffin, threw it in the Nile, then later cut the body of Osiris into fourteen pieces scattered throughout Egypt. But Isis collected them with one regenerative exception, and, in some versions of the story, resuscitated Osiris. Nevertheless, according to American legal opinion, Osiris is not alive and well and living in San Francisco. In 1982 in that city, Lieutenant George La Brash was on duty guarding the Tutankhamun exhibition. He suffered a stroke, and subsequently sued his employers for £9,700 in wages lost during his recovery. He claimed that his injuries were caused in the line of duty, since he was struck down by Osiris. The judge ruled otherwise, and the suit was unsuccessful.

OSTRICH

(*Struthio camelus*) The largest living bird.

A 20-stone man can stand on an ostrich egg without breaking the shell. A single such egg, if you do manage to crack it, makes an omelette sufficient to feed twelve men. If you prefer a boiled egg, leave it for between forty minutes and 1½ hours according to taste.

☐ See also: *swimming.*

OTTAWA

City and capital of Canada.

☐ See **BEE.**

OTTER

(*Lutra*) Aquatic carnivorous fur-bearing mammal of the family Mustelidae. When the sea otter settles down to sleep, it ties itself in seaweed in order to avoid being swept away by currents. The dolphin has another way of avoiding being woken up with a nasty surprise: it sleeps with one eye open.

☐ See also: *English, nasal sex, seal, yak.*

OVERCROWDING

Stoats are more likely to suffer from overcrowding than weasels. Whereas each weasel family needs 10 acres of hunting land, a family of stoats requires 100 acres.

OVERQUALIFICATION

Charlie McCarthy has been awarded an honorary degree by Northwestern University. Mr McCarthy is a ventriloquist's dummy.

OWENS, Jesse (1913–80)

American sprinter, winner of four gold medals at the 1938 Olympics.

☐ See **SPEED.**

OWL

Order of nocturnal birds of prey (Strigiformes).

☐ See **HAWAII, HINTING, HOSPITAL, NIGHTINGALE, RATTLESNAKE, WHOOPING COUGH.**

OX

(From the Old English: *oxa*, plural: *oxan*.)
Male of any species of *Bovidae*.

☐ See **ASTHMA.**

OXFORD

County town of Oxfordshire, England, an
home of the oldest University Press in th
world. Readers in the Bodleian Library i
Oxford are obliged to take an oath that the
will not kindle a fire in the library.

☐ See also: ***films, wedding customs.***

OYSTER

(*Ostrea*) A bi-valve mollusc. The theatrica
days of the oyster seem now to be over, bu
Molly the Whistling Oyster was a grea
success at Drury Lane in 1840. Whether sh
always answered to the name 'Molly' is
matter for some speculation, since oyster
are ambisexual, starting life as males the
changing back and forth between the tw
sexes.

You can be fined for maltreating a
oyster in Maryland.

☐ See also: ***Casanova, Duncan, economics***
jet lag, gluttony, Jamaica, last words,
starfish.

P

PACIFIC

(From the Latin: *pax, pacis*, peace; *facere*, to make.)

☐ See **BELGIUM, BOLIVIA, OCEAN, PANAMA.**

PACIFISM

☐ See **EISENHOWER.**

PADEREWSKI, Ignace Jan (1859–1941)

Polish politician and pianist whose last word was 'please', in reply to an offer of some champagne.

☐ See **POLAND.**

PAGANINI, Nicolo (1784–1840)

Composer and violinist, Paganini would probably not have been so successful had he not suffered from Marfan's syndrome. The symptoms of this condition include a tall, thin body, underdeveloped muscles, hyper-mobile joints and long arms and fingers.

PAKISTAN

☐ See **UMPIRING.**

PALINDROME

(From the Greek: *palin*, back; *dromos*, running.) A word or phrase reading the same backwards or forwards.

☐ See **FINLAND.**

PALMERSTON, Henry John Temple, 3rd Viscount (1784–1865)

Lord Palmerston is the oldest British ex-Prime Minister to be cited as co-respondent in a divorce case. He was 78 at the time. When he died three years later, his last words were: 'That's article 98; now go on to the next.' It is believed that he was re-living his role as Foreign Secretary.

PAMPERED PETS

In Imperial China, royal pekinese puppies were suckled by human wet-nurses. The Roman poet Virgil did not go that far for his favourite pet fly, but he did spend the equivalent of £50,000 on its funeral. There was, however, sound financial sense behind this investment. He was able to declare the burial area a cemetery, thereby avoiding payment of a land tax.

PANAMA

Central American republic. Twenty thousand Frenchmen died of malaria while working on the construction of the Panama Canal. The painter Paul Gauguin was one of those who survived. Perhaps the delirium of malarial fever is to blame for the curious circumstance that the Atlantic entrance to the Panama Canal is further west than the Pacific entrance. This means that any ship wanting to cross from the eastern ocean to the western, would have to travel east along the canal. With such potential confusion in the air, it is a comforting thought that Panama Disease only affects bananas.

PANDA

The panda, or wah, (*Ailurus fulgens*) is, as might be expected, smaller than the giant panda (*Ailuropus melanoleucus*), though the newborn giant panda may be smaller than a mouse. Pandas are praised in the Gulf of Pohai, China, where one gave warning of an impending earthquake by holding its head and screaming. Other pieces of animal behaviour which the Chinese watch for as signs of an impending earthquake are turtles becoming agitated, and tigers, swans and yaks lying down.

There were earthquakes in London in February and March 1750 (with rather few pandas or yaks around to give any warning). When a scaremonger predicted another tremor in April, brisk business was done on the streets of the capital sellin 'earthquake pills' to alleviate the effects o the disturbance.

PAPUA, New Guinea

☐ See **POSSUM**.

PARACELSUS (c. 1492–1541)

Working name of Swiss physicia Theophrastus Bombast von Hohenheim.

☐ See **JULIUS CAESAR**.

PARACHUTING

(From the Italian: *parare*, to ward off; an the French: *chute*, a fall.) The first eve human descent by parachute was made i 1797 by André Jacques Garnerin. Ove come by the sense of occasion of thi historic jump, his first act on landing safel was to throw up.

☐ See also: ***christening, misprint***.

Onan looking shameful

*ARAGUAY
Country in South America.
□ See **BOLIVIA.**

*ARALYSIS
□ See **APOPLEXY, ROOSEVELT, F. D.**

*ARANOIA
(From the Greek: *para*, beside, beyond; *noos*, mind.) Czar Nicholas I established a commission to investigate all the music written and played in Russia, to look for signs of coded conspiracy. Statistics show that schizophrenics and manic depressives are most likely to be born in January, February or March.

*ARÉ, Ambroise (1510–90)
French surgeon, expert on gunshot wounds, and the first to use ligatures to stop patients bleeding to death after amputations.
□ See **ARTIFICIAL LIMBS.**

PARKER, Dorothy (1893–1967)
American writer and wit. Dorothy Parker's dog was called Cliché. She also had a pet parrot which she named Onan because it spilt its seed on the ground. In Ohio, domestic animals must wear tail-lights if out after dark.

PARROT
Psittacine bird with zygodactylic feet.
□ See **GEORGE V, MODESTY, PARKER, SQUID.**

PARSEE
(Inhabitant of Pars, or Persia.) The Parsee religion (found mainly in India) does not admit converts. When a Parsee dies, the body is taken to the entrance of the Towers of Silence. The corpse-bearers, the only men permitted beyond the entrance, then carry it to the Towers, where the body is left to be picked clean by vultures.
    This Parsee ritual is not explained totally by altruism towards vultures. There is also a

belief that the practice helps to release the soul more quickly. Burning or burying a corpse would, in any case, defile the elements, since the body is impure.

The oldest recorded vulture lived to the age of 117, but as the Parsee population is declining, a vulture food shortage may be imminent.

Vultures at the Parsee take-away

PARSLEY

Biennial herb (*Carum petroselinum*) of the natural order Umbelliferae. There are over 2,000 different species of parsley, compared with about 1,000 species of bat, and 600 ways to make love. The latter are listed in the Marquis de Sade's *100 Days of Sodom*. Oddly enough, 600 is also the approximate number of species of spider found in Great Britain.

PARTHENOGENESIS

(From the Greek: *parthenos*, a virgin; *genesis*, production.) Reproduction from an unfertilised ovum.

☐ See **LESBIANISM.**

PARTY SPIRIT

Four guests on their way to a wedding somewhere in Uttar Pradesh, India, took along some drinks for the journey and decided to share them with their transport,

an elephant. The intoxicated pachyderm later blundered into a power cable, electrocuting itself and killing its four passengers. The Indian police have never been known to breathalyse an elephant.

PASSION

☐ See **ANTONYMS, BEANS.**

PASTEUR, Louis (1822–95)

Louis Pasteur refused to shake hands with acquaintances for fear of infection. He had sound reason; more germs are transmitted in a handshake than in a kiss. Pasteur's policy on kissing is not known.

PATERNITY

Paternity suits were unknown in the days of Henry VIII, but the regulations for his Officers of the Bedchamber did state that 'Such pages as cause the maids of the King's household to become mothers shall go without beer for a month.'

PATIENCE

The sheep tick drops off its host after a meal and may wait for up to four years before the next sheep – and meal – comes along.

PAUL I, Czar of Russia (1754–1801)

Son of Catherine the Great and Peter III, who despised him so much that he refused to acknowledge his existence. Not surprisingly, Czar Paul grew up to be a sensitive character, not least on the subject of his own baldness. Anyone mentioning it was liable to be flogged to death.

PAVLOVA, Anna (1881–1931)

Slim Russian dancer who gave her name to a fattening dessert.

☐ See **LAST WORDS.**

PEA

(*Pisum sativum*) Annual climbing herb of the natural order Leguminosae.

☐ See **MEASLES.**

PEACH

(*Prunus Persica*)

☐ See **JOHN,** King of England.

PEANUT

(Also known as ground nut or monkey nut.) In 1981 a fossilised peanut more than 100,000 years old was found in China. (But probably the 'sell by' date on the packet had already expired.) In eighteenth-century Ireland, innkeepers did not have dry-roasted, or even ordinary salted peanuts behind the bar, but they did keep a pair of duelling pistols handy for customers who had forgotten their own and had sudden need of them. Lermontov and Pushkin were both killed in duels.

PEAR

Fruit of the pear tree (*pyrus communis*).

☐ See **ORANGE.**

PENGUIN

The penguin was the name originally given to the now extinct great auk. The excrement of the Gentoo penguin is pink. The Gentoo penguin itself may be unaware of this phenomenon, since penguins are in general extremely short-sighted on land, though they do see well underwater. That is fortunate, perhaps, since sitatunga antelopes can sleep underwater and a collision with a penguin would doubtless be a nasty shock for both of them.

☐ See also: **astonishment, Henry III, Mongolia.**

PENICILLIN

(From the Latin: *penicillus*, paint-brush; diminutive of *penis*, a tail. The name refers to the tuft-like appearance of the penicillin mould.)

☐ See **GUINEA PIG.**

PENIS

☐ See **BEDBUG, BRASSIERE, EMU, GORILLA, HYENA, IMPOTENCE, PERFUME, SCULPTURE, SLEEP, TOULOUSE L'AUTREC.**

PEPIN THE SHORT, King of the Franks (*d.* 768)

☐ See **BREEDING.**

PEPYS, Samuel (1633–1703)

Diarist and admiralty official, his diary was not deciphered until more than a century after his death.

☐ See **NECROPHILIA.**

PERFUME

Aleister Crowley, black magician known as The Great Beast, developed his own Perfume of Immortality. One part ambergris to two parts musk and three parts civet, it fulfilled its purpose of attracting women to him. It also attracted horses, which would whinny after him in the street. A stallion's penis can be 2 ft 6 in. long, only one foot longer than that of a pig.

PERJURY

☐ See **LEPROSY**.

PERON

Eva, Juan and Isabel. First family of **ARGENTINA**.

PERPETUAL MOTION

The tuna fish swims at a speed of 9 mph and never stops moving.

PERSPIRATION

When working in a mild climate, a human being will average 5 pints of sweat in a day. A hard-working miner, however, can drip 13 pints on a shift, while an Indian toiling in the sun can lose up to 20 pints a day. The champion sweater is the oak tree which, fully grown, can evaporate over 6 tons of water vapour from its leaves on a hot summer's day.

☐ See also: *Caroline, potoroo.*

PERU

The sun worship of the Incas lives on in Peru in a more modern form: the currency is called the sol. Some Peruvian Indians believe that the smell of llama urine is effective in warding off evil spirits. Babies are even washed in it to keep them pure.

Despite such quaint customs, Peru is the world's fourth greatest fishing nation (though admittedly 90 per cent of the catch is used as fishmeal for livestock).

☐ See also: *artists, milk powder.*

PERVERSITY

☐ See **BUCKINGHAM PALACE**.

PETER I, Czar of Russia (1672–1725)

Known as Peter the Great, son of the Czar Alexis. Peter the Great became Czar at the age of 10. Too young for such responsibility, one might think, but Miss Lima Medina, aged 5 years 8 months, gave birt to a healthy baby in Lima, Peru, in 1939 With such a rate of prepubescent procrea tion, Benedict IX could have been grandfather when he became pope at th age of 12. He was later to be expelled fo vice and moral corruption anyway. *Be Hur*, incidentally, was the first work o fiction to be blessed by a pope.

☐ See also: *alcohol, hair.*

PETER III, Czar of Russia (1728–62)

Grandson of Peter the Great, husband o Catherine II, who plotted his downfall an succeeded him.

☐ See **BURIAL**.

PETER THE HERMIT (died c. 1115)

Wandering medieval preacher and trave courier from Cologne to Constantinopl during the first **CRUSADE**.

PETS

The British spend twice as much on pe food as on baby food. Despite the fact tha it is illegal to sell a pet to anyone under th age of 12 in Britain, there are 5.2 millio dogs, 3.7 million cats, 3.3 million budgies 10.5 million tropical fish, 5 million goldfis and one million rabbits kept as domesti animals in the United Kingdom. The land i also shared by as many rats as there ar people and an amazing 200,000 billio (2×10^{14}) spiders. The wolf spider ha eight eyes.

☐ See also: *Hitler, musical composition, pampered pets, Parker, Pompadour.*

PHILATELY

Between 1870 and 1891, postmasters in th Afghanistan postal service were required t cancel letters by biting the corners off th stamps. The nutritious value of this diet i doubtful, but it may be significant that eve today the Afghans eat fewer potatoes an nuts than any other race.

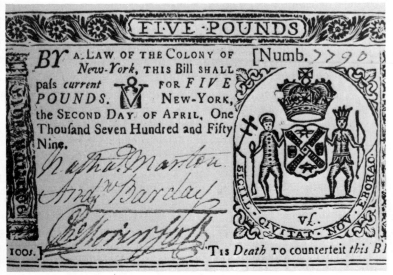

An American £5 note from the time of Czar Peter III of Russia

HILEMON (c. 360–263 BC)

Greek comic poet who generally won the prizes ahead of his great rival Menander, not through the quality of his work, but because his friends were better at fixing things.

❒ See **HUMOUR.**

HILIP I, King of Spain (1478–1506)

Known as Philip the Handsome.

❒ See **BEDTIME.**

HILIP II, King of Spain (1527–98)

Married Mary of Portugal in 1543, then on her death married Mary Tudor, Queen of England, in 1554. When she too died, he offered his hand to Queen Elizabeth, was declined, so married the French princess, Isabella.

❒ See **SAN MARINO.**

HILIP IV, King of Spain (1605–65)

Philip IV of Spain had six children by his first wife and one by his second. Nevertheless, he is reputed to have smiled only three times in his entire life.

PHILIP IV, King of France (1268–1314)

Known as Philip the Fair, he was the son of Philip III of France, known as Philip the Bold. Only the Bold deserve the Fair.

☐ See **BEAUTY, CLOTHES.**

PHILIPPINES

One of the strangest fish in the world, *Anthias squamipinnis*, lives in the waters of the Philippines. In any colony of these fish, the females heavily outnumber the males. But the females can apparently change sex at will. Experiments have shown that if a number of males are removed from any colony, exactly the same number of females will change their gender to re-establish the same number of males as before.

☐ See also: ***salivation, yo-yo.***

PHILOSOPHY

According to Sir Alfred J. Ayer, Wykeham Professor of Logic at Oxford from 1959–78, it is not necessarily inconsistent for a logical positivist to be a supporter of Tottenham Hotspur Football Club.

☐ See also: ***beans.***

PHOSPHORUS

(From the Greek: *phosphoros*, light-bringing.) Chemical element (P: atomic number 15).

☐ See **BODY.**

PHOTOCOPYING

(From the Greek: *xeros*, dry.)

☐ See **CIVILISATION.**

PHOTOGRAPHY

It is hard to take a photograph of a trio of Japanese. They have a superstition that being photographed in the middle of a group of three is an omen of death. Perhaps Haydn had the Japanese market in mind when he wrote seventy-seven string quartets and only some forty trios.

PHYSICS

The word 'Dord' is not a synonym f density. It appeared as such by mistake the 1934 Merriam–Webster Internation Dictionary. The intention had been indicate that 'D' or 'd' is used as abbreviation for density. Later dictionari copied the word in its misprinted sta taking the meaning on trust.

PI

One of the greatest examples of wast effort and dedication, is that of the Engli mathematician William Shanks who, 1873, completed his calculation of the val of pi to 707 decimal places. It had taken hi fifteen years, and subsequent calculatio revealed that the last hundred or so dig were incorrect.

Exactly 100 years later, the value of was calculated to a million decimal plac by computer and the result published as 400-page book. Not the most grippi reading, and quite unnecessary when o bears in mind House Bill No. 246 of t General Assembly of Indiana in 1897 whi decreed a totally different, rational val for pi.

PIANOFORTE

(From the Italian: *piano*, soft; *forte*, loud The world record for underwater pia playing was claimed by students of t Middlesex Hospital in 1982 for a submari recital lasting 110 hours. Anyone trying beat this record will need a great deal water, but there is certainly enough to round. If all the oceans of the world we divided equally among the people, would each get 110 billion gallons. It however, impossible to boil water in paper bag.

PICASSO, Pablo (1881–1973)

On Picasso's ninetieth birthday, nine children released ninety doves from t steps of an art gallery. His last words wer 'Drink to me.'

☐ See **ARTISTS.**

The sea-horse can be a problem for an underwater pianist

IG

(From the Middle English: *pigge*.) The pig has a long history of criminal behaviour. In 1457 in Lavegny, a sow and six piglets were put on trial for killing and partly eating a child. The sow was condemned to death, but the piglets escaped with their bacon, thanks to the court's decision that their responsibility was diminished by reason of their youth. In 1572 another pig was sentenced to death for the murder of a child. It appeared at the trial dressed in human clothes.

Respect for the pig had evidently declined considerably since the days of ancient Greece, where the greatest delicacy which could be served was a pig which had died of overeating.

☐ See also: *garbage disposal, goat, mumps, perfume, pigtail, weasel, yak, Yugoslavia.*

PIGEON

(Birds of the order Columbiformes, including the dodo.) Contraceptive birdseed cut the pigeon population of Paris from 750,000 to 20,000 in four years. A female pigeon cannot lay eggs unless she sees another pigeon or her own reflection in a mirror.

☐ See also: *dancing, envy, Henry Frederick.*

PIGTAIL

In Imperial China, slaves wore their hair in pigtails as a form of identification. One unusual attraction in Imperial Britain, at the Great Exhibition of 1851, was a pigtail organ. The 'music' came from pigs whose squeaks had been specially selected to cover the necessary range of notes. Each pig had its tail connected to an organ key by a mechanical device which ensured that the pig's tail was pinched when the key was

Parisian pigeon delivering a French letter

played. Tunes could thus be produced in the usual manner.

Such is the speed of progress that it was only one year later, in 1852, that the first public lavatory was opened in London. It proved at first not much more popular than the pigtail organ, but has lasted better.

PILLORY

The Statute of the Pillory, 1266, ordained its use as punishment for 'forestallers and regrators' (those who buy up goods and sell them at higher price, nowadays known as retailers), users of false weights, perjurers and forgers. As well as having head and hands locked in the wooden device, the criminal's ears were liable to be nailed to the wood.

☐ See **LEPROSY.**

PINKNESS

☐ See **ELIZABETH I, Empress of Russia, FLAMINGO, PENGUIN.**

PIN MONEY

☐ See **JANUARY SALES.**

PIRANHA

Unfriendly South American fish.

☐ See **FLORIDA.**

PISSARRO, Camille (1830–1903)

French painter.

☐ See **ARTISTS.**

PITT, William (1759–1806)

Known as Pitt the Younger, William Pi was the younger son of Pitt the Elder, ali the 1st Earl of Chatham. As treatment fe his gout, Pitt's doctor assured him that th affliction would be cured if he drank bottle of port a day. Following this advi (sometimes even going two bottles over th recommended dose) Pitt died of cirrhosis the liver. Michelangelo, Luther, Calvin an Darwin were also gout sufferers. So we Charlemagne and Alexander the Grea out they were not great port drinkers. In his youth Alexander the Great had been taught by Aristotle, whose views on port are not known, but he liked a good syllogism.

LACENTA

From the Latin: *placenta*, a flat cake.)

☐ See **ALEXANDRIA, OBSTETRICS.**

LAGUE

(From the Latin: *plaga*, a blow.) An estimated 75 million people died from the Black Death in the middle of the fourteenth century, including a quarter of the population of Europe. Between 1603 and 1665, however, they knew how to treat it: Pluck the tail feathers from a live pullet and place the bird's bare bum on the carbuncle to draw the venom. Repeat until the last bird escapes contagion. This must have worked wonders because by 1978 there were only eleven cases of plague in the United States and only two of those were fatal.

PLATO (*c.* 427–348 BC)

Plato's original name was Aristocles, but they called him Plato because he had large shoulders. He recommended that everyone should be encouraged to be ambidextrous and should learn to play the lyre from the age of 13. He died on his eighty-first birthday. King Harold also died on his (Harold's) birthday. Henry VIII died on the birthday of Henry VII.

PLATYPUS

(From the Greek: *platys*, broad; *pous*, foot.) The duck-billed platypus (*Ornithorhynchus anatinus*) is the only mammal with poisonous glands. It eats more food relative to its weight than any other mammal. Despite having no nipples, the mother weans the infant platypus on milk which seeps through pores in her abdomen.

☐ See also: ***yak.***

The Great Plague

The Duck-billed Platypus

PLINY THE ELDER (AD 23–79)

Gaius Plinius Secundus was probably the greatest swot of all time. He hated to waste a single minute, and even had servants read to him while he was eating so that the time would not be lost. He once censured his nephew, Pliny the Younger, for going for a walk, on the grounds that the time could have been more profitably occupied.

Having travelled to watch and study the eruption of Vesuvius at Pompeii, he stayed on too long and got too close. His body was found three days later and was buried by his nephew.

☐ See also: *Alexandria, baldness, fingerprints, hyena, lactation, rabies, sex, snakebite, weasel.*

PLINY THE YOUNGER (61–113)

Highly respected Roman consul, writer and orator, Pliny the Younger (Gaius Plinius Caecilius Secundus) cut taxes and stopped persecuting the Christians, whom he deemed meek and inoffensive. He was adopted by his uncle, **PLINY THE ELDER.**

PLUTO

God of the Underworld, pipe-line unde the ocean, cartoon dog.

☐ See **INDIVIDUALITY.**

PNEUMONIA

(From the Greek: *pneumon*, a lung.) Acut infective disease of the lung.

☐ See **DESCARTES, FOOTWEAR.**

POETIC JUSTICE

Hugues Aubriot, Provost of Paris, built th Bastille only to find himself charged wit heresy and the first man to be confine therein.

The Earl of Salisbury was responsible fo the introduction of cannon into warfare. H was also the first Englishman to be killed b a cannonball.

Dr Joseph-Ignace Guillotin (1738–181ᵃ introduced the feminised version of h name to France. He died of a carbuncle c his shoulder at the age of 76.

☐ See also: *stocks.*

*OETIC LICENCE

When Tennyson wrote, 'Every moment dies a man, every moment one is born,' he received an irate letter from mathematician Charles Babbage, who clearly thought that he deserved to have his poetic licence endorsed. If the statement were true, argued Babbage, we would have zero population growth. The correct version should read, 'Every moment one and one-sixteenth is born,' according to Babbage.

*OGO STICK

Bouncing around Eaton Square on a pogo stick was described as 'unbecoming to a Greek scholar and a gentleman' by an opposition spokesman in the House of Commons in 1962. The remark was offered in criticism of the then Minister of Health, Enoch Powell, who had performed the feat described.

As far as can be ascertained, opposition policy on pogo sticks and their use in the vicinity of Eaton Square has not substantially altered since that statement.

*OISON

☐ See **CUCKOLDRY, EDWARD VI.**

*OLAND

The only country to have had a concert pianist as premier. Ignace Jan Paderewsky headed the Polish Government in 1919 and was head of the government in exile at the beginning of the Second World War. Although he was a very successful concert performer, he may have been encouraged to take up his secondary career as politician and statesman by the remarks of his piano teacher, who told him that he would never be a good pianist because his middle fingers were too short.

☐ See also: *birthday, dancing, flax, Montez.*

*OLAR BEAR

Eskimo women never comb their hair on the day a polar bear is to be killed. All polar bears are left-handed. Albert Schweitzer was also left-handed, but was often forced to write with his other hand because his cat, Sizi, had the habit of falling asleep on his left arm.

☐ See also: *bequests, Henry III, vitamins.*

POLITENESS

Surveys indicate that politeness is far more prevalent on the London underground railway than in those of other capital cities. In England's capital, 70 per cent of travellers say 'please' and 'thank you' when buying tickets compared with 50 per cent in Tokyo, 30 per cent in Hamburg, and 10 per cent in New York.

☐ See also: *proposal.*

POLO

(From the Tibetan: *pulu*, a ball.) A **SPORT** played on horseback.

☐ See **GENGHIS KHAN.**

POLO, Marco (*c.* 1254–1324)

One of the first travel writers.

☐ See **DEBT.**

POLYDACTYLISM

(From the Greek: *poly*, much, many; *daktylos*, a finger.) Having more than the usual number of fingers or toes.

☐ See **FRANCE.**

POLYGAMY

(From the Greek: *poly*, much, many; *gamos*, marriage.) Having more than the usual number of wives. King Abdul Aziz Ibn Saud of Saudi Arabia married 300 wives between 1932 and 1953. Nowadays in Saudi Arabia, a bride costs £5,000 if she is a virgin, or £3,500 second hand. Assuming that the good king would not have considered shop-soiled goods, the bill comes to £1½ million at today's prices.

The fourth Mogul Emperor Jahangir between 1605 and 1627 had 300 wives too, but he also had 5,000 mistresses and 1,000 young men. Whether the young men were employed to ease the King's burden, or to give him something to do on Sundays, is not related by history.

POMEGRANATE

(From the Latin: *pomum*, a fruit, an apple; *granatum*, having many grains.)

☐ See **CONSTIPATION.**

POMPADOUR, Madame de (1721–64)

Jeanne Antoinette Poisson, Marquise de Pompadour, mistress of Louis XVI, was the first person in France to have a pet goldfish.

POMPEII

First holiday resort to be wrecked by bank holiday disturbances, AD 24 August 79.

☐ See **PLINY THE ELDER.**

POPCORN

The Public Health Service of the Food and Drug Administration in the United States does not permit the sale of popcorn to the public if, in six 10 oz samples, there is found either one rodent pellet or one rodent hair in each sample. But you are perfectly free to sell Smarties, except, of course, for the red ones which are banned because the dye used (Red Dye No. 4) has not been passed safe for human consumption.

POPERY

On the death of a pope, the Papal Secretary must call his Christian name three times before he is officially declared dead. He also has to tap the dead pope's head with a silver hammer. Twenty-six popes have been assassinated.

On meeting a live pope, do not succumb to the temptation to kiss his toe. Papal toe-kissing was abolished in 1773 after having been the custom for more than a thousand years.

POPPAEA (died *c.* AD 65)

Poppaea Sabina married Rufus Crispinus, was carried off by Otho, a favourite of Nero, but the Emperor then sent Otho off to govern a province and married Poppaea himself. When the honeymoon had worn thin, Poppaea died after being kicked by Nero when in an advanced state of pregnancy. She had 500 asses kept for the sole purpose of providing milk for her daily bath.

☐ See **COSMETICS.**

POPULATION

Every minute approximately 240 people are born and just over 100 die. Every minute twelve cars are made in the United States. That means that every time a car is made in the United States, eight-and-a third people die. There are half a million more cars than people in Los Angeles.

☐ See also: *demography.*

PORCUPINE

(From the French: *porc*, pig; *épine* prickle.)

I could a tale unfold whose lightest word
Would harrow up thy soul, freeze thy young blood,
Make thy two eyes, like stars, start from their spheres,
Thy knotted and combined locks to part
And each particular hair to stand on end,
Like quills upon the fretful porpentine.

It is not known whether the ghost, thus addressing Hamlet, knew that a porpentine, fretful or not, has 36,000 quills. Part of the mating ritual of the tree porcupine involves the male drenching his partner in urine. This is not so much to show her who is boss, as to deter possible rival suitors.

PORNOGRAPHY

(From the Greek: *porne*, a whore; *graphein*, to write or draw.) At a trial in Glasgow in 1982, the judge and jury found it necessary to view an allegedly obscene film. The entertainment had been running for ten minutes before it was realised that the film was being run backwards.

*ORSON, Richard (1759–1808)

Scholar (Eton and Trinity, Cambridge) with a phenomenal memory. Indolent and intemperate, he nevertheless impressed enough to be elected Regius Professor of Greek at Cambridge.

☐ See **MILTON.**

*ORT

Fortified wine shipped from Oporto, Portugal.

☐ See **PITT, VOLTAIRE.**

*ORTUGAL

In 1755, Lisbon, the capital of Portugal, was destroyed by an earthquake and a tidal wave. At the time this disaster was attributed to Benjamin Franklin's invention two years previously of the lightning rod. God and nature were assumed to be revenging themselves on this sacrilegious attempt to divert the power of the clouds and avert divine wrath.

It has been calculated that if all the population of China jumped up and down together in a synchronised manner, the resulting vibrations would cause a tidal wave large enough to engulf America.

☐ See also: *Czechoslovakia, hearing, pregnancy.*

*OSSLQ

Realising that language was not keeping pace with sociological practice, the US Census Bureau added the acronym Posslq (pronounced Possle-Q) to its list of replies to indicate marital status. It stands for 'Person of Opposite Sex Sharing Living Quarters'.

Despite a brief vogue in California, the word does not seem to be spreading into general usage. 'Bedfellow' was the term in olden days for much the same thing, but would seem to exclude posslqs with twin-beds.

POSSUM

Colloquial aphetic form of opossum, a small marsupial. 'Eat More Possum' is the motto of the Possum Growers and Breeders Association of America. Possum meat, like kangaroo meat, has the healthy advantage of being totally free of cholesterol. A potential hazard, at least according to the Hua tribe of Papua, New Guinea, is that eating possum can cause pregnancy in men. This belief is not given great publicity by the PGBA of America.

☐ See also: *vole.*

POSTMEN

☐ See **CHIENS.**

POTATO

(*Solanum tuberosum*) 'Let the sky rain potatoes,' exclaims Falstaff in Shakespeare's 'Merry Wives of Windsor' (Act V, Scene 5). But at the time the play was set, the potato had not yet been imported into Europe from Peru.

It has never actually rained potatoes, but in 1921 Gibraltar was hit by a shower of frogs, while a storm of thousands of these same small beasts hit Brignoles in southern France in 1973. Perhaps the strangest weather of all was experienced in Arkansas in 1974 when frozen ducks pelted down, killed by a sudden belt of freezing-cold air across their flight path.

Had Falstaff had the foresight to order it to rain with ducks and potatoes, he might have had a good meal in prospect.

☐ See also: *asthma, leprosy, philately, productivity, rheumatism.*

POTOROO

The potoroo, smallest member of the kangaroo family, does not drink water and sweats through its tail. Dogs sweat through their paws; cows sweat through their noses.

POWELL, John Enoch (*b.* 1912)

☐ See **POGO STICK.**

PRAGMATISM

Thomas Sprat (*d.* 1713), the Bishop of Rochester in Kent, was a Puritan under Cromwell's rule, became High Church when Charles II was king, switched his allegiance to the Roman Catholic Church for James II, became a Lutheran during the reign of William and Mary, and ended his career in the bosom of the Church of England under Queen Anne. He is buried in Westminster Abbey.

PRAWN

Stalk-eyed crustacean (*Leander serratus*) of the family Palaemonidae.

☐ See **SWIMMING**.

PRAYING MANTIS

Orthopterous insect.

☐ See **RALEIGH**.

PRECOCIOUSNESS

(From the Latin: *prae*, in front of, beforehand; *coquere*, to ripen or cook.) Margaret Beaufort (1443–1509) was married, bore a son (later to achieve fame as Henry VII) and was widowed all before she was 15 years old. Her grandson, Prince Arthur, died seven years before she did. She outlasted Henry VII by a few months.

☐ See also: *incest, Nicaragua, Peter the Great.*

PREGNANCY

According to Mexican folklore, it is dangerous for a woman to catch sight of monkeys, bears, elephants or any wild animal in a zoo, while she is in the first four months of pregnancy. By doing so, she would run the risk of the foetus taking the form of the animal sighted. And she should not go swimming or boating either, unless she wants the child to look like a fish.

Portuguese fishermen have no particular taboos about taking pregnant women aboard their boats, but they do paint eyes on the bows of their vessels to help them find the way towards shoals of fish.

☐ See also: *possum, salamander, Tyburn.*

PRE-MARITAL SEX

In Malaysia recently a 117-year-old man was fined 80 dollars for living with his 40-year-old lover without marrying her, thus breaking Moslem law. The couple were later married. Malaysia clearly believes in taking a firm stand on issues of contemporary morality; they have even banned video games as unhealthy.

In Britain, promiscuity has reached such depths that many of the lionesses in wildlife parks are now on the pill.

☐ See also: *posslq.*

PRESLEY, Elvis Aron (1935–77)

☐ See **NEANDERTHAL MAN**.

PROCRASTINATION

If a job's worth doing, it's worth doing slowly. Though Mozart had only thirty-five years of life in which to compose all his works, the task of cataloguing these 624 or so pieces of music took Ludwig von Koche twelve years. A pretty snappy piece of work when you consider that it took 579 years to build Milan cathedral.

PROCREATION

To ensure that an act of human love making results in pregnancy, all you have to do (according to ancient Roman beliefs) is the following: Knot together the hair plucked from the tail of a she-mule, while a stallion is covering her.

Whether the knotting has to be done before, during or after the human love making is not made clear. If in doubt, it might be wise to grab three hanks of mule hair just to be on the safe side.

☐ See also: *pregnancy.*

PRODUCTIVITY

The industries of the world produce enough

each day for everybody on earth to have 2 kg of coal, ½ pint of milk, one potato, 2 cigarettes, ½ kg of steel and a weight of fish equal to about half a sardine.

PROMISCUITY

(From the Latin: *pro*, a prefix of intensiveness; *miscere*, to mix.) Dr Joyce Brothers calculates that the average American girl kisses seventy-nine men before marriage (cf. **PRE-MARITAL SEX**).

PROPHYLAXIS

(From the Greek: *prophylaktikos – pro*, before; *phylax*, a guard.) When scorpions make love, both partners have to take prophylactic measures. Since each knows that the other is liable to kill and eat it, given half a chance, the mating ritual involves the two scorpions facing one another at arm's length, with pincers tightly linked together. The male then deposits his sperm on the ground and drags his mate over it to permit insemination to take place.

Sea-horses are much more friendly. The female lays her eggs in a pouch which the male has near his tail. The male incubates the eggs until they are hatched. Sea-horses have prehensile tails.

PROPOSAL

When proposed to, only 8 per cent of girls ask for time to think it over. If, after thinking it over, she should then decline, it will probably be done with considerably more politeness than an unwillingly propositioned female echidna. This nasty little marsupial has the habit of saying no by prodding her spines at the genitals of her suitor.

PROSTITUTION

(From the Latin: *prostituere*, to set up for sale.) In the town of Siena in Italy, prostitutes are forbidden to have the name Mary. The Virgin Mary has, however, appeared a record ten times on the cover of *Time* magazine, more than any other woman. There's nothing wrong with being a cover-girl.

☐ See also: **knackers.**

PROTEIN

Complex nitrogenous substance essential to food.

☐ See **CANNIBALISM, GIRAFFE, RABIES.**

PROUST, Marcel (1871–1922)

French novelist.

☐ See **BEETHOVEN.**

PRUDERY

However lewd, suggestive, or just plain disgusting the rest of the picture may be, Chinese paintings never show a woman's feet uncovered. A further step towards decency was made on 7 December 1911, when the pigtail was outlawed in China. Egypt has less pigs than any other country.

PRUSSIA

☐ See **BAKING, FREDERICK THE GREAT, REPARTEE.**

PSYCHIATRY

The suicide rate among American psychiatrists is reported to be twice as high as that of their patients. This might seem to cast doubt upon the value of psychiatry, but according to recent evidence that value can now be assigned a precise figure. In 1982 a gunman holding hostages in a Memphis hospital negotiated the release of one of his captives, a psychiatrist, in return for five hamburgers, five cheeseburgers and a packet of crisps.

☐ See also: **paranoia, tattoo.**

PSYCHOANALYSIS

Sigmund Freud used cocaine for many years. Despite this stimulation to his mental processes, he never learned to read railway timetables and for that reason would never travel alone on trains.

PSYCHOKINESIS

. The power of the human mind to influence inanimate objects.

☐ See **COMPENSATION.**

PTOLEMY XIII, King of Egypt (61–47 BC)

Eldest son of Ptolemy XII and first husband of **CLEOPATRA.**

PTOLEMY XIV, King of Egypt (*d.* 44 BC)

Younger brother of Ptolemy XIII and second husband of **CLEOPATRA.**

PTOLEMY (*fl.* AD 127–151)

Claudius Ptolemaius was the most esteemed astronomer of his day in Egypt, and the founder of the Ptolemaic system, accounting for the movement of stars and planets. About 1,800 years after his death, it was discovered not only that he had probably stolen his reported observational data from Hipparchus, but that he had also bent the figures to fit his theory that the earth was the centre of the solar system. If this is right he must have been as egocentric as his theories were geocentric.

PUBERTY

In Iran, girls may be executed at the age of 9. One 9-year-old girl was shot in 1981. Edward VI of England was King at the age of 8 and dead at 15 (cf. **PRECOCIOUS-NESS**).

PUBLIC LAVATORY

☐ See **LIZARD, PIGTAIL.**

PUBLIC TRUSTEE OFFICE

☐ See **JESUS CHRIST.**

PUMPKIN

A plant (*Cucurbita pepo*) of the gourd family. The 1983 Championships of the World Pumpkin Federation were held in Colins, near Buffalo in New York State. The world's biggest pumpkin in 1982 had been Canadian, produced by Mr Howard Dill of Nova Scotia and weighing in a 493½ lb.

PUNISHMENT

In medieval Spain, dancing the sarabande was illegal. Girls found so doing were liable to be exiled, while their male partners were sentenced to six years in the galleys. This might seem to be a primitive over-reaction to an insignificant offence, but it should be compared with the more modern case o Ellsworth P. de France. Mr de France wa released in 1903 from Sioux Falls prison New York, after serving a fifteen-yea sentence for the theft of a penny postage stamp.

☐ See also: *execution, hanging, stocks,* etc

PUNK

There is strong evidence to suggest tha punk hair styles may have originated among the Zulu Kaffirs.

PURCELL, Henry (*c.* 1658–95)

The piece of music long known as 'Purcell'

Trumpet Voluntary' was written by Jeremiah Clarke, organist at St Paul's Cathedral. Quite apart from having to wait more than two centuries for the credit for that composition, Jeremiah Clarke had a life full of ill-fortune. After being jilted, he tossed a coin to decide whether to kill himself by drowning or hanging. The coin stuck on its edge in the mud, so he shot himself.

URITANS
☐ See **CHOCOLATE, CHRISTMAS.**

USHKIN, Alexander Sergeyevich 1799–1837)

Russian poet whose mother was a granddaughter of Abraham Petrovich Hannibal, negro favourite and godson of Peter the Great.
☐ See **PEANUT.**

UTREFACTION
☐ See **MONET.**

PYGMY

(From the Greek: *pygme*, a measurement of the distance from elbow to knuckle, approximately equal to 13½ inches.) President Albert Bernard Bongo of Gabon is less than 5 feet tall, wears platform shoes, and has banned the use of the word 'pygmy' in his country.

PYJAMAS

The only president of the French Republic ever to fall off the Orient Express clad only in his pyjamas was Paul Eugene Deschanel, in 1920, when on his way to Lyons. He was still in office at the time of the accident and was unharmed apart from the damage to his dignity. He resigned four months later.

PYRAMID

The Great Pyramid of Cheops, standing 480.9 feet high, was the tallest structure in the world for over 4,000 years, f. om 2580 BC until AD 1548 when the central tower of

Python hunters

Lincoln Cathedral finally overtook it. There is enough mortar and stone in the Egyptian pyramids to build a wall 10 feet high and 5 feet wide from Calais to Baghdad. But anyone considering attempting the scheme should be warned that planning permission would be extremely difficult to obtain.

☐ See also: *scorpion.*

PYTHAGORAS (born *c.* 582 BC)

After proving the forty-seventh proposition of the first book of Euclid's elements (you know it, the one about the square on the hypotenuse), Pythagoras is said to have made a sacrifice of a hecatomb (100 oxen) to the gods. But since the philosopher and mathematician disapproved of spilling blood, the gods probably had to be satisfied with wax oxen that day.

☐ See **BEANS.**

PYTHON

Large serpent of the boa family. When capturing a python, a useful rule to remember is that it is considered advisable to have one man present for every 4 or 5 feet of snake. Four or 5 feet is also the average length of the human large intestine. The large intestine is shorter than the small intestine, which unwound averages three or four times the height of its owner.

☐ See also: *Borneo.*

Q

QUETZAL

The quetzal is a tropical bird of the trogon group. The middle two plumes of a quetzal's tail may be as much as 2 metres in length. The quetzal is the national emblem of Guatemala and is also its unit of currency. To avoid having to carry cumbersome tropical birds around, the Bank of Guatemala mints its own quetzals.

Quetzalcoatl was an ancient Mexican god, not on any account to be confused with Popocatepetl, which is a mountain. Axolotl comes from two Aztec words, *atl* and *xolotl*, meaning servant of the sea.

QUINSY

(From the Late Latin: *quinancia* which in turn derives from the Greek: *kyon*, a dog; *angkein*, to throttle. The word appears in English in two forms: quinsy and cynanche. It means a disease of the throat.)

□ See **ELDRED, SEURAT.**

QUIZ

The word 'quiz' was invented by a theatre manager named Daly in 1780 in order to win a bet that he could introduce a new word into the language. He scrawled it all over the walls of Dublin, causing intense bewilderment. The meaning stuck.

A less successful gambler was rock musician Terry Kath who played Russian roulette with a pistol in 1978. His last words were: 'Don't worry, it's not loaded.'

R

RABBIT

(Yctolagus cuniculus) The rabbit is a gnawing mammal (of the order Rodentia) and one of nature's most prolific defecators, dropping pellets at a rate of 360 an hour. It differs from the hare in that the rabbit is born bald, the hare with hair. The Belgian hare is a rabbit.

☐ See also: **bravery, goat, myxomatosis, pet, umbrella.**

RABIES

(From the Latin: *rabere*, to rave.) The cure for rabies decreed by law in eighteenth-century Ireland was to smother the patient between two feather beds and get a 'sufficient number' of neighbours to lie on it until he is out of danger.

According to Pliny the Elder, just one taste of mother's milk is enough to prevent a dog from ever falling victim to rabies. Cow's milk has twice as much protein as human milk, but it does not come in such attractive containers.

RACCOON

☐ See **HYGIENE.**

RACEHORSE

Caligula, who made his horse Incitatus a senator, was not the only Roman emperor who treated these animals with respect. Nero awarded pensions to retired race horses, which were dressed in huma clothing for the ceremonies of presenta tion.

RADIO

(From the Latin: *radius*, a rod, spoke radius or ray.) There are two radio sets pe person in the United States. In Afghanista there are 1,000 people per radio set. I would therefore take on average 12,00 Afghans to get together before they coul manage a performance of John Cage 'Imaginary Landscape No. 4' (1953), musical work scored for twelve radio tuned at random.

Abdur Rahman Khan, Amir of Afghan istan, had no known opinions on radio sets but his parting sentence before he die in 1901 was: 'My last words to you, m son and successor, are never trust th Russians.'

☐ See also: **media.**

RADIUM

A radioactive metallic element, symbol Ra currently occupying the number 88 spot i the atomic table. Pierre and Marie Curi refused to take out a patent on thei radium-making process, on the highl altruistic grounds that it belonged to th world and no one should profit from financially.

William Hunt was less altruistic about his invention of the safety pin in 1849. He sold the idea to pay off a debt of $15. The safety pin, however, may not have been original; the Etruscans had a gold version in the seventh century BC.

RAILWAY

William Huskisson (1770–1830), statesman and economist, was secretary of the treasury (1804–6 and 1807–9), secretary of the colonies (1827) and the first man to be killed in a railway accident (1830). He was run over by Stephenson's *Rocket* at the opening of the Liverpool and Manchester Railway. At the time of the accident, Mr Huskisson was imprudently crossing the tracks to have a word with the Duke of Wellington.

☐ See also: *Argentina, careers, eagle, excursions, psycho-analysis, Rossini, Wellington.*

RAIN

You can tell when a storm is imminent because the wool on a sheep uncurls. This must be especially easy in Wales, where there are over 5 million sheep ready to be consulted on the matter. Catgut comes from sheep.

☐ See also: *birth, flood, gormlessness, Sahara, sloth, Sri Lanka.*

RAINCOAT

The mackintosh was invented by Mr C. Macintosh. The 'k' appears to have slipped in for purely euphonic reasons, though it might be conjectured that the extra 'k' helps keep the rain off.

RALEIGH, Sir Walter (*c.* 1552–1618)

Walter Raleigh was granted a patent on tobacco and potatoes in 1584, which he held until it lapsed to the crown in 1603. After he was executed in 1618, his widow had his head embalmed and kept it in a red leather bag which she carried with her everywhere until she too died twenty-nine years later. There is a clear analogy here with the behaviour of the female praying mantis which, after mating, also takes a fancy to its mate's head and is liable to bite it off.

☐ See also: *spelling.*

RAMESES III, King of Egypt (reigned *c.* 1200 BC)

The sarcophagus of Rameses III is in Paris, but its lid is in the Fitzwilliam Museum in Cambridge, and the mummy itself is in Cairo.

☐ See **INDUSTRIAL DISPUTE.**

RAPE

The old Viking law for rape was simple and founded on an undeniable logic: rape was a capital offence, but only if the woman screamed as soon as she was touched. Their divorce laws were equally well considered. A woman was agreed to have sufficient grounds for divorce if her husband wore women's clothing or did not fulfil his conjugal duties.

☐ See also: *sexism, spelling.*

RASPUTIN, Grigori (1873–1916)

Born Grigori Novikh, he started life as a fisherman, but also showed talent as a drunkard and thief. His friends called him 'Rasputin', meaning 'immoral one'. He liked the name and adopted it. Taking time off from his trade as Russian court guru, he once had a contest with Count Louis Hamon in which each man tried to hypnotise the other. The match ended in a draw, but the Count won the girl – he became Mata Hari's lover after reading her palm. Polite to the end, Mata Hari's last words before she was shot were: 'Thank you, monsieur.'

RAT

Under the Rat and Mouse Act of 1921, British householders were obliged to destroy rats and mice in their premises under penalty of a £20 fine. In a controlled experiment in Cambridge in 1982, only or rat out of eight preferred a Mars bar t cheddar cheese.

☐ See also: *Cameroon, English, genius, industrial accident, Mozart, pets, Richard III, Siberia, Wordsworth.*

RATTLESNAKE

The rattlesnake (*Crotalus*) has two senso organs between its eyes and nostrils whic enable it to detect the heat from a mouse body at a distance of 15 cm. An owl can e: ten mice in one meal.

If you are afraid of mice and do not hav a pet owl (cf. *Nightingale*) handy to eat an that may cross your path, try calling upon ' Gertrude. She is a patron saint of travelle: and also protectress against mice and rats

☐ See also: *Cyprus, Forsdyke-Smith.*

RAZOR BLADE
☐ See **SNAIL.**

EAGAN, Ronald Wilson (*b.* 1911)

❏ See **KENNEDY**.

ECYCLING

In nineteenth-century Manchester in a single year, 13 tons of dead cats were found in the city's dustbins. They were not wasted; their fat content was broken down and used in the manufacture of oleo margarine. The cat fat fetched £24 a ton.

EFRIGERATOR

❏ See **ESKIMO**.

EINCARNATION

Being born again in another form. In 1983, Tom Gribble, aged 62, of Bristol, wrote a will stipulating that on his death he be cremated and the ashes put in an egg-timer so that he 'will be of some use again one day'.

　　In Britain 64.85 per cent of all funerals are by cremation, a higher proportion than in any other Christian country.

❏ See also: ***metempsychosis.***

EINDEER

The reindeer (*Cervus tarandus*) is the only deer to have been successfully domesticated. If you really care about your food, however, smoked tongue of reindeer is the only part worth eating. Prior to having its tongue smoked, a reindeer likes to munch its way through a mouthful of duck droppings, its staple diet. Nowhere in the whole of the Old Testament is there any explicit reference either to a duck or a reindeer.

ELATIVITY

The Theory of Relativity was officially rejected in China between 1970 and 1978 as a 'reactionary, idealistic and metaphysical world view'. White is the colour of mourning in China.

EMARRIAGE

After divorce or widowhood, a man is twice as likely to remarry as a woman in England. The last time a widowed Queen of England remarried was in 1547, when Catherine Parr took Lord Seymour of Sudeley to be her fourth husband. Mary Queen of Scots had only three husbands.

REPARATIONS

At the end of the Second World War, England was offered the Volkswagen business as part of reparations. The offer was declined on the grounds that no car with the engine at the back could possibly be a commercial success.

REPARTEE

The ultimate in repartee must surely have been the last sentence of King Frederick William I of Prussia. In reply to the priest's words: 'Naked came I out of my mother's womb and naked shall I return', the King corrected: 'No, not quite naked, I shall have my uniform on'. And, with his uniform on, he died.

REPRODUCTION

Between 1849 and 1957, parents giving birth to triplets in England were entitled to a royal payment of £3. Never properly rewarded, the hippopotamus gives birth underwater, the first act of the newborn being to float to the surface for its first breath of air.

RHEUMATISM

A combination of three folk remedies might be tried for this painful complaint. Rub fried garlic over the affected parts (Mexico), while leaning against a bellows (West Sussex), with a raw potato in your pocket (Britain).

RHINOCEROS

(From the Greek: *rhinos*, of the nose; *keras*, horn.) Plural, rhinoceroses (the forms rhinocerot and rhinocerotes are now obsolete), adjective, rhinocerotic.

❏ See **LOST PROPERTY, MUSICAL APPRECIATION, SOUTH AFRICA**.

RIB

(From the Old English: *ribb*, a rib.)

☐ See **CHLOROFORM, INDECENCY, SLOTH.**

RICE

A grass (*Oryza sativa*) of the natural order Gramineae.

☐ See **FASHION.**

RICE PUDDING

☐ See **DENMARK.**

RICHARD I, King of England (1157–99)

Affectionately known as Coeur de Lion, the Lionheart, Richard I is the nearest thing England has ever had to an absentee landlord. He spent only six months of his ten-year reign actually in England, and his Queen, Berengaria, is the only English Queen never to have been in England. Wounded while besieging the castle of Chaluz in 1199, Richard need not have died had not the surgeon 'so rankled the wound' in trying to extract the arrow, that it 'mortified and brought on the end'.

Hip, hip, hooray was originally a battle cry of the Crusaders. The 'hip' (originally 'hep') was an abbreviation of 'Hierosylma est perdita' (Jerusalem has fallen) and the 'hooray' was a corruption of a slavonic curse Hu-ray (to paradise).

RICHARD II, King of England (1367–1400)

The reputed inventor of the handkerchief is King Richard II, though something very similar was in use in Roman times. The preferred dimensions of Richard's handkerchief are not recorded (cf. *handkerchief*) but the longest recorded human nose was that of Thomas Wedders (1709–77) at a magnificent 7½ inches.

RICHARD III, King of England (1452–85)

Successful usurper of the throne of England, King Richard III was born with teeth. So were Napoleon Bonaparte and King Louis XIV. Rats' incisors grow at a rate of 5 inches a year.

☐ See also: ***Henry VII, hunchback.***

RIGHT OF CLERGY

From the time of William the Conqueror until 1827, Right of Clergy (or Benefit of Clergy) was a privilege available to the educated classes in English law. Any member of one of the seven classes of clergy (which in effect meant anyone who could read) could escape a death penalty by claiming Right of Clergy to be tried by an ecclesiastical court, where the death sentence could not be ordained. When Ben Jonson killed another actor in a duel in 1598, he was tried, but escaped through Benefit of Clergy. This escape hatch was closed with its abolition in 1827, though peers retained the privilege (probably through an oversight) until 1841.

RIN-TIN-TIN (1916–32)

Dog star.

☐ See **ACTING, CHIENS, MALI.**

RIOTOUS BEHAVIOUR

Under the Riot Act of 1715, magistrates have the power to apprehend as felons persons to the number of twelve or more who refuse to disperse within an hour after the reading of a proclamation bidding them to do so. But it only takes three to riot (a violent disturbance of the peace by not less than three persons).

☐ See also: ***Fawkes, mumps.***

RITZ

César Ritz (1850–1918), founder of the famous hotel in Piccadilly which bears his name, once earned his living feeding elephants in a Paris zoo. A change of career in the other direction, away from the hotel and catering trade, was that of Ho Chi Minh who in 1911 worked under Escoffier in the kitchen of the Carlton Hotel in London.

As César Ritz probably knew, a good way to estimate the height of an elephant at the shoulder is to measure the distance round its foot and double it. (Strictly speaking this applies more particularly to Indian elephants.)

OAD SAFETY

Julius Caesar banned wheeled vehicles in Rome during the hours of daylight because of traffic congestion. In the United Arab Emirates, free-ranging camels are fitted with fluorescent jackets to cut down accidents. While this may increase the feeling of self-importance among trendy Arab camels, they can hardly approach the self-esteem of Israeli cows, which are issued with identity cards. Cattle can be identified by their nose-prints.

had had numbers since 1463. Evidently the Londoners thought that 300 years was a fair trial period for a French innovation. It was a typical piece of American creative thinking which gave us odd numbers on one side of the street and evens on the other.

☐ See also: ***theft.***

ROBIN

(*Erithacus rubecula*) A song bird of the thrush family.

☐ See **WORM.**

ROCKING CHAIR

☐ See **BIFOCALS.**

A device to avert collisions on the railways

OBBERY

In 1971, the house at number 10 Jardin Street, London SE5, was stolen, brick by brick, over a period of time. One of the security devices which prevents the same thing from happening to number 10 Downing Street, London SW1, is the absence of a keyhole on the outside.

Houses only began to be numbered in London in 1764, though Parisian addresses

ROGERS, Roy (*b.* 1912)

☐ See **BENTHAM, Jeremy.**

ROGERS, Samuel (1763–1855)

British poet and conversationalist.

☐ See **WORDSWORTH.**

ROLLER-SKATING

☐ See **VIOLIN.**

ROMAN NUMERALS

Crossword clue: 1200
Answer: Marylebone Cricket Club.

☐ See also: *Iraq.*

ROME

Capital city of Italy, traditionally founded in 753 BC.

☐ See **DECENCY, NEW YORK, OHIO.**

ROOK

A common bird (*Corvus frugilegus*) of the crow family.

☐ See **CHESS, GOAT.**

ROOSEVELT, Franklin Delano (1882–1945)

A recent survey indicated that F. D. Roosevelt was a long way out when he stated that 'the only thing we have to fear is fear itself'. Fear itself did not in fact feature among the top four in a table of what young men are most afraid of today. The top fears are: 1. Cancer, 2. Impotence, 3. Paralysis, 4. Insanity. In Britain, thirty-five times as many women as men are confined in mental homes, but exactly the reverse ratio exists among inmates of Her Majesty's prisons.

The fear of fear is correctly termed phobophobia.

ROOSEVELT, Theodore (1858–1919)

American president whose last words were: 'Please put out the light.' Theodore Roosevelt once gave an 'electric picnic' in which a turkey was killed by an electric shock, cooked on a primitive electric stove, while being turned on an electric spit.

☐ See also: *barrel-organ.*

ROSSINI, Gioachino Antonio (1792–1868)

Rossini had written thirty-eight operas by the time he was 37, then spent the rest of his life enjoying himself. In his remaining years until his death at 76, he wrote only two more full-scale musical works. As a tribute to his early success, he was given a state pension at the age of 38 and the job of

'Inspector General of Singing in France (He had by then settled in Paris after h Italian childhood.) He was born on Lea Year Day, 29 February 1792, and wou never travel by rail.

☐ See also: *celibacy.*

ROULETTE, Russian

☐ See **QUIZ.**

ROUSSEAU, Henri (1844–1910)

French painter.

☐ See **ART.**

ROWING

The May races in Cambridge, like the Ma balls, take place in June. The Octobe Revolution in Russia took place in Nove ber, but they were a bit confused about th calendar at the time.

☐ See **MONACO.**

ROYALTY

Princess Anne was reported to have bee the only woman competing at the 197 Olympic Games in Montreal not to hav been given a sex test. The Emperor Ner is believed to have been the only winner an Olympic gold medal without actuall winning an event. He was defeated in th competition, but awarded the gold b popular acclaim.

RUBBER

A rubber company in Ohio in 1983 bega the task of making two artificial flippers fc a crippled 350-lb turtle which had come o second best in a battle with a shark. Afte spending more than $20,000 on research they finally performed the operation i January 1984. The patient was a 50-year-ol lady turtle, named Lucky.

The starfish is luckier; it can regro broken arms.

RUBIK CUBE

☐ See **DISEASE.**

RUM

Bill McCoy was a rum runner between the British West Indies and the United States. So far superior were his goods to the booze the Americans could obtain from other sources, that his name gave us the expression 'the real McCoy'.

The first firm to make Cow gum was started by Mr Peter Cow.

RUMANIA

The Rumanians prefer Rumania to be spelt Romania. Do not be surprised to see 'crap' on a Rumanian restaurant menu. It is the Rumanian for carp.

RUPERT, Prince (1619–82)

Son of the Elector Palatine, Frederick V, and Elizabeth, daughter of James I of England. Prince Rupert introduced into England the mezzotint process of engraving.

☐ See **THESPIANS.**

RUSSELL, Jane (*b.* 1921)

Look at **BREASTS**.

S

SACRILEGE
☐ See **PORTUGAL**.

SADE, Donatien Alphonse François, Marquis de (1740–1814)

The Marquis de Sade was sentenced to death in 1772 for immoral practices, but the sentence was commuted to imprisonment.

☐ See **PARSLEY**.

SAHARA

The Sahara desert of North Africa is as large in area as the whole of Europe and larger than the combined area of the next nine largest deserts on earth. On 18 February 1978, there was a snowstorm in the Sahara desert, the first in living memory. When it rained in 1971 in the Atacama desert in Chile, it broke a drought which had been continuing for at least 400 years. It is more than 700 years, however, since we last saw a Welsh-born Prince of Wales. The last such was Llewelyn, who died in 1282.

SAINTS

St Joseph is the patron saint of both Canada and Belgium. In the event of a dispute between those two nations, he is believed to favour a position of strict neutrality.

St Nicholas is the patron saint of parish clerks, Russia, Aberdeen, pawnbrokers and thieves. Might these last two perhaps explain whence Santa Claus acquires those sacks of toys? (Father Christmas is a fence.) St Nicholas is also accredited with the miracle of restoring to life three boys who had been cut up and pickled in a salting tub to be served as bacon.

In order to become a saint, one must first be dead, then beatified, and finally, after producing evidence of two first-class miracles, canonised. Here are a few of our favourite saints:

St Brigid of Ireland, the sixteenth-century abbess of Kildare, who transformed her bath water into beer for visiting clerics.

St Elvira, who died at the age of 12, after a lifetime busying herself in a daily ritual which involved catching the fleas which lived in her blankets, counting them, separating the males from the females, and finally releasing them ready again for the next day.

St Peter Arbuez, the Grand Inquisitor, who was canonised after his lifetime's zeal had sent 40,000 to be burnt at the stake.

St Simeon the Younger, who spent the last forty-five years of his life sitting on a column.

St Augustine of Hippo, the patron saint of brewers. (He must have just pipped Brigid for the job.)

St Paula the Bearded, a Spanish saint of uncertain date, who fled to the refuge of a crucifix in order to escape the attentions of a pursuing man. Immediately a beard and moustache appeared on her face, disguising her and saving her from the would-be ravisher. Whether she later shaved the miraculous growth, or kept it as a souvenir, is not recorded.

The patron saint of hatters is St William, of librarians, St Jerome. Pontius Pilate is a saint, but only in the Ethiopian church.

ALAMANDER

A genus of tailed batrachians. The female salamander is rather a shy and prudish creature; she inseminates herself from jelly dumped by the male. Alpine salamanders remain pregnant for over three years. But it's worth waiting for: they always have twins.

☐ See also: *knowledge.*

ALISBURY

English city on the River Avon. The clock in Salisbury Cathedral has no face. If you want to know the time you must wait for it to chime. Actually the whole building is a piece of shoddy workmanship; the spire is 2 feet off perpendicular too.

SALIVATION

Everyone produces between 2 and 3 pints of saliva every day. This should be disposed of thoughtfully; there is a statutory fine ranging from $66.50 to $133 written into the Philippine basketball rules, for players who spit at the referee.

SALMON

(*Salmo salar*) Eskimos do not suffer from heart disease. One research study recently attributed this healthy sign to their diet of salmon, which reduces the level of blood cholesterol. British doctors, however, are still reluctant to prescribe salmon on the National Health Service.

South African witch doctors have a nice code of ethics which precludes their charging a fee if the patient is going to die.

SALT

(Chloride of Sodium; NaCl.) An autopsy was performed on the exhumed body of Charles I by Sir Henry Halford, the royal surgeon, in 1813. After completing the

Salisbury Cathedral

task, he took away as a souvenir the ex-King's fourth cervical vertebra, which had been completely detached by the executioner's axe. For the next thirty years he surprised dinner guests by using the bone as a salt cellar. The bone was eventually returned to the coffin on the express instructions of Queen Victoria.

☐ See also: *kidney, suicide.*

SANDWICH

John Montagu, 4th Earl of Sandwich (1718–92), gave his name not only to the sandwich but also to the Sandwich Islands.

☐ See **OHIO.**

SAN FRANCISCO

☐ See **NERO, OSIRIS.**

SAN MARINO

Found, if you search hard enough, in central Italy, the republic of San Marino is the third smallest country in the world, covering 62 sq. km. With a fitting lack of pretension, its national anthem is only four lines in length. But it does have words, which is more than can be said for the Spanish national anthem. On the other hand, King Philip II of Spain did have the largest heart of any known man.

SARABANDE

Stately dance of Hispano-Moorish origin, once performed as a solo by Cardinal Richelieu before Anne of Austria.

☐ See **PUNISHMENT.**

SARDINE

A young pilchard most commonly found tinned in oil.

☐ See **NIGER, PRODUCTIVITY.**

SATIE, Eric (1866–1923)

French composer among whose works for piano are 'Flabby Prelude for a Dog' and 'Things seen from Left to Right Without Spectacles'. His first work was entitled

'Opus 62', and he generally exhorted the audience to talk while his music was being performed. In this respect, he deserves to be remembered as the spiritual father of Muzak. Gustav Mahler's last word before he died was 'Mozart'.

☐ See also: *Vexations.*

SAUCE BÉARNAISE

(Also known as Béarnaise Sauce.) According to an article in the scientific journal *Nature*, the secret of a successful Béarnaise sauce is to obtain 'a stable colloidal suspension consisting of a hydrophobic phase suspended in a low pH aqueous base'.

What this means, in technical terms, is that if it curdles the best thing to do is add a few drops more vinegar, or if that fails to help, then allow it to cool, then beat it drop by drop onto a teaspoon of boiling water in a clear basin.

SAUDI ARABIA

Saudi Arabia covers 830,000 sq. miles, but has no rivers. It imports both camels (from North Africa) and sand (from Scotland). They just cannot breed enough camels of their own, while their sand, though plentiful, is not of sufficiently high quality for building work.

China is the largest producer of camel hair in the world. Camel hair paint brushes, however, are mostly made from squirrel. The 'Camel' in the name is that of Mr Camel, who designed them.

☐ See also: *polygamy, skull.*

SAUSAGE

The Frankfurter sausage was invented in China. What provided the inspiration for this innovative foodstuff is unknown, but it might have been a grasshopper; both the Chinese and Japanese used to take caged grasshoppers to work with them in order to listen to their music.

SCANDERBURG of Albania (c.1403–67)

Warrior king of Albania, the son of an

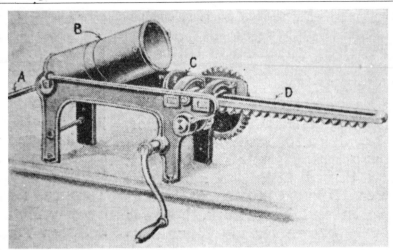

A sausage machine

Albanian prince and a Serbian princess, born George Castriot Swinamed. Also known as Scanderbeg.

☐ See **EXECUTION.**

SCARBOROUGH

In January 1948, the residents of Scarborough were completely fooled by Mr Hezekiah Johnson's impersonation of a cuckoo. 'I used to do the nightingale,' explained Mr Johnson, a road-cleaner, 'when I had my teeth in.'

SCARF

Item of neckgear.

☐ See **AUSTRALIA, DUNCAN.**

SCARLATTI, Domenico (1685–1757)

Composer son of Alessandro Scarlatti.

☐ See **MUSICAL COMPOSITION.**

SCHOENBERG, Arnold (1874–1951)

Composer Arnold Schoenberg was highly superstitious about the number thirteen. He expected to die, as indeed he did, at the age of 76 (7+6=13). In fact he conked out on Friday the thirteenth at thirteen minutes to midnight. Schubert was not superstitious about the number thirteen, but he was the thirteenth child of fourteen in his family, and he died at the age of 31. By the time Keats was 31, he had already been dead for six years.

Triskaidekaphobia is the proper term for fear of the number thirteen.

☐ See also: *Mozart.*

SCHUBERT, Franz Peter (1797–1828)

Schubert studied musical theory under Antonio Salieri (1750–1825) who claimed to have poisoned Mozart. Schubert himself died when he was only 31 years old. By the time Shelley reached that age, he had already been dead for two years.

☐ See also: *Schoenberg, Siamese twins.*

SCHWEITZER, Albert (1875–1965)

☐ See **POLAR BEAR.**

SCIATICA

(From the Greek: *ischion*, the hip joint.) Painful affection of the sciatic nerve for which an old Russian remedy prescribes the wearing of long red woollen underpants at all times. Whether the colour of the underpants is essential to the efficacy of the cure, or merely a political statement, is unclear. Those who incline to the other wing of the political spectrum should be advised that the Irish bilberry is the only naturally blue food.

SCIENCE

The Aztec, Toltec, Inca and Mayan civilisations all functioned without the use of the wheel.

Until 1840, the English language functioned perfectly well without the word 'scientist'. The first appearance of 'sociology' had been two years previously, in 1838.

SCORPION

Order (Scorpiones) of the class Arachnida in the phylum Arthropoda. If a drop of whisky is squirted onto the back of a scorpion, it will sting itself to death. If, as we must reluctantly conclude, experimenters have been going round irritating scorpions in this manner, it is hardly surprising that 20,352 people were killed by scorpions in Mexico between 1940 and 1949.

The world's biggest pyramid is in Mexico, at Cholula de Rivadabia, only 100 km, as the scorpion crawls, from Mexico City.

□ See also: *prophylaxis.*

SCOTLAND

A clan of Scottish cannibals in the fifteenth century are believed to have killed and eaten over 1,000 people. Their leader and head of table was Sawney Beane who lived with his wife, eight sons, six daughters and numerous grandchildren in a cave on the Galloway coast. It is not known whether they had any preference towards light or dark meat, but strong feelings in their gastronomic choice might account for the fact that the Scottish Highlands now have the highest proportion of redheads in the world – 11 per cent.

Blonde beards, incidentally, grow more quickly than dark ones.

□ See also: *bequests, pornography, Saudi Arabia.*

SCOTLAND YARD

Former headquarters of the Metropolitan Police in London, Old Scotland Yard was built on a site once the residence of Scottish kings visiting London.

□ See **DARWIN.**

SCOTTISH GATHERING

L. BOGLE Del. Ro.

SCROFULA

(From the Latin: *scrofulae, scrofa,* a sow supposedly liable to the disease.) A tubercular disease formerly known as the King's Evil from the belief that the touch of a monarch could cure it. Touching for the King's Evil was a regular ceremony from the time of Edward the Confessor until Queen Anne. (Though the Jacobites denied the healing power of William III and Anne, because they had no divine hereditary right.) The last person touched in England was Dr Johnson in 1712, when he was 2½ years old. Edward I is said to have cured 1,736 of the disease in the year 1300, but the record is held by Charles II who touched 2,983 sufferers in 1669. Throughout his reign, his healing fingers were bestowed upon 92,107. It is not known how many recovered.

❏ See also: *menstruation.*

CULPTURE

A useful guide towards dating a Greek or Roman sculpture of a naked male is the relative size of the testicles (always assuming no prude has stuck a vine leaf over them, of course). Before about 600 BC the beauty of symmetry held sway and testicles would be carved of equal sizes, but later the school of realism took over and the left was depicted larger and lower. If the tubes inside a testicle, which carry the sperm to the penis, were uncoiled, they would stretch more than 20 feet.

CYTHIA

Ancient region around the top right-hand side of the Black Sea. Favourite foods of the Scythians in the seventh century included soured mare's milk and ox haggis.

❏ See **HEAD.**

EA

The least salty sea in the world is the Baltic. The Sargasso Sea has plenty of salt but no shoreline. It is surrounded entirely by the Atlantic Ocean. Nowhere in Great Britain is more than 75 miles from the sea, but there are some towns in Scotland for which the nearest railway station is in Norway.

EA-HORSE

(*Hippocampus antiquorum*)
❏ See **PROPHYLAXIS.**

EAL

(From the Anglo-Saxon: *seol.*) The seal never sleeps for more than 1½ minutes without waking up again. When travelling

in boats, seals have been known to show symptoms of seasickness. The footprint of an otter is called a seal.

❏ See also: *famine, fountain, soup.*

SEASIDE

If you do like to be beside the seaside, try Canada. It has the longest coastline of any country, six times that of Australia. Canada also has the world's longest street, Yonge Street in Toronto. If you find yourself at the wrong end, you could be in for a walk of more than 1,000 miles. Should you pass through Quebec on your way to or from Yonge Street, do remember that it is illegal to sell anti-freeze to the Indians there.

SEA URCHIN

(From the Latin: *ericius*, a hedgehog.) Spiny echinoderm.

❏ See **BELIZE, BUTTERFLY.**

SEAWEED

❏ See **BARBADOS, OTTER.**

SECRETS

In 1957 after four years' work, the United States Air Force finally completed their task of recharting the North Atlantic. When questioned about the width of the Ocean, the answer was withheld for security reasons. It was stated that the Air Force would like to disclose whether Europe and America had grown nearer or further apart since the last survey, but such information could be of great military value to the Russians.

❏ See also: *bestseller, lobster.*

SECURITY

After an attempt on her life, Queen Victoria (cf. *hunchback*) had some of her sunshades lined with chain mail. The 'lace' curtains which hang in the windows of numbers 10 and 11 Downing Street are bulletproof.

SEDATIVE

Régine Le Guilloux, a mother of seven grown-up sons, was sent for trial in Paris in October 1983. She was accused of putting sleeping pills in her husband's soup every night so that he would not want sex. Over-excited male baboons have been seen trying to mate with foxes, cats, dogs, and even snakes.

SEDUCTION

(From the Latin: *se-*, aside; *ducere*, to lead.)

☐ See **EDGAR, SHAW, WASP, XYLOCOPID.**

SEGREGATION

The peninsula of Mount Athos in Greece (*Ayion Oros*) is inhabited solely by monks. No woman, or any other female creature, is allowed there. The monastery was founded by Athanasius around AD 369.

The word 'lady' derives from an Old English word *hlaefdige*. *Hlaef*, a loaf; *dig-*, the stem of a verb meaning to knead. Hence a lady is one who kneads loaves. Had Athanasius known that, he might have allowed them onto his peninsula. It is now known that the Athanasian Creed was not written by Athanasius.

☐ See also: *apartheid.*

SEURAT, Georges (1859–91)

Impressionist painter. His father was a one-armed bailiff who lived away from home and indulged in 'strange religious practices'. He returned to dine at his wife's table every Tuesday, when he would screw the knives and forks into the end of his artificial arm. He died of septic quinsy.

SEX

According to Pliny the Elder, sexual intercourse is remedial for pains in the loins, dimness of sight, insanity and melancholia. The consensus of modern opinion would not dispute the last of these.

According to a recent study on the benefits of different forms of exercise, single act of making love expends the sam amount of energy as 1½ hours playir cards, 45 minutes of frisbee throwing, 7½ hours standing around at cockta parties. But standing around at cockta parties can cause pains in the loins.

☐ See also: *aural sex, nasal sex, pre-marital sex,* etc.

SEX CHANGE

The first recorded sex-change operatic was on 1 December 1952 in the USA whe George Jorgenson, formerly of the arme forces, became a woman. The first perso to serve in both the men's navy and th women's navy in the United States w Joanna (née Michael) Clark in 1969.

The nipples of the female whale are c her back.

☐ See also: *Philippines.*

SEXISM

Out of a sample of 200 fairy tales by th brothers Grimm, there were found to be 1 wicked mothers or step-mothers, compare with only 3 such fathers or step-father: there were 23 wicked female witches an only 2 wicked male witches; and 13 wome killed their husbands or lovers, compare with only one such dastardly deed commi' ted by a male. These proportions are qui the opposite of those reflected by real-lif crime. For example, in Britain in 1970 c 305 persons convicted of rape, only one wa a woman.

☐ See also: *Somalia.*

SEXUALITY

The Dani tribe of Grand Valley, Ne Guinea, is the only known human society t have no interest in sex.

SHAKESPEARE, William (1564–1616)

William Shakespeare had red hair and spe his surname eleven different ways.

See also: **bequests, Bohemia, boxing, Cervantes, potato, starling, thespians, tin, turkey.**

HARK

Primitive fish with cartilaginous skeleton. In Bermuda, shark liver oil is used to forecast the weather. Kept in an airtight jar, it turns cloudy before a storm and forms peaks and ridges before heavy winds. The best results are obtained by using the oil from the liver of a puppy shark. The oil from nurse or hammerhead sharks seems to be no good for this purpose, though it is useful in the treatment of colds. The shark has one of the largest livers of all animals. Its liver can account for 10 per cent of its total body weight.

☐ See also: **beaver, Mansion House, musical appreciation, obstetrics, rubber, smell.**

SHAVING

Napoleon Bonaparte always shaved with an English razor, he would trust no other. In 1820 an auction was held of some personal effects of Napoleon which had been taken by the Prussians in Flanders. His shaving brush fetched £3 14s 0d, exactly sixpence more than his toothbrush. A pair of old slippers and a pair of gloves each fetched £1, a handkerchief went for £1 11s 6d, but the star of the sale was a snuff-box for which the bidding reached £166 19s 6d.

☐ See also: **hair.**

Napoleon always made his bids noticed at auction sales

SHAW, George Bernard (1856–1950)

G. B. Shaw was a virgin until he was 29, at which age he was seduced by a widow. The experience was such a revelation to him that he was shocked into a further fifteen years abstinence. When he was 42, he married a virgin (Charlotte Townsend) who stayed that way. He left £367,233.

Tennyson, incidentally, lost his virginity at the age of 41, after his marriage to Emily Sellwood. Their engagement had lasted for fourteen years. The couple produced one child.

SHEEP

A ram can service 40 ewes in 24 hours.

☐ See also: *New Zealand, patience, rain, Tanzania.*

sea creatures as a stimulant of the thyro gland. Shellfish, especially oysters, conta chemicals very similar to the human s hormones. Of all fish, the Japanese fug fish (cf. *zombie*) is probably the most pote aphrodisiac.

SHERIDAN, Richard Brinsley Butler (1751–1816)

Richard Sheridan eloped to France in 17

The journey home after a hard day's servicing

SHEEPDOG

☐ See **TRIPED**.

SHELLEY, Percy Bysshe (1792–1822)

'The pleasure that is sorrow,' wrote Shelley, 'is sweeter than the pleasure of pleasure itself.' He had a remarkably small head.

☐ See also: *Schubert, Sophocles.*

SHELLFISH

In his seventeenth-century work, *Tableau de l'Amour*, Dr Nicholas Venette remarked: 'Those who live almost entirely on shellfish and fish are more ardent in love than others.'

He may have been correct. Later research identified the high iodine content of

with the beautiful Elizabeth Linley, who the time was running away from an impo tunate lover, Captain Matthews. Returnin to England, Sheridan fought two duels wit the wretched Captain Matthews befor finally marrying Miss Linley in 1773. Sh had a beautiful voice, but Sheridan woul not let her perform in public. Painted b Gainsborough and Sir Joshua Reynold ogled by the King when she sang oratorios, Mrs Sheridan died of consum tion at the age of 31. Richard Sheridan wer on to become secretary of the treasury 1783, but went bankrupt and died wit bailiffs in his house.

SHIPWRECK

In 1897, Morgan Robertson wrote a sho novel entitled *Futility* about an unsinkab

Miss Elizabeth Linley

luxury liner named *Titan* which hit an iceberg and sank on its maiden voyage. Fifteen years later the unsinkable luxury liner *Titanic* hit an iceberg and sank on her maiden voyage.

On 5 December 1664 in the Menai Strait, North Wales, a ferry sank with eighty-one passengers on board. There was only one survivor, a man named Hugh Williams.

On 5 December 1785, in the Menai Strait, North Wales, another ferry sank with sixty passengers on board. The name of the sole survivor was Hugh Williams.

Yet a third ferry sank in the Menai Strait on 5 December 1860, and once again a Hugh Williams was the one to return and tell the tale. Of course, probably by that time the only men who would ride on the ferry on 5 December were those named Hugh Williams. The fact that the number of passengers was down to twenty supports this last hypothesis.

SHIVERING

Charles I wore two shirts for his execution. He thought that the cold morning air might make him shiver, and he did not want the crowd to think that he was shaking with fear.

The first recorded judicial execution in the British Isles took place in AD 450.

SHOCK

In 1977 in New York a girl aged 16 was taking her dog for a walk on a metallic lead. The dog died of electric shock and the girl was seriously injured when her pet urinated on a faulty electric sign.

London streets have to cope with 4 tons of dog excrement and 3,000 pints of urine every day. The corrosive properties of the latter are a severe problem for lamp-post designers.

SHOES

There are three landmarks in the history of footgear:
1790 – the invention of the shoelace (buckles had previously been used).
1850 – the popularisation of left shoes and right shoes; until that date each shoe was designed to be worn on either foot. George IV was reputedly the first monarch to wear shoes specially tailored for each foot.
1978 – the Goodyear Tyre Company finally reported the result of years of research: right shoes generally wear out faster than left shoes.

☐ See also: *Louis XIV, love, onion.*

SHOPLIFTING

Shoplifting can damage your health. A Nuremburg woman was recently taken to hospital with suspected brain damage after collapsing at the cash desk of a supermarket. She had been overcome by the effects of the frozen chicken which she was trying to smuggle out under her hat.

☐ See also: *death.*

SHREW

Family of small insectivorous mammals (*Soricidae*). The shrew is a very timid creature, easily terrified. Given a sudden shock its heart rate shoots up to nearly 1,000 beats a minute. Like many nervous characters the shrew eats a great deal, on average it consumes up to two-thirds of its own weight every day.

☐ See also: *heroism, sleep.*

SHRIMP

A small decapod crustacean.

☐ See **FLAMINGO.**

SIAM

Known as **THAILAND** since 1939.

☐ See **CELIBACY.**

SIAMESE TWINS

Siamese twins get their name from Chang and Eng Bunker, born of Chinese parents in Siam in 1811, discovered in their teens by Barnum, of Barnum & Bailey's circus, and exhibited throughout North America. The earliest documented case of conjoined twins, however, was seven centuries earlier with the Biddenden maids, Eliza and Mary Chulkhurst, in 1100 in Kent.

Chang and Eng Bunker owned thirty-three slaves between them. They married two sisters from Yorkshire and slept in a bed for four. Later the sisters moved a few miles away from one another and the boys commuted. They fathered twenty-one children. They died within a few hours of one another at the age of 63 in the year 1874, but Chang had been paralysed from a stroke for his last four years, which condemned Eng to lie in bed with him.

Operations to separate Siamese twins (to break the Thai that joins them, one might say) have been successfully performed, but always carry some risk. The most difficult case is that of craniopagous twins (joined by the head). Bodies so united are ever difficult to carry, but the experience of University College Hospital, London, ha

shown that a cricket bag is ideal for the purpose.

James IV of Scotland had a related freak of nature at his court, a 28-year-old named Jean-Jacques Tocci with two legs, two heads and two chests. He (they?) spoke several languages and played music and chess. A pity, really, that he lived before Schubert wrote his sonatas for four hands.

SIBERIA

An area of Asia covering 4,831,822 sq. miles. Solid blocks of tea were used as currency in eighteenth-century Siberia. If a Siberian felt like a cup, he could just hack off a piece and boil up some water from nearby Lake Baykal, which is believed to hold about 20 per cent of all the fresh water on earth. Rats can survive longer without water (or tea) than camels. Nevertheless, there are more rats than camels in Siberia.

SIBLING RIVALRY

Complex psychological phenomenon affecting the motivations of young people within a family group. For a full discussion, see **CHILDREN.**

SICILY

Largest island in the Mediterranean Sea.

☐ See **FIRE OF LONDON.**

SILENCE

The American composer John Cage wrote a piece entitled '4 minutes 33 seconds' which lasted precisely that length of time, during which no sound is made. Reviewing the work, Igor Stravinsky said that he looked forward to future works of the same composer 'of major length'.

SILKWORM

The moth (usually *Bombyx mori*) whose larva produces silk.

☐ See **INTELLIGENCE.**

SINGAPORE

The capital city of Singapore is called 'City of Singapore'.

☐ See **CULTURE.**

SIRIUS

(From the Greek: *seirios*, scorching.) Brightest star in the sky, also known as Alpha Canis Majoris.

☐ See **MALI, RIN-TIN-TIN.**

SKIN

Tissue of two layers (epidermis and dermis) covering the **BODY**. Double-wrapped to keep all the goodness in, as the advertising men have it.

SKIN DISEASE

☐ See **BEAUTY.**

SKULL

Top bit of a skeleton, when upright; the sconce or noddle. In the Indian Chinook tribe, a flat skull is considered a sign of great beauty. Babies' heads are accordingly strapped to a board for the first year of their lives in order to give them a pretty cranium.

Were this procedure to be adopted in Saudi Arabia, it might make it easier to say you are sorry. Kissing the top of a man's head is a sign of apology in that country.

☐ See also: *Byron, Czechoslovakia, Genghis Khan.*

SLAVERY

Some types of ant steal eggs from the nests of other species and rear the young as slaves after they have hatched. In 1949, it was discovered that ants had eaten through a beam in the ceiling of the bedroom of Cardinal Giovanni Mercati, librarian and archivist of the Roman Catholic Church in the Vatican. The damage was discovered just in time to prevent the collapse of the entire ceiling. For their sins, the ants were not excommunicated, but their nests were destroyed.

Although slavery among both ants and humans was prevalent in biblical times, there is no explicit condemnation of the practice in either the Old or the New Testament.

SLEEP

The desert snail has been known to sleep for three or four years without waking up. This contrasts greatly with the sleeping habits of the short-tailed shrew and the elephant, both of which need only two hours sleep a day. But the elephant's penis may be 5 feet long.

☐ See also: ***brain, colour-blindness, dormouse, horse, knowledge, maternity, otter, penguin, polar bear, seal, sedative.***

SLIMMING

At any given moment 13 per cent of the British population are trying to lose weight. In any single year, one out of every four will have been on some sort of **DIET**. Raw celery provides the eater with less calories than it takes to digest. So a person who eats only celery will, other things being equal, starve to death more quickly than one who eats nothing at all.

SLOTH

The three-toed sloth (*Bradypus*) moves at a rate of between 6 and 8 feet per minute, which is slower than the average tortoise. Nevertheless, it does have six more ribs than an elephant. It only bothers to move at all when food runs out and, according to some authorities, it only defecates in rainy weather. (The raindrops muffle the sound as its droppings pass through the trees.) Neither the three-toed nor the two-toed sloth (*Choloepus*) has any teeth.

Sloth is the collective noun for a group of bears.

SMELL

Dogs are far from being the best creatures to use for tracking purposes. Eels have a

much keener sense of smell than dogs. Or if you are looking for something with blood in it, the shark may be your best bet; a shark can smell one part of blood in 100 million parts water. The human nose is not a bad close-range sniffer; it can distinguish approximately 10,000 different smells.

NAIL

A gastropod mollusc with an external shell. Before 1914 snails used to be eaten by Bristol glassblowers to improve their lung power.

Thanks to the sticky carpet exuded in their wake, snails can crawl along the edge of a razor blade without coming to any harm.

□ See also: *discipline, sleep, tuberculosis.*

NAKE

(From the Anglo-Saxon; *snaca*, a snake.) During the Second World War, the unique collection of pickled snakes at London's Natural History Museum was evacuated to the safety of caves in Surrey. A snake, even before it has been pickled, can go for a whole year between meals. They are totally deaf, but can pick up vibrations with their tongues.

□ See also: *barrel-organ, Cyprus, eyelid, hedgehog, Hitler, Madagascar, python, sedative, vinegar.*

NAKEBITE

The testes of a hippopotamus taken in water in doses of one drachm (or thereabouts) is a cure for snakebite according to Pliny the Elder. The raw materials might well be obtained from Hungary, which exports more hippopotamus than any other European country. Their health-giving mineral springs have been given the credit for the great hippo boom in Hungarian zoos.

More deaths in Burma result from snake-bites than from road accidents. The Burmese should perhaps consider importing more hippo testes from Hungary. Those hippopotamic Hungarian juggernauts would have every chance of altering the statistics back in favour of road accidents.

In times of acute hippo shortage, fear not! For the genitalia of a stag taken in wine is an equally potent antidote to snakebite.

□ See also: *bee, sport.*

SNEEZING

If you want to sneeze, first inhale deeply, then momentarily close the glottis and contract the abdominal muscles strongly, pressing the viscera against the diaphragm, thus raising the pressure in the lungs. Finally open the glottis, and a strong current of air may be directed through the nose.

The thirteenth-century astrologer and magician, Michael Scot, gave detailed rules for interpreting the predictive nature of sneezes made in the course of a business venture: if you sneeze twice or four times, you must get up and walk round if you want your scheme to be successful; one sneeze after a contract is made indicates that it will be kept, but three sneezes means that it will be broken. If you sneeze twice in the night on three successive nights, a death in the house is predicted. (Modern medical opinion inclines more towards diagnosis of a common cold in this last case.)

□ See also: *handkerchief.*

SNORING

A British patent was taken out in 1955 for an alarm to waken snorers. A microphone on the head board above the sleeper's nose would detect the snore and set a hinged board shaking beneath his pillow. Unaccountably it was never a commercial success. Gorillas never snore.

□ See also: *knowledge.*

SNOW

Ten inches of snow provides as much water as one inch of rain. If you only require one teaspoon of water, it is wise to remember that there are as many molecules in a

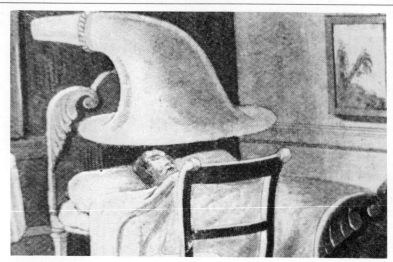

Servant listens for His Master's Snore in the next room

teaspoon of water as there are teaspoons of water in the Atlantic. There are also as many stars in the Milky Way as people who have ever lived.

☐ See also: ***Antarctica.***

SNUFF

☐ See **BURIAL.**

SOAP

Cleanliness was next to lasciviousness as far as Demetrius Poliorcetes, King of Macedonia (337–282 BC), was concerned. He instigated a tax on soap specifically to provide the funds to enable him to afford the services of a particularly expensive courtesan.

According to a 1984 survey, the average Frenchman uses only two bars of soap a year. Worse still, half of them never use a toothbrush and 31 per cent change their underwear only infrequently. The women are not so bad, but 10 per cent still make a habit of wearing dirty knickers.

☐ See also: ***body, Einstein, Netherlands.***

SOCIAL DEMOCRATIC PARTY
☐ See **LENIN.**

SOCIOLOGY
☐ See **POSSLQ, SCIENCE.**

SOCKS
(From the Anglo-Saxon, *socc*; Latin: *soccus*, a small shoe.) The highest ever laundry bill for a sock was the estimated £800 for cleansing a woollen sock thrown away by a tenth-century Viking warrior. The sock had been preserved in bogland in York, England, until discovered in 1983. It is generally believed that the average Viking could, in fact, have had a pair of socks cleaned for less than £1,600, but after 1,000 years without a wash, they can get pretty filthy. Albert Einstein hated wearing socks.

☐ See also: ***trousers.***

SOLOMON ISLANDS
☐ See **COCONUT, WEALTH.**

SOMALIA
Until 1973 Somali was only a spoken, not a written language. In graveyards in Somalia, only the male corpses are allowed to have headstones. They are, however, more generous with their camels, having about six camels for every ten people. The comparable rate for automobiles works out at about one car per 200 camels. Somalia has 32 per cent of the world's camels.

SOOTHSAYING
When a soothsayer is asked to predict the hour of his own death, he has to be very careful. Martius Galeotti, soothsayer to King Louis XI of France, answered this tricky question by announcing that he would die 'twenty-four hours before Your Majesty'. This bright response earned his careful protection from his master. It seems that he borrowed the answer from an old soothsayers' trick book. Thrasullus gave an identical reply to the Emperor Tiberius, with equally protective results.

SOPHOCLES (495–405 BC)
Accused by his children of insanity, Sophocles' defence in the Athens court was to read his recently finished play *Oedipus at Colonus*, asking the judges whether the author of such a performance could be mad. He was acquitted and lived to the age of 91.

Sophocles' own children may not have appreciated him, but Shelley certainly did. Drowned in a sailing accident in 1822, Shelley's body was found with a volume of Sophocles in one of his pockets and some of Keats's poetry in the other. Byron was at the funeral.

SORCERY
The last time a cow was publicly hanged for sorcery (or indeed for anything else) was in 1740 in Paris.

SORE THROAT
☐ See **FOOTWEAR, HERRING, TOAD.**

SOUP
Seal-hunting vessels in Newfoundland are obliged by law to serve soup on Saturdays. Fortunately there is no similarly mandatory tureen in New Jersey, where it is illegal to slurp soup in a restaurant.

☐ See also: ***eucalyptus.***

SOUTH AFRICA
Each year South Africa moves 2 inches further away from South America. This is usually ascribed to continental drift, but some part may also be played by the use of rhinoceros urine as a disinfectant in South Africa. The male rhino urinates in a highly pressurised spray. The female rhino has a gestation period of 560 days.

SPACE INVADERS
☐ See **DISEASE.**

SPAGHETTI
(Italian, meaning little ropes.) Kentishman

John Blakesley won a return trip for two to New York's Little Italy when he ate 100 yards of spaghetti in a London restaurant in a time of 1 min 31 sec. The competition must have been short of top class since his winning time was more than a minute outside the world record.

☐ See also: *genius, Uruguay.*

SPAIN

☐ See **ANDORRA, BRAVERY, HOMOSEXUALITY, MISOGYNY, SAN MARINO, YUGOSLAVIA.**

SPECTACLES

(From the Latin: *spectare*, intensive form of *specere*, to look at.)

☐ See **INDUSTRIAL ACCIDENT, SATIE.**

SPEED

The Cuban land crab can scuttle at speeds of up to 20 mph. Not bad for a crustacean, but in 1970 a runaway deer in Manchester registered 42 mph on a police radar trap. A cheetah can accelerate from zero to 45 mph in two seconds. Its top speed is over 60 mph, but it can only keep up the pace for about 300 yards. In 1936, Jesse Owens beat a racehorse over a 100-yard race. The falcon, however, is faster than any of them. At full pelt, in a dive, it has been known to touch 300 mph.

SPELLING

There are 127 recorded different ways of spelling the surname 'Raleigh'. In 1592, Sir Walter Raleigh was imprisoned, not for spelling his name 127 different ways, but for misbehaviour with Elizabeth Throgmorton, one of the maids of honour to the Queen. Sir Thomas Malory wrote his *Morte d'Arthur* while in prison on a rape charge.

☐ See also: *Edward VIII, Shakespeare.*

SPERM

The sperm of the mouse are longer than those of men, bulls, elephants or whales. The sperm of the human male are worse swimmers than those of any other animal.

SPERMICIDE

The death rate among sperm is staggering. Every sexually potent man produces some 200 million a day. Each year in England and Wales approximately 177,181,200 billion sperm are ejaculated in heterosexual activity alone, and almost all of these are doomed to give their lives in vain.

SPIDER

Arthropod of the order Araneidae of the class Arachnida. The total weight of insects eaten each year by the world's spiders exceeds the combined weight of all human beings on earth.

The harvestman spider distracts predators by detaching one of its legs. The freed leg continues twitching to keep the predator interested, while its former owner scuttles away on all sevens.

☐ See also: *gorilla, Mauritania, parsley, pets.*

SPIRITUALISM

☐ See **BURIAL.**

SPITTING

(From the Old Norse: *spyta*, to spit.) Among the Masai tribesmen of Kenya spitting is considered an act of friendship and trust. Meeting, bidding farewell, and making bargains are all marked by salutatory spit.

Spitting upon a finger and pressing it behind one's left ear is part of an old Worcestershire treatment for burns.

☐ See also: *melon, salivation.*

SPONGE

A lowly animal of the zoological phylum Porifera. Often found in colonies, the solitary sponge is also sometimes found in sea or **BATH.**

POONERISM

The butterfly was originally called the flutterby, a more logical descriptive name. Nobody is sure how the change happened.

PORT

The horsemen of northern Afghanistan play a version of polo in winter, but without the inconvenience of polo stick or ball. Instead the riders carry the headless body of a calf, trying to deposit it in the opponents' goal. Players are allowed to whip and kick the man with the calf, but off-the-calf fouls are frowned upon. The game is called Buzkashi.

On the whole, the Burmese are easier to keep amused. A popular pastime for them is to put two fish in a jar and watch them fight. Burma has the world's highest mortality rate from snakebite.

☐ See also: *Israel.*

SQUASH

(From the Old French: *esquacer*, to crush.) Trendy game.

☐ See **CHAMPAGNE.**

QUID

A ten-armed cephalopod. The giant squid is the largest living creature without a backbone. Its eyeball is over a foot in diameter. No giant squid has ever been taught to talk, but when a parrot talks its (the parrot's) eyes contract.

QUINTING

The most influential squint in English history may well have been that of Sir John Trevor, Speaker of the House of Commons between 1690 and 1694. Until his time, when the Speaker wished to call a Member to say his piece, he would indicate by pointing. So confusing was Sir John's squint, however, that when he pointed two Members would frequently rise together. Thanks to this, the rules of the House were changed and all subsequent Speakers have had to learn the names of all Members in order to call them to deliver their oratory.

SQUIRREL

(From the Greek: *skia*, shadow; *oura*, tail.)

☐ See **ENGLISH.**

SRI LANKA

The Tamils of Sri Lanka (formerly Ceylon) inhale the fumes of crushed red ants as a cure for the common cold. Before a rainstorm, ants move to higher ground. There is some reason to believe that this behaviour might be an attempt to escape from any Tamil who catches cold in the rain.

STALIN, Josef Vissarionovich (1879–1953)

Born Josef Dzhugashvili, he changed his name to Stalin. *Stal* in Russian means steel; Dzhugashvili, in his native Georgian, had connotations of worthlessness. Not only Stalin's name was a cosmetic embellishment; the pipe on which he was always meditatively chewing in photographs was only there to give him a homely, avuncular image. In private he would chain smoke cigarettes. Molotov is the Russian for Hammer.

☐ See also: *doodling, Lenin, Marx.*

STAMMERING

Arnold Bennett, Somerset Maugham and Nevil Shute were all stammerers. So was Demosthenes, but he cured his affliction by training himself to speak with a mouthful of pebbles. He grew to become the greatest orator of his time. A more modern treatment for stammering recommends learning to substitute words beginning with labial consonants for those beginning with the plosives which set off the stammer. But one cannot help feeling sorry for the poor boozer who has to settle for a half of mild when he wants a pint of bitter.

STARFISH

The starfish is the only animal able to turn

its stomach inside out voluntarily. It has an eye on the end of each arm and can exert a constant pull of 3 lb. This is a superb piece of design, since that is just the force required to open an oyster.

☐ See also: *rubber.*

STARLING

(*Sturnus vulgaris*) Insectivorous bird with black plumage with green and purple reflections. In 1890, Eugene Scheillfin began a project to introduce into America all birds mentioned in the works of Shakespeare. The starling occurs only once (*Henry IV*, Part One, Act I, scene iii; Hotspur: 'I'll have a starling shall be taught to speak . . . '). Starlings were consequently set loose in New York's Central Park and now there are millions all over America.

In 1945 Big Ben in London lost five minutes because of the weight of a flock of starlings which had perched on the minute hand.

☐ See also: *musical composition.*

STATUE

You can tell from the statue of a mounted horseman (if it has been constructed in the traditional manner) how the rider met his death. If all four of the horse's feet are on the ground, he passed away from natural causes; three on the ground and one raised signifies that he died of wounds sustained in battle; two legs raised and two down means that the rider died in action. There are no known statues of horses standing on one leg. A statue by Joseph Wilton of George III on horseback, erected in Berkeley Square, London, was made of such a heavy mix of lead and zinc that the weight of the rider made the horse's legs go bandy. The whole structure was hastily removed.

☐ See also: *Austria.*

STATUE OF LIBERTY
☐ See **EIFFEL.**

STERILITY

(From the Latin: *sterilis*, barren.)

☐ See **HYENA.**

STEVENSON, Robert Louis (1850–94)

Born Robert Lewis Balfour Stevenson, th novelist chose to alter the spelling of h second name and to drop the third. H father was a lighthouse engineer. R. L Stevenson liked to use cocaine to stimula his creative processes. He is buried on th summit of Mount Vaea, near Apia, th capital of Western Samoa.

STILTS

(From the Middle English: *stilte*, a stilt.)

☐ See **ALBERT I, King of Belgium.**

STIRRUP

(From the Anglo-Saxon: *stirap* or *stigra* from *stigan*, to climb; *rap*, a rope.) Assis ance in mounting and riding horses.

☐ See **COWBOY, MANURE.**

STOAT

Carnivorous mammal of the weasel tribe whose winter coat gives us ermine.

☐ See **OVERCROWDING.**

STOCKS

The first man in Boston to be sentenced t be locked in the stocks was their construc tor, a Mr Palmer. His bill to the Bosto authorities for building the device in 163 was considered to be excessive.

The last use of the stocks in England wa in Newbury on 11 June 1872, when Mar Tuck, 'an incorrigible bacchanalian', wa sentenced to four hours in the stocks fc insobriety and creating a disturbance in th parish church.

Stocks, which hold a man by his leg should not be confused with the pillor which clams head and arms.

☐ See also: *kissing.*

TOKER, Bram (1847–1912)
☐ See **TANZANIA.**

TOMACH ACHE
This ailment can have a number of causes. When one Lateef Daramola was taken to hospital complaining of stomach pains, X-rays revealed thirty-two keys, one padlock, one ring, a wristwatch (complete with band), some pieces of broken bottles, some nail-cutters, earrings and coins, and two safety pins.

TOPES, Marie Carmichael (1880–1958)
The first marriage of birth control pioneer Marie Stopes left her a virgin divorcee. Later she found less restrictive ways to plan families and produced a son after marrying again at the age of 38. She did not like the idea of getting old, so always celebrated her twenty-sixth birthday. On her 45th twenty-sixth birthday, at the age of 70, she demonstrated her fitness and agility by sticking her big toe in her mouth. According to a recent estimate, over 15 per cent of Americans secretly bite their own toenails.

TORK
Family of large birds (Ciconiidae) of the heron tribe. In northern Germany there is a belief that no fire will ever damage a building upon which there is a stork's nest. Storks are therefore allowed, and indeed encouraged, to build their nests everywhere.

In 1831 a boy aged 9 was hanged in England for arson. The building to which he was accused of setting fire is believed to have had no stork's nest on it. Statistics show that arson in Britain is most commonly committed seven days after a new moon.

☐ See also: *Aborigine.*

TRACHEY, Giles Lytton (1880–1932)
'The horror of getting up is unparalleled, and I am filled with amazement every morning when I find that I have done it' (Lytton Strachey).

☐ See **LAST WORDS.**

STRAVINSKY, Igor Fedorovich (1882–1971)
Russian composer.

☐ See **SILENCE.**

STRAWBERRY
The white or yellow five-petalled flowers of the strawberry plant (*Fragaria*) are unisexual.

☐ See **BREASTS, MACARONI.**

STRING
(From the Anglo-Saxon: *streng.*) The correct word for a morbid fear of string is linonophobia. General Gebhard von Blücher was a brave soldier who could laugh in the face of a piece of string, but he did have a morbid fear that he would give birth to an elephant.

Gebhard von Blücher

SUBMARINE

☐ See **PIANOFORTE**.

SUGAR

The Bulgarians are the greatest consumers of sugar ($C_{12}H_{22}O_{11}$) in the world. Cats, on the other hand, cannot taste sweet food at all. They would therefore probably be unimpressed by the serendipity berry, discovered in Nigeria in the 1960s, which is 1,500 times sweeter than sugar. Serendip was the old name of Ceylon, now Sri Lanka.

SUICIDE

Spring and summer are the most common seasons for suicide, in the afternoon rather than the morning, during times of peace rather than war, and when unemployment is high. More women than men attempt suicide in most countries, but doctors kill themselves at twice the average rate. Unemployed female doctors on a peaceful spring afternoon are considered to be at great risk.

A popular method of committing suicide in ancient China was to eat a pound of salt.

☐ See also: *astrology, bargaining, cookery, lobster, marriage, Marx, psychiatry, Purcell, traffic.*

SULLIVAN, Sir Arthur Seymour (1842–1900)

☐ See **GILBERT**.

SUNDAY TRADING

The British laws regarding Sunday trading have a perhaps unjustified reputation for complexity and inconsistency. Simply expressed, they allow you, in England on a Sunday, to buy soft pornographic magazines and aspirin, but not a toothbrush or a Bible. If desperate, you can buy a Bible at an airport on a Sunday. In Scotland, you can buy what you like, but you cannot get your hair cut by a barber.

SUPPER, The Last

☐ See **ORANGE**.

SURGERY

(Originally chirurgery, from the Gree *cheirourgos – cheir*, hand; *ergon*, a work The Barber-Surgeons Company w founded in 1461 when blood-letting ar other minor operations were the provin of the versatile barbers. Almost three ce turies passed before, in 1751, the fin break came between the Barbers' and Su geons' trades. The barber's pole is symbo of a bandage wrapped round an arm pri to blood-letting. In Hong Kong the sam pole is used as a sign of a brothel.

SURVEYING

☐ See **CONVEYANCING**.

SURVIVAL

A blue whale can survive for six months its own blubber without eating. This approximately 5 months 29½ days long than a mole can go without a meal, sin moles must eat at least once every twel hours. A human being deprived of slee will die more quickly than one deprived food.

☐ See also: *bedbug.*

SWAN

Small genus (*Cygnus*) of large birds.

☐ See **FEATHERS, NAPOLEON I**.

SWEARING

Under the Profane Oaths Act of 174 labourers could be fined one shilling p oath, but those under the degree of gentl men (but not labourers) had to pay tw shillings, and gentlemen or above forfeit five shillings for every oath uttered. Wome could swear for nothing.

It is still illegal to swear in the Roy Parks.

SWEDEN

Although Sweden has more old people p head of population than any other count (one in six is over 65), Albania claims t highest rate for women over 50 giving birth. In 1967, Albania became the first officially atheist state in the world.

☐ See also: *body, coffee, compensation, Descartes, discipline, fertiliser, Gabon, geography, Gustav III, louse.*

SWIMMING

Hippopotamuses, gorillas and elephants cannot swim, though the elephant can use its trunk as a snorkel and the hippo is jolly good at running along the sea bed while holding its breath. Ostriches and moles can swim (one mole was once spotted enjoying a dip 1½ miles offshore in a Scottish loch). Prawns walk forwards, but swim backwards. Flies take off backwards, but fly forwards.

☐ See also: *crocodile, Henry VIII, ocean, pregnancy, sperm.*

Quite apart from the beautiful sound of cowbells, Switzerland can offer the world's first hang-gliding taxi service.

☐ See also: *Australia, chocolate, discipline, witchcraft.*

SYPHILIS

(Originally the title of a 1530 Latin poem by Fracastoro, of which the hero, *Syphilis*, had syphilis.) Sixteenth-century astrologers believed this disease to be caused by the conjunction of Saturn, Jupiter and Mars in Cancer, which did terrible things to corrupt the air. Petrus Maynardus, who taught medicine at Padua, said that only men born under Scorpio, the sign which rules the genitals, were subject to this disease. He further predicted, incorrectly as it turned out, that syphilis would totally vanish after a conjunction in 1584.

The hazards of swimming

SWITZERLAND

Swiss citizenship is not the easiest to obtain. In December 1983, Vit Stupak, a Czechoslovakian, was refused Swiss citizenship after a village meeting at his home town of Adligenswil in Switzerland. The village council considered that his dislike of cowbells showed that he was not properly assimilated, despite having lived there for fourteen years.

It used to be believed (and still is among some Italian peasants) that a man could be cured of syphilis by having intercourse with a virgin.

☐ See also: *Antigua, aural sex.*

SYRIA

The only battle in history which featured elephants on both sides was fought during the fourth Syrian War in 217 BC. In battle, or just going about its normal daily chores, an elephant will generally use only one of its tusks. Some elephants are right-tusked, others left-tusked. Jack the Ripper and the Emperor Tiberius were both left-handed.

☐ See also: ***hamster.***

T

TABLE MANNERS
☐ See **ETIQUETTE, NASAL SEX.**

TABOO
(From the Tongan: *tabu*, holy, unclean, to be shunned.) The Malagasy Indians, indigenous natives of Madagascar, have a number of strange taboos. It is considered terribly bad form for a pregnant woman to eat eels or to wear a hat, while there is little worse a man can do than eat an animal's rump while his father still lives. A son is also strictly forbidden to grow taller than his father; should he wish to do so, he must first pay the sum of one ox to buy the right.

TAFT, William Howard (1857–1930)
William Taft, President of the United States 1908–12, weighed 350 lb, which bulk caused him to become stuck in his bath at the White House, wedged tight. Following his rescue, he diagnosed the true cause of his misfortune and promptly ordered the installation of a bigger bath.

TAIWAN
Taiwan (capital Taipei) is the largest exporter of mushrooms in the world, but Madagascar produces most vanilla.

TANZANIA
The Masai tribesmen of Tanzania like to drink the blood from the jugular vein of sheep or cattle. They shoot special arrows into the neck of the creature in order to tap the blood. The Nuer tribe of the upper Nile also like a quick swig of blood occasionally, but they boil it first in order to add to the thickness. In the Second World War, the milk from young coconuts was successfully used as a substitute for blood plasma in transfusions. Vampire-creator, Bram Stoker, attributed the idea for *Dracula* to a nightmare following his dining on crabs.

☐ See also: *dove, war.*

TARANTULA
In America, the tarantula is venomous and catches birds; in Africa it bites, but is not venomous; in Australia it is harmless (but the red-back and funnel-web are killers); in southern Europe, it comes from Taranto in south Italy (hence the name), its bite was believed to cause the hysteria known as tarantism, but it could be cured by dancing a tarantella. The tarantula cannot spin a web.

TASTELESSNESS
(See illustration overleaf) cf. **KITSCH.**

TATTOO
During the Second World War, a tattooed man was 1½ times more likely to be

A hall-porter's chair

rejected for service in the US Armed Forces than a man without illustrations. Of the tattooees rejected, the reason given in 58 per cent of cases was neuro-psychiatric abnormalities. This was all reported in a study by Captain Joseph Lauder and Corporal Harold M. Kohn in the *American Journal of Psychiatry*, where they further noted that a man with a nude tattoo was more likely to be rejected as abnormal, than a man with a flag or landscape adorning his person.

If tattooee is a real word (authorities differ on this point), then it is one of the only three English words with three consecutive pairs of double letters. Bookkeeper and bookkeeping are the other two (and spoil-sports spell them with a hyphen to ruin the effect).

☐ See also: **Maori.**

TAX

Income Tax was first levied at 3 per cent in the United States in 1864 to help finance the Civil War. It was declared unconstitutional by the Supreme Court thirty years later, but finally made inevitable by the sixteenth amendment in 1913. Anyone who sells his blood for research or biological purposes in the United States has the profit taxed just as though he were disposing of any other liquid asset.

Told, on her deathbed in 1820, that nothing was as certain as death, Elisa Bonaparte, sister of Napoleon I, expired after uttering the words: 'Except taxes'.

☐ See also: **Gilbert, hedgehog, pampered pets.**

TAXI

(Abbreviation of *taxicab*)

☐ See **FREDERICK WILLIAM I of Prussia, SWITZERLAND.**

TAYLOR, Elizabeth (*b.* 1932)

In the contest for 'Most Memorable Eyebrows of 1976', Miss Elizabeth Taylor was runner-up. The title was awarded to the dog, Lassie. In third place was Vice-President Walter Mondale.

The whale does not have memorable eyebrows, but its eyeball is fixed in position in its head. If it wants to change its line of sight it must move its whole body.

TEA

Beverage brewed from the leaves of the tea plant (in Chinese: *cha*).

☐ See **APOPLEXY, BUILDING, CEYLON, COFFEE, HAZLITT, SIBERIA.**

TEAPOT

Vessel for brewing the leaves of the tea plant.

☐ See **TOULOUSE-LAUTREC.**

TEARS

In ancient Persia, the tears of mourners were saved and bottled. They were believed have the power to cure a number of diseases. The tears of a hippopotamus form the staple diet of a type of small worm, exclusive to the hippo, which lives under its eyelids.

] See also: *witches.*

CASING

According to a 1943 American survey, there are 151 different ways of teasing a child aged less than 6 years.

TECHNOLOGY

Michelangelo designed the tunics which were worn by the Swiss Guard at the Vatican. This design remained unchanged for 450 years before it finally had to be amended to keep pace with the white-heat of the technological revolution. The necessary modification was a pocket to carry tear-gas grenades.

] See also: *Curie.*

TEETH

(Plural of tooth. From the Anglo-Saxon: *toth-* plural *teth-*, a tooth; as for example in *toth-wyrm*, a tooth-worm.) The early Spaniards used to clean their teeth in urine. George Washington, however, preferred to soak his false teeth in port at night to improve the flavour. He had several sets fashioned from various materials which may help to explain why the taste needed to be improved. Elephant tusks, lead, and the teeth of cows, hippos, humans and something thought to be a walrus all took their place amid the Washington gums. When he became president in 1789, he still had two of his own teeth, plus another one which had fallen out but had been remounted on a denture.

☐ See also: *Apollonia, beaver, bombing, butterfly, Cameroon, Elizabeth I, extraction, Fiji, hair, Kenya, Liechtenstein, Montez, mosquito, Richard III, Scarborough, turtle, umbrella, wealth.*

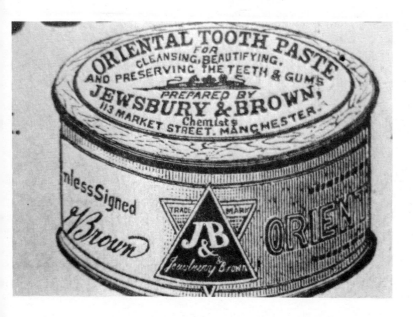

TEL AVIV

Commercial capital of Israel.

☐ See **NEW YORK, NUDITY.**

TELEPHONE

(From the Greek: *tele*, afar; *phone*, sound.) Alexander Graham **BELL**, inventor of the telephone, set a world water speed record of 70 mph in a boat driven by a hydrofoil in 1919. In 1963, a giraffe in Chester Zoo was discovered to be the cause of many wrong numbers in the city. It had developed a playful habit of reaching up and grabbing with its tongue the telephone wires above its enclosure. It would then twang the wires back, release them and watch them all tangle up. Normal telephone service was resumed when the telegraph pole was raised 4 feet.

☐ See also: *civilisation, Denmark, Iceland, interment.*

TELEVISION

In a recent survey, it was found that 44 per cent of American children between the age of 4 and 6 years prefer the television set to Daddy.

☐ See also: *Grenada, media.*

TELEX

☐ See **CIVILISATION.**

TEMPERATURE

On a hot day the Eiffel Tower may expand to a height 6 inches above its normal cold position. The temperature cricket also chirps faster when it is warmer. The precise temperature may be caculated by timing the noises of this insect. If c is the number of chirps per minute, the temperature in degrees fahrenheit is given by the formula: $\frac{1}{4}c + 40$. If this is really accurate, the poor insect begins to produce negative chirps as the temperature approaches freezing point.

TENNIS

The game of Lawn Tennis was first played in 1879. Thirteen years later it was intr duced to Korea with an exhibition mat played on the courts of the British Legati in the presence of Queen Min and Ki Kojong. The Queen was heard to comme of the players: 'These Englishmen a becoming very hot. Why do they not ha their servants do it?'

One hundred years after the birth tennis, Elizabeth Ryan, holder of ninete Wimbledon titles, died at the age of 87. H death came on the same day that Billie-Je King overtook her record by winning h twentieth title, 6 July 1979.

☐ See also: *breathing, Charles VIII.*

TENNYSON, Alfred, Lord (1809–92)

Tennyson's last words, when he died 6 October 1892, were: 'I have opened i Nobody has the faintest idea what he w talking about.

☐ See also: *Shaw, Wordsworth.*

TENPIN BOWLING

The origin of tenpin bowling stems from an eighteenth-century law in Connecticut which made it illegal to bowl at nine pins. To evade the law a tenth pin was added to the traditional game. In Minnesota, it is illegal to hang male and female underwear on the same washing line.

TERMITE

From the Latin: *termes, termitis*, a woodworm.) The termite produces a substance which will rust steel, burn through lead and disintegrate glass. With such an inherently scandalous nature, it is hardly surprising that the courtship of a royal couple of termites is also a violent affair. They seal themselves into the nuptial cell and fore-play consists of eating between one and five segments from each other's antennae; they copulate three days later.

☐ See also: *aardvark, navy, Uganda.*

TERRAPIN

'Terrapin' is a North American Indian word meaning 'edible'. In ancient China stewed turtle or tortoise were among their favourite delicacies, but so were wolf breast, dog liver and fried great crane, so they were perhaps not really too fussy about their food.

TESTICLE

Diminutive of the Latin, *testis*.)

☐ See **ABORTION, BOTSWANA, FOX, ORCHID, SCULPTURE, TRANSPLANT, WEASEL.**

TEXAS

The state of Texas appears to be the source of more folk remedies for sore throat than anywhere else on earth. Among them are the following:

(i) tie nine knots in a piece of black thread, dip it in turpentine and wrap it round your neck;

(ii) attach a piece of string to a strip of bacon. Swallow the bacon, then pull it back up by the end of the string;

(iii) have a complete stranger blow into your mouth;

(iv) tie a bag of red ants round your neck. When they are all dead, the sore throat will be gone.

☐ See also: *boils, wealth.*

THAILAND

Any white elephant found in Thailand must be given to the king; it is a sign of good luck.

☐ See also: *Bangkok, celibacy.*

THATCHER, Margaret (*b.* 1925)

☐ See **CLEOPATRA.**

THEATRE

In ancient China, descendants of leading actors were not allowed to enter for public examinations for three generations. The British monarchy viewed this behaviour with total apathy, since Charles II was the first British king to go to the theatre.

☐ See also: *thespians.*

THEFT

A million cars are stolen every year in the United States. If you are looking for a car to steal, Los Angeles is a good place to find one. Over a quarter of the free ground area of Los Angeles is covered by cars.

☐ See also: *artistic appreciation, Boleyn, Burma, punishment, robbery.*

THEODOSIUS I (346–395)

East Roman Emperor forced by St Ambrose to do public penance after ordering the massacre of some 7,000 in Thessalonica, after a Roman officer had been killed in the town.

☐ See **ALECTRYOMANCY.**

THEOLOGY

One goddess worshipped by the Romans was named Robigo (or Rubigo). She was the goddess who protected crops from mildew. The festival of Robigalia was celebrated on 25 April and it was customary to offer her the entrails of a sheep and of a dog.

According to the table of permissible defect levels published by the US Food and Drug Administration, asparagus must not be sold to the public if 10 per cent of the spears are infested with six asparagus beetle eggs, or if there are found to be 40 thrips or 5 insects in a 100 g sample.

THESPIANS

(From Thespis, a Greek poet of Attica, supposed to be the inventor of tragedy around 536 BC.) Until 1660 all women's parts in the English theatre were played by men. The first major performance by a woman on the London stage was that of Margaret Hughes, on 8 December 1660, in the role of Desdemona in *Othello*, played in Clare Market. Margaret Hughes was the mistress of Prince Rupert, the grandson of James I. In 1662 Charles II passed a law legalising the practice of women appearing on stage. In 1899 Sarah Bernhardt pushed forward new frontiers by playing the role of Hamlet. She had her leg amputated fifteen years later. The role of Hamlet contains 11,610 words.

THOMAS, Dylan Marlais (1914–53)

Dylan Thomas once drank eighteen straight whiskies. It was practically the last thing he did.

THOTHMES III, King of Egypt (sixteenth century BC)

Son of Thothmes II, grandson of Thothmes I, nephew of Hatshepsut who was also his stepmother. He married his half-sister. If his mummy is to be trusted he was less than 5 feet tall.

□ See **CLEOPATRA**.

THRACE

Ancient state in the Balkans. When a Thracian warrior died, his wives would fig for the privilege of being killed and buri alongside him. This touching display marital fidelity was normal practice I tween about 1300 BC and 500 BC.

THURBER, James Grover (1894–1961)

□ See **CARTOONS**.

TIBERIUS, Emperor of Rome (24 BC–AD ?

The Emperor Tiberius declined the offe put to him by the Senate, to have the mor November named after him, as Julius a Augustus had given their names to t months of their own births. 'What will y do when you have thirteen emperor was his rhetorical reply. Until the la eighteenth century, the accent on July English was on the first syllable.

□ See also: *soothsaying, Syria.*

TIBET

□ See **ETIQUETTE, WEDDING CUSTOMS**.

TIERRA DEL FUEGO

(From the Spanish: Land of fire.)
□ See **FAMINE**.

TIGER

(*Felis tigris*) Although cats are said to ha nine lives, the Nepalese tiger is allow only three. In Nepal it is permitted to sho and kill a tiger only after it has be responsible for the deaths of three peopl

□ See also: *carpentry, panda.*

TIN

Metallic element, chemical symbol: (from the Latin: *stannum*, tin). Worki flat out, a Cornish tin mine pump co raise 19,000 gallons of water while fuell by 12 bushels of coal. This is the origin the expression '19 to the dozen'. It w impossible to hurry before the time Shakespeare. The best one could do wh pushed for time was to make haste, sin

Felis tigris

Shakespeare's writings are the first recorded instance of the verb 'to hurry'.

TINTORETTO (1518–94)

Italian painter whose real name was Jacopo Robusti. When he painted his 'Israelites Gathering Manna in the Wilderness', Tintoretto depicted Moses' men as having shotguns slung over their arms. The shotgun was not in fact invented until 1326.

TIPPING

In the eighteenth century, it was customary for a nobleman to tip the executioner between £7 and £10 before the latter lopped off his head. This act of generosity helped to ensure that the man would at least sharpen his axe before coming to work.

One explanation of the derivation of the verb 'to tip' is that it is an acronym for 'to insure promptness'. Perhaps in the case of an execution, the tipper might welcome a delay.

TOAD

A cure for sore throat dating back to 1855 recommends taking three toads, tied together by their legs, and leaving them in the sun to dry and decay. When that process is sufficiently advanced, the string is worn around the neck of the sufferer.

Take care when selecting your toads. The male midwife toad carries eggs laid by the female.

☐ See also: ***boils, eye.***

TOE

(From the Anglo-Saxon: *ta*, plural *tan*, a toe.) An old Texan remedy for ingrowing toenails is to tie a lizard's liver to a leather thong and attach it to the left ankle. The nail will be cured in nine days. For pigeon toes, an Australian remedy recommends wearing a pair of shoes one size too large, put on the wrong feet and kept on in bed. It is a common misapprehension that this is the way most Australians behave even without ingrowing toenails.

☐ See also: ***popery, Stopes.***

TOILET

☐ See **BRAILLE, BUMPH, CHIENS, CHILE, GENIUS.**

TOLSTOY, Count Leo Nikolayevich (1828–1910)

The Moscow Society of Velocipede Lovers gave Tolstoy a present of a bicycle when he was 67 years old. He had never ridden one before, but took lessons and learned quickly. There are over 500 characters in *War and Peace*, a fat book by Tolstoy. 'Tolstoy' is the Russian for 'fat'.

☐ See also: ***excursions.***

TONGA

(Also known as the Friendly Islands.) Polynesian divers in Tonga used to hold underwater walking races. The capital is called Nuku'alofa.

TONGUE

☐ See **CHAMELEON, REINDEER.**

TONSILLITIS

☐ See **BANANA, VINEGAR.**

TOOTHACHE

When Homly the Elephant had toothache at Bloemfontein Zoo in South Africa in 1981, a team of seventeen doctors and dentists was called into action, armed to the teeth with enough anaesthetic to kill seventy men. The tooth was drilled and packed with £100 worth of amalgam. It was the first such dental work performed on an elephant. The main problem according to the dentists was that its big tongue and flappy cheeks obscured the view inside its mouth.

The cause of the toothache in the first place was not clearly identified, but it was probably not doughnuts, considered by dental researchers to be the least harmful of sweets. Fudge and plain chocolate are the worst for encouraging tooth decay.

☐ See also: *abortion, Apollonia, trousers, vinegar.*

TORONTO

Capital of the province of Ontario, Canada.

☐ See **OHIO.**

TORTOISE

Name given to the land species of the order Chelonia of the reptiles.

☐ See **EARTHQUAKE, SLOTH, TERRAPIN.**

TORTURE

A sale of instruments of torture at Sotheby's of London in 1968 attracted a great deal of interest and fetched a total of £6,752. The strangest enquiry, according to Sotheby's staff, came from a telephone caller who wanted to know whether they were offering for sale a set of branding irons with his initials on them.

TOTTENHAM HOTSPUR

English professional Association football club, founded by boys from a Tottenham Presbyterian school in 1882.

☐ See **PHILOSOPHY.**

TOUCAN

Family of birds (Rhamphastidae) of the sub-order Picidae (woodpeckers).

☐ See **ARTIFICIAL LIMBS.**

TOULOUSE-LAUTREC, Henri de (1864–1901)

At the age of 13, Toulouse-Lautrec tripped

Under the hammer at Sotheby's

over and broke a leg. To prove it was no fluke, a year later he did the same with the other leg. The long-term result of the damage was to stunt his growth. Another of his physical problems was hypertrophy (exaggerated growth) of the penis. He lived in a brothel where he was nicknamed 'teapot'.

TRAFFIC

Over a million people have been killed by cars in the past thirty years in the United States. In that same country, one person commits suicide every twenty minutes. That works out at 788,940 suicides in thirty years. It seems probable, therefore, that more people are killed in automobile accidents than commit suicide, but we cannot make any definitive deduction without knowing how many people kill themselves by throwing themselves under cars.

More than 400 people are killed every year in the United States by lightning. Even some of these may have been suicides,

deliberately standing out in the rain hoping for a passing bolt to strike them down.

☐ See also: *dentistry, Melbourne, road safety.*

TRAFFIC LIGHTS

The first traffic lights in history were erected at the corner of Bridge Street and New Palace Yard outside the Houses of Parliament in London in 1868. Lit by a gas cylinder, they blew up the following year, severely injuring the policeman operating them. They were removed in 1872.

May 1982 was a vintage month for traffic offences in the west of England. The traffic lights at Combwich in Somerset were stolen, while down the road at Newton Abbot two council workmen had a parking ticket stuck on their lorry while they were round the corner painting double yellow lines to prohibit parking in the street.

TRAFFIC OFFENCE

The first man to be sent to jail for a traffic

offence was N. J. Cugnot, a captain in the French army. He had, in fact, been responsible for the design of the first ever mechanical road vehicle, a steam-powered tractor which was used for pulling cannon in 1769. Unfortunately the good Captain had the bad luck to drive it into a wall.

It has been calculated that courts in the United States now spend more than half their time dealing with cases involving cars.

TRAFFIC WARDEN

☐ See **KISSING.**

TRAINING

A Pentagon report to the American Congress in 1977 announced that it takes thirteen months to train a jet pilot, but fifteen months to train a military bandleader.

TRANSATLANTIC FLIGHT

The first man ever to cross the Atlantic on, rather than in, an aeroplane was Jaromir Wagner in 1980.

TRANSPLANT

The world's first testicle transplant was performed in 1977 at St Louis. The operation is not worth doing unless donor and recipient are identical twins. Testicular implants have frequently been performed for cosmetic reasons to restore the balance after one of the pair has been lost.

In America 60,000 women a year have breast implants.

TRANSVESTISM

Dr James Barry served for forty years as a surgeon in the army of Queen Victoria, attaining the rank of general. Only on his death in 1865 was it discovered that he was in fact a woman.

There was no secret that Lord Cornbury was a man. In 1702 he was appointed governor (rather than governess) of New York and New Jersey. But he did perform most of his official duties dressed as a woman.

☐ See also: *alcohol, rape.*

Prince Charles of Denmark (b. 1872) at the age of 4, in a fetching off-the-shoulder number

TREACLE

Treacle was originally an antidote to the bites of wild beasts and derives from a Greek word (*theriake*) meaning 'of beasts'. Twenty-one people were killed by a treacle wave which swept through Boston, Mass. in 1919. Two million gallons had been stored in a tank which suddenly ruptured. The resulting 50-foot wave of treacle engulfed eight buildings.

Baked beans were originally tinned in molasses instead of tomato sauce. As far as is known, nobody has yet met his end in a tomato sauce flood.

TREASON

☐ See **KNACKERS.**

George III as his mother remembered him

TREES

The sequoia tree is named after a Cherokee silversmith, Sequoyah (1770–1843), who created an alphabet for the Cherokee language. Thanks to his efforts, the Cherokees had, within seven years, changed into a literate society with a weekly newspaper. As a mark of their respect they named a tree after him.

The smallest tree in the world is the dwarf willow of Greenland, standing a proud two inches high. The last court dwarf in Europe was Coppernin, dwarf of the Princess of Wales, mother of George III of England.

☐ See also: ***Monet.***

TRIAL BY BATTLE

In the 1817 English court case, Thornton *v.* Ashford, Thornton was accused of murdering Mary Ashford. Thornton claimed the right to challenge the plaintiff, brother of the deceased, to wager of battle. Dusting down his old tomes, the judge, Lord Ellenborough, ruled that Trial by Battle was still on the statute books. The suit was allowed, Thornton's challenge refused, and the accused was freed accordingly. This was the last time Trial by Battle was claimed in an English court, since the law was changed the following year.

TRIAL BY FIRE

Until recently, trial by fire was still used to settle disputes in Arabia. The ceremony was conducted by a 'Mobishaa', who opened the proceedings by asking the accused for a confession. If none came, an iron was heated in a fire until white hot. The accused had to lick the iron three times, after which his tongue was examined and the verdict delivered. Both plaintiff and accused paid a sum of about £5 to the Mobishaa; the winner would get his money back.

The principle involved seems similar to that of the modern lie detector. A guilty man will be worried enough to have a dry tongue, which will burn on the iron. The innocent will salivate freely and be protected.

☐ See also: ***Ethelred.***

TRIAL BY JURY

In 1738 Hugh Fowler was convicted of bribery and corruption. The verdict was later quashed when it was disclosed that the jury had reached their decision by tossing a coin.

The old Saxon method of trial seems less open to dispute: the accused held a white-hot iron bar in his hand, and would be deemed innocent if the burns healed within three days.

☐ See also: ***bear.***

TRIGGER

Horse of Roy Rogers.

☐ See **BENTHAM.**

Fake three-legged dog facing disqualification

TRIPED

(From the Latin: *tres*, *tria*, three; *pes*, *pedis*, a foot.) An animal with three legs. A tripedal dog once won a sheepdog trial in California.

☐ See also: *athletics.*

TROGON

☐ See **QUETZAL.**

TROLLOPE, Anthony (1815–82)

British novelist with a long and distinguished career in the postal service. Trollope was responsible for the introduction of the pillar-box. He left £70,000.

☐ See also: *writing.*

TROTSKY, Lev Davidovich (1877–1940)

Assumed name of Bolshevist leader Leiba Bronstein.

☐ See **MARX.**

TROUSERS

The correct mode of donning legwear is important for the prevention of toothache according to old English beliefs. In Sussex the advice is to put on the right sock before the left, and to enter the trousers right leg first. Shropshire lore agrees on the importance of getting it right, but recommends the reverse procedure.

Woodlice have seven pairs of legs and breathe through airholes in the last of these. They neither wear trousers nor suffer from toothache.

Generally right-handed men enter trousers with the right leg leading, left-handed men clothe the left leg first.

☐ See also: *Catherine de Medici.*

TROUT

Freshwater fish (*Salmo fario*) of the family Salmonidae.

☐ See **COW.**

TRUMAN, Harry S (1884–1972)

The S in Harry S Truman did not stand for anything. Both his grandfathers had first names beginning with S, so to avoid an invidious choice he was named Harry S after both of them.

TUBERCULOSIS

An old treatment for tuberculosis was to take a mixture of snail-slime and sugar. The snail, in fact, featured large in medicine. Oribasius, a physician of fourth-century Byzantium, used to treat wounds with a local application of crushed snails mixed with flour dust. But he was very fussy about his flour, which had to be collected from a wall near a mill. If he ran out of snails (or indeed if the snails crawled out on him) he would substitute earthworms.

After taking its slime for the tuberculosis but before crushing it to treat the wound, the snail might be used for an old Cheshire wart-removing recipe: simply rub a child's wart with a snail, then impale the snail on a thorn. The wart will then disappear, but apparently it only works for children.

TULIP

Holland sells more than 2,700 million flowers each year. Tulips, however, do not come from Amsterdam, they originated in Turkey. 'Tulip' is a Turkish word meaning 'turban'.

The Australian bush-turkey builds its nest on the ground. Since such structures have been known to weigh up to 5 tons, this seems a wise decision.

TUNA

The tunny fish.

☐ See **PERPETUAL MOTION.**

TUNNEY, Gene (James Joseph Tunney) (1898–1978)

☐ See **BOXING.**

TURIN

The ancient city of Augusta Taurinorum in Italy, now shrouded in relics.

☐ See **BUSINESS.**

TURKEY

'God's body,' exclaims First Carrier in *Henry IV*, Part One, Act II, scene ii, 'the turkeys in my pannier are quite starved.'

That was one of the bard's little anachronisms, for the action takes place almost a century before the discovery of America, whence came the first turkeys to Europe.

In Turkey, the turkey is called the 'American bird'. The correct collective noun for a gathering of these large birds is a rafter of turkeys.

☐ See also: *cuckoo, gormlessness, Gustav III, knowledge, motoring, tulip, wealth.*

TURTLE

Marine member (*Chelone*) of the tortoise tribe. Turtles have no teeth.

☐ See also: *panda, rubber.*

TUTANKHAMUN (*c.* 1371–1352 BC)

☐ See **OSIRIS.**

TUVALU

Formerly happily together as the Gilbert

and Ellice Islands, Ellice decided to make a go of it on her own and changed her name to Tuvalu in 1978. In Tuvalu, a straying woman is liable to have her nose bitten off by her husband. A male adulterer receives no such penalty; he is set adrift in the Pacific in a canoe with no paddle and no food.

TWAIN, Mark (1835–1910)

Pen-name of American writer Samuel Langhorne Clemens. He claimed descent, on his father's side, from Elizabethan pirates. In 1873, three years before the publication of *Tom Sawyer*, Mark Twain took out a patent for a self-pasting scrapbook, consisting of blank pages covered with gum.

TYBURN

The fee paid to Tyburn hangmen was 13½d plus 1½d for the rope for each hanging. Peers of the realm had the right to demand the luxury of a silken rope if they were to be hanged. Probably this earned the hangman a bonus; it certainly was more comfortable for the victim, since the decrease in friction with a silken rope would have made it more likely to cause death by breaking the neck, rather than a lingering strangulation.

Before the nineteenth century, a woman could have a sentence of hanging postponed if she was more than 4½ months pregnant. But it was strictly a postponement and the sentence would be carried out as soon as practicable after the birth of the child.

TYPEWRITER

'Typewriter' can be typed on the top row of letters of a typewriter.

TYPHOID

(From the Greek: *typhodes*, delirious; *typhos*, a fever; *eidos*, likeness.) The most successful typhoid carrier of all time was Mary Mallon of New York, who managed to start nine outbreaks of the disease before she was finally kept under detention in 1915. She died in 1938. The common housefly is less discriminating in the ailments it spreads; it can transmit thirty different diseases to man. Research indicates that houseflies prefer to breed in the middle of rooms rather than near the walls.

☐ See also: *Henry Frederick.*

TYRRANOSAUR

☐ See **BRONTOSAURUS, ETIQUETTE.**

U

UGANDA

More potatoes and less sugar are eaten in Uganda, per capita, than anywhere else on earth. Some Ugandan surgeons have been known to use African fire ants for sutures. The ant's powerful jaws are used to bite the edges of skin together, then the ant's body is twisted off, leaving the jaws in place.

Ants and termites have been known to burrow to depths of 80 feet in search of water. With their bodies pulled off, however, they are quite harmless.

UGLINESS

King Matthias Corvinus of Hungary ordered all ladies at court to be seated in his presence. His motive was simply that he considered them to be very ugly, and he wanted to see less of them.

UKELELE

Ukelele is the Hawaiian word for flea. In 1670 a plague of fleas (or possibly Hawaiian ukeleles) infested the town of Munster in Germany. So incensed were the inhabitants that the fleas were banned for ten years for disorderly conduct.

UMBILICAL CORD

(From the Latin: *umbilicus*, navel.)

☐ See **VOCATIONAL GUIDANCE.**

UMBRELLA

(From the Latin: *umbra*, shade or shadow.)

The hundreds of umbrellas left each day on trains by Japanese commuters have caused such confusion that the Tokyo authorities display vast adverts reminding passengers not to forget their brollies. In 1969, an Italian was charged with selling as Parmesan cheese a substance later identified on analysis to be grated umbrella handles. Where he obtained his raw materials is not recorded. Probably back in those Tokyo **LOST PROPERTY** offices.

On the whole of the Japanese National Railway network in 1982, there were 1,840,000 articles mislaid, including 156 sets of false teeth, 6 chickens, a rabbit and a beetle.

☐ See also: *barrel-organ, genius, Wellington.*

UMPIRING

The most serious case in a cricket match of players disputing an umpire's decision came in a game in Pakistan in 1976, when an umpire was beaten to death with the stumps by members of the fielding side who disagreed with some of his judgements. Crickets' ears are on their front legs.

UNDERESTIMATION

An assessment falling short of the truth.

☐ See **DIARISTS.**

UNDERWEAR

☐ See **SCIATICA, SOAP, TENPIN BOWLING.**

UNION OF SOVIET SOCIALIST REPUBLICS

☐ See **ABORTION**.

UNIQUENESS

General Eisenhower and Martin van Buren have been the only bald Presidents of the United States. But Richard Nixon was the only president to have been the ninth cousin of an ex-King of Albania (ex-King Leka I). Julius Caesar wore a laurel wreath to disguise his baldness, while Eisenhower boosted his self-esteem by having five pips sewn onto his pyjamas.

Lincoln's fly-away hair gave him endless worries

UNITED STATES OF AMERICA

President James Garfield of the United States could write Latin with one hand and Greek with the other simultaneously.

☐ See also: *automobile, Bible, Chicago, civilisation, motorcycling, murder,*
popcorn, radio, tax, television, traffic, Vietnam.

UNIVERSE

The ratio between the amount of empt space in the universe and that which occupied by matter is about the same as in 20-mile cube containing a single grain o sand.

The number of ways of playing the fir ten moves in a game of chess is as vast as th number of atoms in 3 tons of hydrogen.

☐ See also: *Nut.*

URBAN VIII, Pope (1568–1644)

(Maffeo Barberini)

☐ See **ECLIPSE**.

URINATION

Urinant (from the Latin: *urinari*, to plunge means diving or in a diving posture; th noun is urinator, a diver. These should no be confused with words derived from th Latin *urina*, meaning urine.

☐ See **KNOWLEDGE, LIZARD, PORCUPINE, SHOCK, SOUTH AFRICA, TEETH**.

Giuseppe Garibaldi

URUGUAY

South American republic named after the river of the same name. In Uruguay 10.93 oz of meat is eaten per person per day, more than in any other country. Giuseppe Garibaldi once had the challenging job of selling spaghetti in Uruguay. Better training, one would imagine, than, for example, being distributor of stamps for the county of Westmorland, which is what William Wordsworth did before he took up full-time poetry.

□ See also: *duelling.*

UTILITARIANISM

(From the Latin: *utilis*, useful.) Ethical system which aims at providing the greatest happiness for the largest number.

□ See **BENTHAM.**

V

VAMPIRE

(From the Serbian: *vampir*.) The Hungarian countess Elizabeth Bathory bathed in the blood of peasant girls, which she believed helped to preserve her good looks. Any vampire bat imported into Britain is subject to quarantine for life.

☐ See also: ***Tanzania.***

VAN GOGH, Vincent Willem (1853–90)

Last words of painter Vincent van Gogh were: 'I shall never get rid of this depression.' He then got rid of it by killing himself.

☐ See **ARTISTS.**

VASECTOMY

☐ See **BANGKOK.**

VATICAN

☐ See **HEALING, SLAVERY, TECHNOLOGY.**

VEGETABLES

(From the Latin: *vegetare*, to quicken; *vegetabilis*, animating.) The broad bean is the oldest vegetable known to man. The Brussels sprout loses 90 per cent of its Vitamin C content in cooking. The connection of the Brussels sprout with Belgium seems remote, since it is a native vegetable of Britain. There is, however, a spa named Spa in Belgium from which the word derives.

VENEZUELA

In Venezuela, lovers' letters may be posted at half the normal rate if they are enclosed in special pink envelopes. There are considerable fines imposed on those caught using the special envelopes for non-amatory purposes.

VENICE

(From the Italian: *Venezia*.)

☐ See **ITALY, OHIO.**

VENISON

(From the Latin: *venari*, to hunt.) The flesh of the deer, which should be hung as long as possible to make it tender.

☐ See **CRUELTY.**

VENUS

Planet known to the ancients as Phosphorus and Hesperus.

☐ See **INDIVIDUALITY.**

VERDI, Giuseppe (1813–1901)

Verdi applied to the Milan Conservatorium in 1832, but was turned down for lack of musical ability and for being too scruffily dressed. Sixty-seven years later, the Milan Conservatorium asked Verdi for permission to change their name to the Verdi Conservatorium. The old man had a long memory and refused their request.

☐ See also: ***Duncan.***

VERE, Edward de (1550–1604)

Earl of Oxford.

☐ See **FARTING**.

VERSAILLES

French town 10 miles WSW of Paris. King Louis XIV of France had a diamond-encrusted robe which cost one-sixth as much as the entire palace at Versailles. For fashionable extravagance, he was equalled by Catherine de Medici who had a dress studded with 3,000 diamonds and 39,000 pearls. She wore it only once.

VERTIGO

☐ See **APOPLEXY**.

VESTAL VIRGIN

The task of the vestal virgins in Rome was to tend the sacred fire said to have been brought by Aeneas from Troy and pre-served in a sanctuary in the Forum. Applications were invited from spotless young ladies between the ages of 6 and 10 years. They signed on for a period of five years, during which they were expected to remain spotless. Those who carried out their obligations were free to leave and marry after the five years. Any who lost their virginity during the period of employment were walled up and left to die.

Sucking pig is only on the menu at a Chinese wedding if the bride is a virgin.

VESUVIUS

Volcano in Italy not far from where Pompeii used to be.

☐ See **PLINY THE ELDER**.

VEXATIONS

(From the Latin: *vexare*, to shake or annoy.) 'Vexations' is the title of a composition for pianoforte by Eric Satie, consisting of a ninety second motif and instructions that it be played 840 times without a break. In 1963, American composer John Cage hired a team of pianists to struggle through it in relay. No solo performance has ever been given in public, though the Dutchman, Reinbert de Leeuw, made a gallant attempt in 1963. He had played the theme 117 times before he and his small audience were ejected by a caretaker from Amsterdam's Leidsekade at 1 am.

De Leeuw's recording of 'Vexations' was Phillips' top-selling classical record in November 1983, though the record has to be played thirty-five times for the full effect.

VICTORIA, Queen of Great Britain, Empress of India (1819–1901)

There is some dispute as to Queen Victoria's first act on succeeding to the throne. Some sources say that she removed her bed from her mother's room, others maintain that she washed her favourite dog. The weight of evidence suggests that she washed the dog while having her bed moved, though whether the bed-moving decree was issued before or after the dog hit the water remains a matter for speculation.

☐ See also: ***bedtime, charity, chloroform, hunchback, James I, Mussolini, salt, security, transvestism.***

VIDEO GAMES

A popular way to pass the time.

☐ See **PRE-MARITAL SEX.**

VIETNAM

During the period of the Vietnam War, almost twice as many Americans were killed by guns in the United States as in Vietnam. A new gun is sold on average every 13½ seconds in the United States.

☐ See also: ***bounty hunters, Mexico, Ritz.***

VIKINGS

(From the Old Norse: *vikingr*; probably connected with the Anglo-Saxon, *wicing*, warrior or pirate.)

☐ See **RAPE.**

VINEGAR

The acidic properties of vinegar are utilise in a number of folk remedies, but the mod of application makes all the difference. Fo tonsillitis, it is recommended to wrap you feet in towels moistened with vinegar an cold water, removing the compress onl after it has become warm. For toothache however, a New England cure involve applying to the tooth a snakeskin steepe in vinegar. If you cannot find a snakeskin you can always try a vinegar-free Cornis remedy which recommends simply bitin the first spring fern off right by the ground

Roman ladies used a paste made from vinegar and chalk as a deodorant.

☐ See also: ***goldfish.***

VIOLENCE

In Saxon England, the infliction of persona injuries upon another person was punish able by a system of fines which varie according to the size of wound inflicted. / one-inch gash under the hairline cost on shilling, which rose to two shillings if it wa on the face. Loss of an ear was worth thirt shillings.

VIOLIN

Playing the violin on roller-skates is not t be recommended when a guest at a respec able house. In 1760, one Joseph Mervi tried to do precisely that at one of Mr Cornely's masquerades at Carlisle House i Soho Square. He destroyed a £500 mirro when he crashed into it and sustaine serious cuts.

☐ See also: ***Nero.***

VIPER

Mostly viviparous species of poisonou snake, including the common viper c adder (*Vipera berus*) which is the onl venomous reptile in England. The Gabo viper has the largest fangs of any snake, measuring about 0.5 cm. (There may have been longer ones in prehistoric times but fangs ain't what they used to be.) If all the household rubbish produced each day in Tokyo were divided equally among the population of Gabon, there would be enough for each person to have 25 kilos of garbage.

□ See also: *Cyprus.*

VIRGIL (70–19 BC)

Full name Publius Virgilius Maro.

□ See **PAMPERED PETS.**

VIRGINITY

□ See **INTELLIGENCE, IRAN, MAHOMET, MOUSE, NEWTON, PROSTITUTION, SHAW, STOPES, SYPHILIS.**

VISION

Edison's invention of the electric light bulb did little to improve the foresight of the British Parliamentary Committee set up to investigate its potential value around 1878. Their report described it as: 'good enough for our transatlantic friends . . . but unworthy of the attention of practical or scientific men'. Edison had a collection of 5,000 birds and patented nearly 1,300 inventions.

VISITING CARDS

In polite society, a gentleman's visiting card measures 3 × 1½ inches; a lady's is 3½ × 2½ inches. The surface should be slightly glazed. The edges must not be gilt.

VITAMINS

One of the richest natural sources of Vitamin A is the liver of a polar bear. One nineteenth-century Arctic expedition was totally wiped out after its members had eaten the liver of a polar bear they had killed. They all died of Vitamin A overdose.

VIVALDI, Antonio (1676–1741)

Red-haired priest and composer, music master at the Pieta, a Venetian orphanage for musical girls. Vivaldi wrote over 450 concerti for the all-girl ensembles, including thirty-eight for bassoon.

□ See **DA PONTE.**

VOCATIONAL GUIDANCE

In the Italian town of Perugia, there is a custom to save a small piece of the umbilical cord of a newborn child and to store it in a place relevant to the desired profession of the child. If it is kept in a Bible, the child will become a priest; in a medical textbook, if the parents want it to be a doctor. But there is a grave danger in this procedure: if the cat gets the morsel of cord, then the child will grow up to be a thief. More generally, Italian folklore claims that riches and virility are dependent upon the umbilical cord being cut to the right length.

VOLE

The female meadow vole can reproduce twenty-five days after it is born. It has up to seventeen litters a year, each of between six and eight young. The gestation period of the possum is thirteen days.

VOLKSWAGEN

(From the German: *Volk*, people; *Wagen*, a carriage.) A carriage for German people.

□ See **REPARATIONS.**

VOLTAIRE (1694–1778)

Voltaire's real name was François Marie Arouet. He was born prematurely and drank fifty cups of coffee a day. Dr Samuel Johnson once drank thirty-six glasses of port without moving from his seat.

VULTURE

'If there's one thing above all a vulture can't stand, it's a man with a glass eye' (Frank McKinney Hubbard).

□ See **PARSEE.**

W

WALES

The Roman Emperor Nero used to eat leeks to improve his singing voice. The Welsh, who also sing a lot, also eat leeks. Herein could lie the forgotten secret of male voice choirs.

☐ See also: *Sahara.*

WALRUS

(Originally Scandinavian, meaning whale-horse.)

☐ See **TEETH.**

WAR

Britain and Zanzibar were at war for thirty-eight minutes in 1896. Zanzibar is now part of Tanzania, but 80 per cent of its export earnings still come from the sale of cloves. After the revolution in 1964, a decree was enacted that prescribed a possible death penalty for anyone convicted of smuggling cloves. That punishment is still on the statute books, though no smuggler has yet lost his life for a clove.

WART

There may be a vestige of truth in the old belief that touching a toad could give you warts. The virus which causes warts thrives best in cold clammy places such as the skin of a toad. There seems, however, no scientific reason to believe either of the following folk cures for warts:

(i) On the twentieth day of the moon, go into the country, lie flat on a path, gaze at the moon, reach above your head and rub the warts with whatever your hand first touches.

(ii) Rub the wart with the tail of a tortoise-shell tom cat in May.

☐ See also: *Cicero, tuberculosis.*

WASHINGTON, George (1732–99)

George Washington was the first man to use 'average' as a verb. His dentist pioneered the use of the drill, adapting his mother's spinning wheel to keep it whirring. A tooth which he had personally extracted from the presidential gum was left as a bequest to the dentist's nephew.

☐ See also: *calendar, Churchill, W., teeth.*

WASP

Hymenopterous insect, of which the male has a charming seduction routine. He has been observed to deliver to the female a present of a fly, elaborately gift-wrapped in silk. While his delighted paramour wasp is busily engaged unwrapping the morsel, he takes advantage of the distraction to nip round the back and take advantage of her too.

☐ See also: *honey, humming-bird.*

WATER

Seventy million gallons of water flow over

ne Victoria Falls every minute. This is nough water to satisfy the daily sanitary nd domestic needs of 400,000 Americans, r 1,750,000 Europeans, or 3 million Pakitanis.

Cabbage is 91 per cent water; the human rain is 80 per cent water. Does this mean hat the human brain is nearly 73 per cent abbage?

] See also: *Amazon, bath, body, fishing, Jamaica, love-sickness, pianoforte, Siberia, snow.*

*ATERLOO

The spirit of Waterloo lives on! Mrs Marva Drew, of Waterloo, Iowa, aged 51, typed out all the numbers from 1 to 1,000,000. She did it after being told that it was mpossible. It took her five years.

☐ See also: *Czechoslovakia, dancing.*

'ATERPROOFING

'The thing is not beautiful, although it may still be waterproof,' wrote Woody Allen, not without some profundity. The nineteenth-century newspaper *La Naiade* was indeed waterproof. It was printed on rubber so that it could be read without fear of sogginess in the bath. The venture ran successfully for some years, but finally sank under financial stresses.

ATER-SKIING

Water-skier's syndrome is not in fact anything suffered by the water-skier himself. It is a medical neologism applied to the injuries suffered when someone in the boat which is towing the skier is bounced into the water by its motion and subsequently run over by the skier.

AXWORKS

Miss Mary Fox was the wardress at Lincoln Jail in 1863, when she lent a handkerchief to Priscilla Biggadyke on the morning of the latter's execution. Thirty-two years later, Miss Fox (now retired) was visiting Madame Tussaud's waxworks and saw a model of the unfortunate Miss Biggadyke in the Chamber of Horrors. She was still clutching the borrowed handkerchief.

WEALTH

In 1983 Texas claimed to have six billionaires, including Gordon Paul Getty, 49, estimated to be the richest man in the USA, tipping the scales at a net worth of $2.2 billion.

In 1903 the Czar of Russia had the highest estimated income of any European monarch, calculated to be equivalent to £16.45 a minute. John D. Rockefeller and Alfred Beit both out-earned the Czar, with incomes estimated at £20 a minute.

Runner-up in the European monarch stakes was the Sultan of Turkey at a cool £2 million a year. Dogs' teeth were used as currency in the Solomon Islands until 1850.

WEASEL

Small carnivorous mammal (*Mustela nivalis*). The testes of a weasel or ass, salted and administered in drink, will cure epilepsy according to Pliny the Elder, but only if the sufferer gives up wine for some days before and after. If your weasel has no testes, use its uterus, which is just as effective. (Most weasels will be found to have one or the other.) Or you might try wild boar's testes with mare's milk. But testes of pig, fried and beaten up with sow's milk, are considered by Pliny to be less use.

☐ See also: *cat, overcrowding.*

WEATHER

In the year 1953, 2 June was selected as Coronation Day for Queen Elizabeth II because records showed it to be the most consistently sunny day in the calendar. It rained. But it could have been worse: in 1880, 246 people were killed by hailstones in a downpour in Moradabad in northern India.

☐ See also: *Angola, chess, shark.*

WEDDING CUSTOMS

The Lhopa tribe in Tibet used to celebrate a marriage by eating the bride's mother. The city of Oxford is evidently more restrained in its wedding procedure; in 1975, they refused permission for Miss Cheryl Blabury to have her pet chihuahua Mitzi as a bridesmaid. And Mitzi had even been bought new orange panties and a floral bonnet for the occasion.

☐ See also: *Vestal virgin.*

WEDDING RING

The wedding ring seems to date back to ancient Egypt, where the circle was the hieroglyph for eternity. In England in the sixteenth and seventeenth centuries, wedding rings were worn on ladies' thumbs.

WELLINGTON, Arthur Wellesley, 1st Duke of (1769–1852)

In 1845, Chas Pearson, Surveyor to the City of London, proposed the idea of an under-

ground railway. Wellington wisely rejecte the suggestion on the far-sighted groun that the French army might suddenly arriv on it and take England by surprise.

Of the quarter of a million items left o London Transport in 1941, 47,000 wei umbrellas, but 48,000 were tin hats, rifles o gas-masks.

The umbrella originated in ancient Egy as a symbol of rank in a theocratic societ In the Peninsular War, Wellington issue an order forbidding officers to carr umbrellas into battle. This would perhaj have been totally unnecessary if he had ha the foresight to provide tube trains in th first place on which they could leave thei umbrellas before the battle.

WELLS, Herbert George (1866–1946)

☐ See **LAST WORDS.**

WESTMINSTER ABBEY

☐ See **BURIAL, CAROLINE, PRAGMATISM.**

WESTMINSTER BRIDGE

☐ See **LIBYA.**

WHALE

The order of whales (Cetacea) is divide into two groups: toothed whales (Odor toceti) and whalebone whales (Myst coceti). Not only are whales the bes high-jumpers of all animals, being able t clear heights of up to 20 feet, but th humpback whale has been observed mak ing love in three different positions.

☐ See also: *brassière, compassion, Fiji, kidney, lion, sperm, survival, Taylor.*

WHEEL

(From the Anglo-Saxon: *hweol.*)
☐ See **SCIENCE.**

WHIPPING

The whipping of females in public wa forbidden in England in 1791 (by a curiou coincidence, the year of Mozart's death). All public whippings were abolished in 1817, but they flogged on in the British army and navy until 1881.

WHISKY

(From the Gaelic: *usquebaugh*, water of life.)

☐ See **COMMON COLD, SCORPION, THOMAS.**

WHISTLING

☐ See **OYSTER.**

WHITTINGTON, Sir Richard (*d.* 1423)

Sir Richard 'Dick' Whittington's cat was not a feline creature but a boat. His fortune was made with a fleet of cat-boats, employed to carry coal from Newcastle to London. Many portraits of Whittington with cat were originally Whittington with skull, but the latter was changed to a cat as more cheerful and a nice pun.

Buried in the church of St Michael, his tomb was plundered by the rector, Thomas

Mountain, 'possessed by an ungovernable spirit of avarice and folly'. Finding no valuables in the tomb, the looting rector stripped the body of its lead covering. The good late Lord Mayor was subsequently buried again with all due pomp.

WHOOPING COUGH

(From the Old French: *houper*, to shout.) Remedies for whooping cough (also known as pertussis) vary according to where you are in the British Isles. In Yorkshire, owl broth is recommended, while Scotland prescribed sheep's dung and water (also effective against jaundice). In Ireland, however, passing the sufferer nine times above and below a donkey was thought to do the trick.

☐ See also: *bear-keeping.*

WIFE-HATER

An 1810 edition of the Bible printed in England was known as The Wife-Hater Bible owing to a misprint in Luke, xiv, 26, in which the word 'life' was misprinted as 'wife'. The original should have read:

'If any one comes to me and does not hate his own father and mother and wife and children and brothers and sisters, yes, and even his own life, he cannot be my disciple.'

Fortunately the same misprint was not made also in John, xv, 13.

St Luke was the only non-Jewish author of the New Testament.

WIG

(Short for periwig.)

☐ See **ELIZABETH I of England, FINGERPRINTS.**

WILDE, Oscar Fingall O'Flahertie Wills (1856–1900)

☐ See **LAST WORDS.**

WILLIAM THE CONQUEROR (1027–87)

At 4 ft 2 in. in height, Queen Matilda, wife of William I of England (known as The

Conqueror) was the shortest monarch England has ever had. Attila the Hun, however, was a dwarf. Had William the Conqueror been a dwarf, he would probably not have ridden such large horses, and would thereby have saved himself from the fatal accident in 1087 when he burst open his bowels after being thrown on the pommel of his saddle.

☐ See also: *bachelor.*

WILLIAM I of Hanover
☐ See **WILLIAM II** of Ireland.

WILLIAM I of Prussia (1797–1888)
German Emperor and King of Prussia, second son of Frederick William III of Prussia.

☐ See **BAKING.**

WILLIAM II, King of England (c. 1056–1100)
William Rufus (or the Red King), like his predecessor and father William the Conqueror, met his end in an accident. Out hunting with his friend Walter Tyrrel, the King's last words, on spotting a deer, were: 'Shoot, Walter, shoot; as if it were the devil.' Walter shot, but the arrow ricocheted off a tree and killed the King.

WILLIAM II of Ireland
☐ See **WILLIAM III** of Scotland.

WILLIAM III, King of Great Britain and Ireland (1650–1702)
Little did William III suspect, as he fell to his death, unhorsed by a mole hole on a Saturday in 1702, that he was starting the longest continuous sequence of deaths of European monarchs all on the same day of the week. For he, Queen Anne, and the first four Georges all chose Saturday to conk out.

☐ See also: *barristers, coronation, scrofula.*

WILLIAM III of Scotland
☐ See **WILLIAM IV** of England.

WILLIAM IV, King of Great Britain and Ireland (1765–1837)
The fourth King William of England wa the third King William of Scotland, th second of Ireland and the first of Hanover.

WILSON, Sir Harold (b. 1916)
☐ See **CHURCHILL, R.**

WIND
Farting was banned in China in the sixth century BC. Four centuries later in India Kautilya ruled that men who served the King must not fart. Later still, with the development of more modern scientific understanding, the medical schools o Salerno in the Middle Ages held a more positive view of the value of the fart holding one in was believed to be liable to cause cramp, dropsy, colic or mazed brains.

WINDOW CLEANING
☐ See **MANSION HOUSE.**

WINE
☐ See **APARTHEID, ITALY, KOALA.**

WITCHCRAFT
For many centuries the accepted way to try a woman accused of witchcraft was to bind her right thumb to her left big toe, her left thumb to her right big toe, and throw her in a pond or river. If she floated, she was deemed to be a witch. The procedure was refined by a German archbishop in the ninth century, who added the provision of a rope by which to tow her out if she proved her innocence by sinking.

The logic of the whole procedure was dictated by the belief that witches would have refused the baptismal water, so the water would be bound to reject them. The last European witch was burnt at the stake in Switzerland in 1782.

☐ See also: *annulment, World War II.*

WITCH DOCTOR
☐ See **CRIME, SALMON.**

WITCHES

In the sixteenth and seventeenth centuries, witchfinders received about twenty shillings per witch brought to trial and condemned. The champion witchfinder of the time was Matthew Hopkins, who brought an end to the careers of sixty witches in Essex alone in a single year. Useful signs to look for when hunting witches are: (i) they cannot weep more than three tears, and these only from the left eye; (ii) they cannot repeat the Lord's Prayer without error; (iii) they weigh less than the church Bible. Any of these symptoms could be sufficient to condemn a suspect witch.

WODEHOUSE, P. G. (Pelham Grenville) (1881–1975)

P. G. Wodehouse scored sixty valuable runs for the Authors against the Publishers at Lord's, including one six and ten fours. His bowling also took four Publishers' wickets.

WOJTYLA, Karol (*b.* 1920)

Karol Wojtyla,
Didn't have much joy 'til a
Conclave increased his scope
By electing him Pope.
The first Polish Pope, John Paul II.

WOLF

Member of the dog family (*Canis lupus*).
☐ See **CAREER, DANCING, TERRAPIN.**

WOLFSON, Sir Isaac
☐ See **FILMS.**

WOLSEY, Thomas (*c.* 1475–1530)

English statesman and Cardinal.
☐ See **AURAL SEX, NELSON, WORDSWORTH.**

WOODLOUSE

The woodlouse (*Oniscus*) is a member of the equal-footed crustacea (Isopoda), so all its feet are approximately the same length, and all are used for walking. Curled up woodlice were prescribed for digestive complaints in the Middle Ages, to be taken as pills.
☐ See also: *trousers.*

WOODPECKER

Epileptics had to beware of woodpeckers (Picidae) in the Middle Ages. For when

Matthew Hopkins

they went gathering peonies (believed to be a certain cure for the disease) a woodpecker in sight was a sure sign that the sufferer would go blind.

WOOL

The large number of deaths from the Great Plague was a factor in helping the ailing wool trade in Britain in the seventeenth century. Feeling, no doubt, that every plague must have a silver lining (or a woollen one at least) parliament in 1666 decreed that all bodies must be wrapped in a woollen shroud for burial. The Act was not repealed until 1814.

WORDS

The English word with the highest proportion of consonants is 'strengths' with but one vowel in its nine letters. In writing the most common word is 'the', but this is overtaken in speech by the frequency of the pronoun 'I'.

No English word rhymes with 'oblige'.

WORDSWORTH, William (1770–1850)

For his investiture as Poet Laureate, William Wordsworth wore the same suit as had Tennyson for the same ceremony. They had both borrowed it from Samuel Rogers. Poetry was held in high esteem in the nineteenth century, though it must be admitted that in 1857 the Queen's rat-catcher earned more than the Poet Laureate. Wordsworth did not in fact write any poetry in his seven years in the post, though the catcher of the royal rat is believed to have trapped several rodents. During his fifteen years as Archbishop of York, Cardinal Wolsey never once visited the city.

☐ See also: *Uruguay.*

WORLD WAR I (1914–18)

☐ See **CABBAGE, DACHSHUND, EXCURSIONS.**

WORLD WAR II (1939–45)

Few realise the decisive part played in the

Sir Walter Scott declined the poet laureateship, perhaps because he too lacked a decent suit to wear

Second World War by a coven of English witches. They prevented an invasion of Britain by directing at Hitler's brain the thought that he could never successfully cross the Channel. Hitler attacked Russia instead, but the effort had been so great from the witches that all those involved became weak and died within a few years.

In 1659 James Howell wrote: 'Wear the inside of thy stockings outside to scare the witches.' Had Hitler heeded this advice, the whole course of history could have been altered.

☐ See also: *asthma, Chopin, illiteracy, reparations, Tanzania, tattoo.*

WORMS

A worm-eating contest at Rialto College California, saw a new record of twenty

'Your Country Needs You' poster for witches

eight set by Rusty Rice. A young robin, however, can consume 14 feet of earthworm a day.

In a cooking with worms competition sponsored by the North American Bait Company, the winner was a recipe for Earthworm Applesauce Surprise Cake. In Mexico, they just eat them plainly grilled on toast.

Though not particularly noted for their mental agility, earthworms do learn faster between the hours of 8 pm and midnight.

☐ See also: **aphrodisiac, tears.**

WREN, Sir Christopher (1632–1723)

Christopher Wren's first profession was that of astronomer; in 1657 he became professor of astronomy at Gresham College, and in 1660, Savilian professor of astronomy at Oxford. His first design for St Paul's Cathedral was rejected in 1673.

☐ See **HOBBIES.**

WRESTLING

(From the Anglo-Saxon: *wraestlian*.)

☐ See **ROYALTY.**

WRIST

The joint (*Carpus*) which separates the arm from the hand.

☐ See **BONE**.

WRITING

Anthony Trollope had a precise schedule of writing, beginning at 5.30 every morning and writing 250 words every fifteen minutes. Graham Greene is said to write exactly 200 words a day.

X

XAVIER, St Francis (1506–52)

St Francis Xavier founded the first Jesuit mission in India in 1542 in Goa, where his mortal remains are still kept. Sadly all that remains of the remains is a toe, which is preserved as a holy relic and brought out for adoration only once every ten years.

XYLOCOPID

The xylocopid, or carpenter bee, when in the mood will try to seduce anything that flies. They have been seen making advances towards dandelion seeds, birds and aircraft. The xylocopid is the largest of all bees, but the distance between the wingtips of a Boeing 747 is longer than the inaugural flight made by the Wright brothers.

Y

YAK

The yak (*Bos grunniens*) has the skeleton of a bison, the hair of a goat, the head of a cow, the tail of a horse and it grunts like a pig. Only very rarely, if ever, has a yak been mistaken for a platypus, which has the fur of an otter, the tail of a beaver, the feet of a duck and no nipples. If you still have doubts, the one which lays an egg is sure to be the platypus.

☐ See also: ***panda.***

YEMEN

☐ See **HAIRCUT.**

YOGA

Robert Antosczyck at 29 became so adept at sitting in the lotus posture and slowing his pulse rate, that one day he succeeded in stopping his heart entirely and dying.

YORICK

There is no 'well' in the line: 'Alas! poor Yorick. I knew him, Horatio: a fellow of infinite jest.'

☐ See **BEQUESTS.**

YORK

☐ See **WORDSWORTH.**

YORKSHIRE

☐ See **BIBLE, CAREERS.**

YO-YO

The yo-yo was originally a Filipino jungle weapon, designed to be a returnable projectile which could be hurled at its target, then brought back for re-use.

YUCATAN

When the Spaniards landed in Yucatan, they asked the native Indians what the place was called. The Indians replied 'Yucatan' and the name stuck. In the local language, Yucatan means 'What do you want?'

YUGOSLAVIA

If you are spending New Year's Eve in Yugoslavia, it is wise to have a pig about the house. Holding onto the tail of such an animal as the clock chimes midnight is considered to bring good luck throughout the year. There is a similar superstition in Spain involving the consumption of twelve grapes before the chimes have finished.

Danish pig breeders have produced a pig with two extra vertebrae in order to give more best back bacon. It is not known whether such an extension would promise any extra good fortune to any New Year tail-holding Yugoslav.

☐ See also: *cormorant.*

Z

ZAIRE

Zaire (or the Belgian Congo as it then was) saw a riot of 10,000 in Leopoldville (or Kinshasa as it now is) caused by a Czech sculptor named Foit in 1950. He was threatened by the mob, who accused him of night-time kidnapping raids, and of turning his victims into corned beef for export. The misunderstanding seemed to arise from the terracotta heads and bodies seen in his lorry, and a particular brand of corned beef which had as its trade mark the head of a negro (as we then called them).

☐ See also: *chemistry.*

ZANZIBAR

(Now **TANZANIA.**)

☐ See **WAR.**

ZBOJNICKI

☐ See **DANCING.**

ZEBRA

Lord Rothschild, the naturalist, had a carriage drawn by zebras. If he looked at them closely he would have realised that their stripes were white, not black, and that no two zebras have the same pattern.

☐ See also: *cuckoo.*

ZIP

When the zip was invented in 1891, it inventor, Whitcomb L. Judson, gave it th really zippy title: 'Clasp Locker and Un locker for Shoes'. Japan now produces a quarter of the world's zips.

ZOMBIE

(From the West African: *zumbi*, a fetish. The puffer fish, or fugu, is a great delicac in Japan but kills about 200 people each year through a deadly poison in its guts. Only specially licensed chefs are allowed to prepare it in restaurants. The poison is called tetrodotoxin and it paralyses the nervous system.

There is a theory that a very similar poison is used by Haitian witch doctors to produce evidence of zombiism. A highly potent cocktail including tetrodotoxin could be administered to produce the symptoms of death, but the 'corpse' could be revived as a zombie. At least two cases are known of people poisoned by fugu recovering at their own funerals. Harvard ethnopharmacologists believe that this is the cause of the zombie phenomenon.

ZOROASTER

Also known as Zarathustra, he flourished around the seventh century BC in north-west Persia. While founding the Zoroastrian religion, he lived on nothing but cheese for fifty years. Zoroaster would probably have liked the Dutch town of Hoorn, which has a market selling only cheese. The French eat 40 lb of cheese per capita each year. There are more than 240 different types of cheese made in France.

ZYGODACTYL

A very useful word when talking about the **PARROT**. It means having four toes, two in front and two behind, on each foot.

Also available in Unwin Paperbacks

A DICTIONARY OF EUPHEMISMS
Judith S. Neaman & Carole G. Silver

This book brings together more than 4,000 expressions used to avoid saying what we mean about sensitive subjects. It includes other ways of talking about sex, sin, death, the body, war and government.

After reading or dipping into this book you will be able to converse with bureaucrats, criminals, soldiers and sailors – whether you are in Britain, Australia or North America – in the correct manner.

'a fascinating reference book that will provide years of browsing.'
Daily Mail

ACCIDENTAL TIMES

Compiled by Jane Lambert
Illustrated by Bill Tidy

Accidental Times offers a fascinating insight into the lives of the Victorians. Theirs seems to have been a world infinitely more hazardous than our own: poisons were freely available, guns were universally owned, gunpowder was used to clean kitchen stoves, horses were continually running off with their carriages and, at the theatre, the footlights were still naked flames. And yet, paradoxically, the Victorians seem to have been more reckless, more carefree, more enterprising. You will meet people who carry nitric acid in their pockets, drink unknown substances with dire effects, shoot themselves with their own guns and go bathing when they can't swim. You will find the bizarre and the poignant, absurd feats, miraculous escapes and monumental bad luck stories. Above all, you will discover a delight in prurient detail which is ill-concealed. It all testifies to the strange mixture of the sensational and the coy, which characterizes the Victorian outlook.

AMAZING TIMES!
A selection of the most amusing and amazing articles from *The Times*

Chosen by Stephen Winkworth
Illustrated by ffolkes

The kangaroo which stole a five pound note, the soldier who stowed his girlfriend in his kitbag, artificial icebergs, the penicillin black market in Berlin, the golden eagle which travelled in a laundry basket, how the Vatican was invaded by white ants, the elephant that water-skied, the couple who lived in a tree, the 101-year-old lady who slid down banisters, the curry which turned a girl pink ... Add to that Lucky Luciano's funeral, the last days of Nijinsky, Casanova's autobiography, Picasso's painting machine, the curse of the Hope diamond and the founding of the Order of the Mosquito ... and you have *Amazing Times!*

'wry effectiveness ... the human interest is rich.'   *The Observer*

THE FIRST CUCKOO
Letters to *The Times* since 1900

Revised Edition

Chosen and introduced by Kenneth Gregory
Foreword by Bernard Levin

The first edition of witty, entertaining and memorable correspondence
to *The Times* was greeted with great critical enthusiasm and went on to
become a best-seller. Now Kenneth Gregory has brought up-to-date
his selection of the most witty, amusing and memorable letters to *The
Times* since 1900. Among the 'top people' whose eloquence fills these
pages figure a host of writers, artists, sportsmen, statesmen and public
personalities. There is Conan Doyle on a military invention, Neville
Chamberlain on the grey wagtail, Winston Churchill on corporal
punishment, Bernard Berenson on art forgeries, H. G. Wells on strike-
breaking, T. S. Eliot and Malcolm Muggeridge on television, Vita
Sackville-West on stamps as wallpaper, Field-Marshal Montgomery
on skiing.

   Among the letters he has chosen from the past five years are ones on
toads, tea-boys, triremes, gnomes, postage stamps, British Rail,
chamber-pots, knitting, foreigners and trade unions – from correspondents as diverse as Kenneth Clark, Beverley Nichols, Professor
Hayek and Graham Greene – and of course more about the sighting of
the first cuckoo in Spring.

'Wholly fascinating ... there is no end to the astonishments.'
Arthur Marshall – New Statesman

'The most enjoyable anthology for many a day.'
E. S. Turner – The Listener

'Hilarious.' *Alistair Cooke*

THE SECOND CUCKOO
A New Selection of Letters to *The Times* since 1900

Chosen and introduced by Kenneth Gregory

A totally new selection of letters to *The Times* – among them ones by Evelyn Waugh on earning an honest dollar, Sir Thomas Beecham on tempo, Reginald Bosanquet on Army nicknames, Patience Strong on 'God Save the Queen', Marie Stopes on pocket money, Agatha Christie on Shakespeare, A. L. Rowse on General de Gaulle, Katharine Whitehorn on how to end a letter, Joyce Grenfell on 'glamoramas', John le Carré on the Foreign Office, Iris Murdoch on the selection principle in education, Robert Graves on the bliss of being ignored, John Betjeman on old churches, Ravel on *Daphnis and Chloë*, Rebecca West on the Prince Consort's death chamber and many, many more.

This time he has been able to include running correspondence on trouser turn-ups, the origin of marmalade, the whereabouts of Ruritania, hygiene and the Communion cup, military nicknames and perfect manners – and individual letters on topics as diverse as hip baths, top hats, how to get a message to an express train, *Brideshead Revisited*, oarswomen's dress, war in the Falklands, Oliver Cromwell's head, the sinking of the Titanic – and cuckoos à la Beethoven.

'Editors and proprietors may fall, but the letters page of *The Times* still furnishes a welcome nest for the committed as well as the cosy. In this second collection its contributors are again in full throttle.'
The Observer

A Dictionary of Euphemisms *Judith S. Neaman &*
   Carole G. Silver   £2.95 ☐
Accidental Times *Jane Lambert*   £2.95 ☐
Amazing Times! *Stephen Winkworth*   £2.95 ☐
The First Cuckoo *Kenneth Gregory*   £2.95 ☐
The Second Cuckoo *Kenneth Gregory*   £2.95 ☐

All these books are available at your local bookshop or newsagent, or can be ordered direct by post. Just tick the titles you want and fill in the form below.

Name ....

Address ....

....

....

Write to Unwin Cash Sales, PO Box 11, Falmouth, Cornwall TR10 9EN.
Please enclose remittance to the value of the cover price plus:
UK: 55p for the first book plus 22p for the second book, thereafter 14p for each additional book ordered to a maximum charge of £1.75.
BFPO and EIRE: 55p for the first book plus 22p for the second book and 14p for the next 7 books and thereafter 8p per book.
OVERSEAS: £1.00 for the first book plus 25p per copy for each additional book.

Unwin Paperbacks reserve the right to show new retail prices on covers, which may differ from those previously advertised in the text or elsewhere. Postage rates are also subject to revision.

THE ULTIMATE ~~IRRELEVANT~~ ENCYCLOPAEDIA

'inspired by entries which flit chaotically from one revelation to another with delightfully tenuous links.'

THE GUARDIAN

'Fascination for trivia throws up a splendid flotsam, mostly to do with sex or human pride . . . Slightly absurd but very funny.'

MAIL ON SUNDAY

'a collection of fascinating, obscure facts.'

WEEKEND

'Delightful book of useless information but utterly fascinating collection of the bizarre.'

YORKSHIRE EVENING POST

Cover designed by
Taylor Grunfeld

GB £ NET   +003.50

ISBN 0-04-827148-9 NZI

00350

UNWIN PAPERBACKS
HUMOUR

£3.50

9 780048 271488